KU-449-673

Mark Hix

British REGIONAL FOOD

A *cook's* tour of Britain and Ireland

Photography by Jason Lowe

QUADRILLE

This edition published in 2006 by
Quadrille Publishing Limited,
Alhambra House,
27-31 Charing Cross Road,
London WC2H OLS

Editorial Director: Jane O'Shea
Creative Director: Helen Lewis
Editor & Project Manager: Lewis Esson
Art Director: Lawrence Morton
Photography: Jason Lowe
Food Styling: Mark Hix
Styling: Cynthia Inions
Production: Bridget Fish

Text © Mark Hix 2006
Photography © Jason Lowe 2006
Edited text, design & layout © Quadrille
Publishing Ltd 2006

The rights of Mark Hix to be identified as
the Author of this Work have been asserted
by him in accordance with the Copyright,
Design and Patents Act 1988.

All rights reserved. No part of this book
may be reproduced, stored in a retrieval system
or transmitted in any form or by any means,
electronic, electrostatic, magnetic tape,
mechanical, photocopying, recording
or otherwise, without the prior permission in
writing of the publisher.

Cataloguing in Publication Data:
a catalogue record for this book is
available from the British Library

ISBN-13: 978-184400-234-4
ISBN-10: 1-84400-234-9

Printed in China

CONTENTS

Introduction

I knew as soon as I set out on this project that in order to do the subject justice I really needed to take about two or three years off my day job and probably fill several volumes with what I found. Of course, that was impractical, so I decided right from the start that all I could really do was just to try to seek out what took my fancy all over the country, and write about that in the hope that it would give readers sufficient feeling of what is out there that they would want to find out more for themselves.

I apologize wholeheartedly to those I have omitted… perhaps next time… and to those I have included but have not mentioned all their products or spelled something wrongly, or not included the latest developments (I did start researching this book back in early 2005), I have tried my best - as has my redoubtable editor, Lewis Esson - to get it as right as we could.

I do have to thank my friend and photographer Jason Lowe, not only for accompanying me to many of the places I have visited and for taking such beautiful pictures for the book, but for leading me to so many fascinating places, producers and personalities.

If we have managed to convey just a fraction of the interest and excitement we came upon in our travels around these beautiful islands, then I am sure you will forgive me any errors or omissions, and that you will get almost as much enjoyment from reading this book as we did from making it.

Mark Hix

London 2006

LONDON

PRICE INCLUDE	% VAT	
1 LARGE PIE & MASH	300	ALL
1 SMALL PIE & MASH	250	PRICES
2 LARGE PIES & MASH	500	ARE TO
2 SMALL PIES & MASH	400	EAT IN
VEGETARIAN PIES	120	SHOP
SMALL EELS & MASH	350	
LARGE EEL & MASH	600	
JELLIED EELS	S 250 L 500	
FRUIT PIE & ICE CREAM	125	
DRINKS 60		
TEA 50		TRAYS 20
COFFEE 60		
		LILY

AS THE MAIN PORT INTO WHICH CAME all the heady spices of the Orient, and the tea, coffee and chocolate of the Far East and Americas, London has long been a dynamic centre of food fashion. It is no surprise then that these made their mark on the great city – not only in evocative place names like Cinnamon Wharf, but in the city's bustling inns and coffee and chocolate houses, the smoky bonhomie of which spawned great institutions like the gentleman's club and the Stock Exchange, as well as industries like insurance. Local manufacturers also used the rich reservoir of flavourings available to create condiments that are still staples of the British table, like HP Sauce and Gentleman's Relish. The city's position as the world's trading centre also made it increasingly multicultural, so Cockney pie and mash shops, whelk stalls and jellied eel stands were soon vying with the salt beef and bagel shops of Jewish immigrants, who also, surprisingly, gave us that most British of institutions, the fish and chip shop. Later, Limehouse was also to become one of the first 'Chinatowns' in a Western city, and the first Indian restaurant in the West opened in Covent Garden.

London has changed in many ways since Elizabeth David's account of the London food scene back as recently as 1984. I had not long been in London then, but she was absolutely right – there were then no shops to compare with Pec's of Milan or Fauchon of Paris for a combination of high-quality ingredients and quality cooked food. There was nowhere with the energy

You can get a couple of hundred different types of cuisine if you only explore the capital's many ethnic pockets, or read Charles Campion's *The London Restaurant Guide.* Check out things like back-street Turkish and Vietnamese cafés – I love taking visitors to these places. Years ago I took Rick Stein to the Mangal Ocakbashi in Stoke Newington on his return from Turkey, and he reckoned it was the best Turkish food he'd eaten in two weeks.

TOP LEFT The menu board at the current
F. Cooke in Hoxton Street (page 15)
BOTTOM LEFT Andrew Casson's bee hives (page 22)
TOP RIGHT Chelsea buns

ABOVE The interior and window of the original F. Cooke pie and mash shop in Kingsland Road, which is now a Chinese restaurant (right and page 15).

Where I live, you can virtually eat or buy anything at any time of the day, from goat tripe to a pint of milk, and these pockets of London are what make London life really interesting. Many of our small producers' businesses thrive on taking part in the several farmers' markets that are now popping up all over the city, and shopping in these markets can give you a real taste of Britain and what it has now got to offer.

and scope of Dean and Deluca or Balduccis in New York; and where was there to take a foreign visitor to sample skilful English cooking apart from The Connaught or The Dorchester, where neither of the chefs were English, but produced great English food?

Well, I was lucky and worked at the latter for Anton Mosimann, and Elizabeth David was right in saying that the English food in the Grill there was bloody good – I'm still using many of the traditional methods Anton taught us. If Ms David was still around, I'm sure I would bump into her at Borough Market on a Friday or Saturday, as I do most of the other cutting-edge food writers and chefs of today. Chefs and cooks are increasingly understanding the roots of English cooking and it is now not so uncommon to eat English food in restaurants.

Food from far corners of the British Isles makes its way to London now and we don't have to rely on foreign imports any more if we are cooking seasonally and purely British. We still have a few pie and mash shops, which are a fine example of good-value working man's food, although many of them have closed, like the one in Kingsland Road, that has now become a Chinese restaurant. Fortunately, it now serves great Chinese food and they have sympathetically kept the old part of the shop intact, with the original benches, mirrors and mosaic floor tiles, so we can still enjoy that part of the tradition. This, for me, is an example of how London preserves its historic food traditions, because London is as much about Chinese food now as it was once about pie and mash and jellied eels. Now the two food stories still remain in one room, it almost feels like you want to order a bowl of jellied eels with your dim sum.

Whitebait suppers

We have just opened a Rivington restaurant – one of our British-style bistros, the first being in Shoreditch – in Greenwich. There we feature a whitebait supper as a part of our banquet menus, where everyone gets their food in the middle of the table and shares. This area along the Thames has a big whitebait connection. Believe it or not, whitebait suppers were held by the Commissioners of Sewers, who oversaw the engineering projects carried out in and around Dagenham after the great flood that inundated local marshland around the Thames in 1713. Breach House, built for the superintendent of works, became a regular meeting place for the commissioners, who would combine their business meeting with a spot of fishing, and eventually Breach House became a formal fishing club, holding annual whitebait suppers.

The club was apparently damaged beyond repair after a rowdy evening and, after 1812, the suppers were held at riverside inns in and around Greenwich and Blackwall, including the Old Ship Tavern and the Trafalgar Tavern.

During the summers in the 1830s, there were even hourly steamboat sailings, so that civilized gents and cabinet ministers could partake in whitebait suppers.

These annual suppers became very sophisticated and, as well as the whitebait, also featured lobster, stewed eels, a fish soup called 'water souchy', or 'souchy' (pronounced sooky), using the stray fish caught in the nets with the whitebait. The name of this soup was derived from the Dutch word *waterzooi* (a freshwater fish soup). A favourite venue for these grand suppers was Lovegrove's West India Dock Tavern, which would be frequented by politicians and special guests. The last of these grand dinners was recorded in 1894.

Whitebait, the small fry of herrings and sprats, were caught extensively in the mouth of the Thames and sometimes further up, but with the demise of the herring shoals on the east coast, they are now less common and, these days, we have to rely on frozen whitebait, which can be quite acceptable if you buy good quality.

DEEP-FRIED WHITEBAIT *serves* 4

Whitebait are usually sold frozen or recently defrosted and rarely fresh, as they are so perishable. As a young man, working in a pub kitchen in West Bay, I was brought whitebait freshly landed by local fishermen, which I ended up freezing anyway. We've come to live with frozen whitebait, and they still make a perfect comforting starter and snack.

  vegetable oil, for deep-frying

  100g flour

  sea salt

  good pinch of cayenne pepper

  400g frozen whitebait, defrosted

  100ml milk

  lemon wedges, to serve

  tartare sauce, to serve

Preheat about 8cm of oil to 160-180°C in a large heavy-based saucepan or electric deep-fat fryer.

Mix the flour with a pinch of salt and the cayenne pepper. Dust the whitebait in the flour, shake off excess and dip briefly in the milk, then back in the flour. Ensure they are all well coated and shake off excess flour again.

Fry the fish in 2 or 3 batches, depending on how many you're cooking, for 3–4 minutes each batch, until crisp. Drain on to kitchen paper and season with sea salt.

Serve immediately with lemon wedges and tartare sauce.

Fish and chips

Why, you may ask, have fish and chips got a spot in the London section of a modern regional food book? You're absolutely right in thinking that our once-favourite takeaway is available all over the British Isles, which it is. However, it was originally a regional food in the working-class areas of the North and London.

Although London had its own kind of food and pies, and 'cook shops' in the Middle Ages, it wasn't until the nineteenth century that fried fish hit the streets, initially without chips. Fish sellers and fried fish shops were all over London in the middle of that century, as there was an abundance of fish available from the fleets working the North Sea. Barking was then an active fishing port, supplying London, and fish like plaice had become so common, and no longer a delicacy, that it would often get tossed back overboard, along with haddock and whiting. Between 1799 and 1823, the supply of North Sea fish reaching Billingsgate Market had increased from 2,500 tonnes to 12,000 tonnes, not including the 500 million oysters brought up from the Essex and Kent coasts.

The freshest fish would get sold immediately and the not-so-fresh would get battered and fried to try to disguise the inferior taste and texture. Deep-frying, as we know it in chippies now, didn't exist then, so the fish would be fried in shallow pans and served occasionally with baked potatoes.

This, incidentally, was around the time of the birth of the baked potato trade; they would be parboiled and

taken to local bakers and then sold on the streets from a kind of four-legged charcoal burner. There was a famous baked potato stall in Shoreditch, which was brass-mounted with German silver, and lamps attached with coloured glass. The potatoes would get served with just butter and salt.

As this way of eating fish became popular, so the fish frying trade developed and, by the mid-1800s, there were around 300 fish fryers in the city. The fried fish would still not have been as we know it now. Fish like dab and sole would be fried whole in a flour-and-water mixture, then just pan-fried in oil. Fish fryers would also trade outside taverns crying 'fish and bread a penny' with painted boxes strung around their necks and fish wrapped in newspaper. These fish sellers would live in communities of their own and garrets, as even the poorest classes objected to taking them in as lodgers, because of the odours of fish and frying.

Between the mid-1800s and 1900, fish shops started opening, some selling just fish and fried unpeeled potatoes, which would be crudely prepared, roughly sliced – even chipped – or, in some cases, small whole potatoes. A Mr Teutten was one of the key figures in the development of chip frying at this time, as he set up a frying range business near Billingsgate in 1869.

One of the earliest recorded proper fish and chip shops with a traceable history was Malins of Old Ford Road in Bow in the East End, which moved a couple of times in its long history, from Cleveland Way and Goldsmiths Row. The family that ran it were originally from Cornwall and the business was thought to have started around 1860. As recently as 1965, they received a plaque from the *Fish Friers Review* and Friers Federation, in recognition of their being the oldest fish and chip shop in the world.

There was, of course, some disgruntlement from some of the Northern fish fryers, who claim to have similar long-standing businesses. Malins has now sadly been scooped up by a larger company, some sort of franchise operation, and is not what you can call a real fish and chip shop any more.

There are a few good examples of quality old-fashioned fish and chip shops still left in London, one of which is Faulkner's in Kingsland Road and the other the Two Brothers in Regents Park Road in Finchley. Sadly, most of the old fish and chip shops have lost their way and have surrendered old tradition to serving fast-food items that have nothing to do with what they were originally all about.

There is, though, a resurgence of modern fish and chip shops, which have the qualities of the old style with a few modern twists, for example frying only in groundnut oil for a healthier product, so keep your eyes open as the real thing may be back on the high street.

Eels, pies and mash

Londoners have always enjoyed eels, as they were once a regular catch in the Thames. They are still there and I have caught many on experimental fishing trips for other species up and down the Thames. They have traditionally been prepared and sold in three different ways, although the eel pie is rarely seen these days.

Eel Pie Island is down near Richmond on the Thames and, back in the mid-1800s, was once a popular place for fairs, picnics and parties. Eel pies were so popular then that the island was named after them. These pies would be made with eels, butter, sherry, parsley and lemon, and covered in puff pastry. I think they need a bit of a revival.

Jellied eels are either loved or loathed, and if you're not an Eastender you may well not appreciate them. They have the appeal of something like tripe, I suppose, and a similar texture, and I love both. Jellied eels would be sold at fish stalls outside pubs in the East End and you do occasionally see this old tradition, except many of them sell imitation fish these days, like crab sticks and prawn shapes, which are quite disgusting and badly let down the old tradition.

Eel shops do still exist but, sadly, their numbers are dwindling rapidly, and the best preserved one of all in the Kingsland Road, Hackney, that was the original F. Cooke, is now a Chinese restaurant, although thanks to English Heritage they have kept the lovely interior, including mirrors with eels carved into the frames and beautiful mosaic tiles on the floor. It always feels odd, sitting at the same old wooden benches and marble tables from which people used to eat their pie and mash.

The remaining F. Cooke in Hoxton Street, has been in Joe Cook's family for 80 years and things haven't changed there, except perhaps for the range of canned drinks on offer. There is something wonderfully comforting about a steaming plate of hot eels with mash and liquor, or one of their crisp homemade pies with the same mash and liquor. You wouldn't want to get on the wrong side of Joe's wife Kim, I'll tell you, whether you are staff or a customer. I've been there a couple of times with Ellie and Lydia, and they are as well behaved there as I've ever seen them in restaurants.

In the good old days, you would see the eels swimming in tanks, ready for the chop, these days, sadly no more. The eel and pie shop is a great formula, but as times move on, I can't see the younger generation keeping the eel business alive.

London clubs

If you walk around Pall Mall and St James's, you will only be subconsciously aware you are walking amongst buildings that are a major part of London's culture. There are no signs inviting you in or even saying what the buildings are. Occasionally you may spot a doorman holding a door open for someone leaving one of these discreet establishments. These are the gentleman's clubs of London. You can't enter them unless you are invited by a member and if you try to get a membership, you could well be on the waiting list for the rest of your life.

Inns have existed in London for the last two thousand years or so, and we can assume they existed in some form or other long before that. Coffee houses, believe it or not, appeared in the middle of the 1600s and the best known was owned by a Turkey merchant named Mr Edwards, in 1652, who had brought his Ragusan servant with him from Smyrna to make coffee for him every morning. This was such a hit with Edwards' friends that he set up his servant, Pasqua Rosee in a coffee house in St Michael's Alley, Cornhill. As well as being a popular beverage, coffee was regarded as a cure for dropsy, gout and scurvy, and, as Rosee said, 'it will prevent drowsiness and make one fit for business'.

It cost a penny to go into a coffee house, and the behaviour rules were stricter than those for taverns. Coffee induced conversation rather than drunkenness, snacks like mutton pies were on sale and newspapers were provided. Some coffee houses were not 'dry', however; Garraways was famous for its Champagne and its anchovy toasts, as well as being said to be the first such establishment to sell tea. Within fifty years, there were almost three thousand coffee houses in London.

As time went on, particular coffee houses began to be frequented by gentlemen with common interests and they became like clubs. Some began attracting certain professions, like Jonathan's for stock jobbers, Truby's for clergymen, the St James and the Smyrna for Whig politicians, and the Cocoa Tree for Tories. The city-based ones were for businessmen, the Fleet Street and Long Acre ones for lawyers and artists, and St James's for the political and social. This led to the formation of gentleman's clubs as we know them today.

Records show Whites, which started as a chocolate house, is the oldest of the actual London gentleman's clubs, founded around 1736. Its founder was Franciso Bianco, who was apparently a man of great taste for people, food and drink. These original clubs set the scene

in the nineteenth century for more specific clubs for certain types of clientele, and the Duke of Wellington was a great supporter, and founder member of most of them.

One club that has a claim to fame in the culinary arena was the Reform Club, and Alexis Soyer was its chef in 1837. He was the original celebrity chef and achieved much acclaim in and out of the club. In June 1838, he rose to the challenge of cooking breakfast for 2,000 people for Queen Victoria's coronation. He designed the kitchens for what was to become the new Reform Club and installed gas ovens, which became a bit of a tourist attraction. Soyer dressed in a non-cheffy way in his kitchens; instead, his work attire was tailor-made, with large lapels and cuffs, and he sported a red velvet chef's hat.

He got involved in various charities, like that to send relief to Ireland during the Great Potato Famine in 1847. He set up soup kitchens and claimed he could provide 100 gallons of soup for a pound, including expenses. He also worked with Florence Nightingale in the Crimea during the war there; designing his own field stove, called the Soyer Stove, which remained in use with the British Army until the early twentieth century.

Soyer was also a great cookery writer and the Elizabeth David of his day. He published *The Gastronomic Regenerator, a simplified and new system of cookery*, which sold 2,000 copies at a guinea each. The book contained the first mention in English of a 'flan', as in an open tart, and contained his invention of what we now know as Cumberland sauce, to go with boar's head. He also published *Soyer's Charitable Cookery*, inspired by his work during the Irish famine, the proceeds of which were all donated to charities. His wife Elizabeth Jones, an artist, sadly died at the very young age of 29 – she was distressed by a thunderstorm, miscarried and died. Aware there was also hunger in London, he later exhibited his late wife's works as Soyer's Philanthropic Gallery, to raise funds for the Spitalfields Soup Kitchen - which, incidentally, was recently converted into flats and I went to look at one there when I was flat-hunting.

By this time, Soyer had left the Reform and gone into business on his own. He invented a 'magic spirit' stove, small enough to cook dishes at the table, and would demonstrate this daily to audiences at his Charing Cross offices. Soyer went on to write many more successful cookbooks, which I've been collecting over the years and I even have several first editions dating back to the early 1800s … nice to have and a piece of London history.

LAMB CUTLETS REFORM *serves* 4

I haven't cooked this dish since my college days, when it was part of the City and Guilds curriculum, and you rarely see it in cookbooks any more. Alexis Soyer invented this dish at the Reform Club in the 1830s. Like many of the old classics, this dish was from a range of ingredients at hand at the time. My theory is that, rather like the Caesar salad, those were the ingredients left in the cold room, and the dish was concocted, perhaps, for a special guest or member; otherwise, who would put lamb, beetroot, egg white, truffle, tongue and beetroot together?

OK, the dish is not strictly British, but it was invented for the British gentry. Most recipes show the garnish in the sauce, but it is probably not a bad idea to serve it as a kind of salad garnish and let your guests do what they want with it.

60–70g fresh white breadcrumbs

50g cooked ham, very finely chopped

1 tablespoon chopped parsley

salt and freshly ground black pepper

8 lamb cutlets, French-trimmed and flattened slightly

2 eggs, beaten

vegetable oil, for frying

good knob of butter

for the sauce

2 large shallots, finely chopped

½ garlic clove, crushed

good pinch of cayenne pepper

60g butter

2 teaspoons flour

½ teaspoon tomato paste

2 tablespoons tarragon vinegar

1 tablespoon redcurrant jelly

300ml beef stock (or half a good-quality stock cube dissolved in that amount of boiling water)

40g sliced tongue or ham, cut into thin 3cm strips

1 small cooked beetroot, about 70g, peeled and cut into similar-sized strips

2 large gherkins, cut into similar-sized strips

white of 1 large hardboiled egg, shredded into similar-sized strips

First make the sauce: gently cook the shallots, garlic and cayenne pepper in half the butter for 2–3 minutes, stirring every so often. Add the flour and tomato paste, and stir well. Add the vinegar and redcurrant jelly, and simmer for a minute, then gradually add the stock, bring to the boil and simmer very gently for 15 minutes. Season to taste and whisk in the remaining butter.

While the sauce is simmering, mix the breadcrumbs with the ham and parsley. Season the lamb cutlets and pass them through the egg and then the breadcrumbs. Heat a couple of tablespoons of the vegetable oil in a frying pan over a medium heat and cook the cutlets for 3–4 minutes on each side until golden, adding the butter towards the end of cooking.

To serve, add the shredded tongue, beetroot, gherkin and egg white to the sauce, or mix and serve separately.

LONDON PARTICULAR *serves 4–6*

This thick and warming soup was given its name by Charles Dickens and referenced in *Bleak House* as 'London Particular', referring to the brown 'fog' from the factories that often used to form a blanket around London, a 'pea souper'. This could well have been the type of soup that Soyer fed the poor in his Spitalfields soup kitchen, although he may have left out the ham.

I find the most economical way to make this soup is to use the stock from a home-cooked ham or ham hock. You then get two or more meals out of it for the cost of a few dried peas. I went in search of dried green peas and they're not as easy to get your hands on these days as you might think. I tried three multiples and several Turkish shops in my part of town, which sell every pulse you can imagine – but not dried green peas. I ended up in an Indian butchers and found tiny dried whole green peas, like petit pois. I bought up his stock, as I didn't want to go through the same saga again. Hopefully, you won't have this problem, but do buy them next time you see them, just in case.

30g butter

1 onion, roughly chopped

a few sprigs of thyme

250g green split peas, or whole ones, soaked overnight in cold water

1.5 litres ham stock, plus a few pieces of the leftover ham meat

salt and freshly ground black pepper

Melt the butter in a heavy-based pan and gently cook the onion for a few minutes until soft, without allowing it to colour. Add the thyme, drained peas and ham stock, checking it's not too salty; if it is, replace some of it with water. Bring to the boil, skim and add some pepper, then simmer for 1 hour. The peas should be soft and beginning to fall apart; if not, simmer for a little longer (you may have to top up with more stock or water as necessary). Cooking times can vary, depending on the peas.

Once they're cooked, blend the soup in a liquidizer or with a stick blender as coarsely or as smoothly as you wish; and add a little water if it is too thick, or simmer for a little longer if too thin. Taste and season again, if necessary. Shred some of the cooked ham trimmings, add to the soup and simmer a minute or so longer before serving.

BOILED SALT BEEF WITH CARROTS AND DUMPLINGS *serves* 4

This dish was a great favourite in London pubs, taverns and eating houses: many old London music hall songs refer to boiled beef and carrots, and it is still one of the city's best dishes. We often serve it on the menu in our restaurants, as it is actually very light. It can be made with other vegetables, like young leeks and turnips, and small onions, according to what's in season.

Salt beef usually comes as brisket or silverside, and is often prepacked in supermarkets, complete with cooking instructions. Don't worry about buying too much; it makes great sandwiches, with dill pickles and mustard served on some soft rye bread, or in a warm bagel. The dumplings can also be adapted to suit; caraway can be added instead of horseradish, or just lots of fresh herbs.

1kg salted silverside or brisket, soaked overnight in cold water

4 small onions, each about 80–100g, peeled

12 young carrots, trimmed and scraped

10 black peppercorns

a few sprigs of thyme

2 cloves

2 blades of mace

1 bay leaf

for the horseradish dumplings

125g plain flour, sieved

1 teaspoon baking powder

½ teaspoon salt

65g shredded beef suet

1 tablespoon chopped parsley

1 tablespoon freshly grated horseradish

Drain the beef and rinse in cold water, then put in a large pan with the vegetables and flavourings. Cover with water to about 5-6cm above the beef and bring to the boil. Skim and simmer gently, covered, for 30 minutes.

Remove the carrots and put to one side. Simmer for another 30 minutes, or until the onions are cooked, remove them and put with the carrots. Continue cooking the beef for an hour or so. Cooking times will vary depending on the size of the beef; if it's prepacked, cooking times will normally be given. When the beef is cooked, remove it from the pan and keep warm.

While the beef is cooking, make the dumplings: mix all the ingredients together with enough cold water to form a sticky dough. Flour your hands and roll the dough into 12 little balls. When the cooked beef has been removed from the pan, remove some of the cooking liquid and poach the dumplings in it for 10 minutes, then remove them, put to one side and discard the liquid.

Simmer the rest of the meat cooking liquor until reduced by about half, or until it has a good strong flavour and skim off any fat. It probably won't need seasoning, as a lot of salt will have come out of the beef.

To serve, reheat the vegetables and dumplings in the reduced liquid. Slice the beef and arrange in a deep plate with the dumplings and veg, and spoon over the liquid.

Neal's Yard Dairy

Neal's Yard Dairy in Neal Street, Covent Garden, has become the temple of British cheeses for both customers and cheese-makers. If you want to buy British cheese – and taste it before you buy – then there's no question that this is the place to go. It has charm and character… and rather a lot of cheese, the best in the British Isles, and staff who know what they are talking about. Our individual cheese boards in our restaurants generally feature three regional cheeses from there, unless I find something that Randolph Hodgson hasn't quite got to yet.

In the late 1970s, after finishing a degree in food science, Randolph got a summer job at a whole food shop in the original Neal's Yard, with its creator Nicholas Saunders, helping make cheese. Neal's Yard then was like a mini farmers' market, with a bakery and greengrocer Fred Baker, who used to push a cart round and pitch up outside Bar Italia every day. The dairy made goats' cheese and curd, and other soft cheeses, crème fraîche and yoghurt.

Nicholas wanted to continue the business, but wasn't interested in running it, so Randolph volunteered to take it on, but had no money. Nicholas put up a few grand for Randolph to get started, and let Randolph just get on with running the business. Randolph initially just sold the cheeses they made on site, then thought he'd experiment by buying in a few farmhouse cheeses, like Hilary Charnley's Devon Garland, but he was still not that well informed with regard to storing and maturing other people's cheeses. He would often visit Alberto at nearby Fratelli Camisa, the famed Italian deli, and rather took a

liking to the Duckett's Caerphilly he used to stock. He bought a few off Alberto for the shop and couldn't get to grips with maturing the cheese, so Alberto let him into a little secret of storing it in a cardboard box, dampened with water every so often.

Randolph began travelling the country in his Citroen 2CV, seeking out small cheese-makers, like Mrs Longstaff, who had only two cows and made only one cheese a day. They, in return, would lead him to the next cheese-maker, and so his repertoire and product list grew. As the business developed in the mid-1980s, he took on a partner, Jane Scotter, who played a big part in developing the business and allowing them to source new cheeses.

He remembers James Aldridge (see page 41) coming into the shop on a regular basis before he got to know him. Aldridge would walk around the shop scribbling the names and addresses of the cheeses on his note pad for investigation and experimentation. This is, of course, where Aldridge got the idea for his washed Duckett's Caerphilly that transformed into his famous Tornegus.

A family chocolate-making business in Shorts Gardens came on the market in 1992. Quickly, Randolph moved in so he could get more than four customers through the door at a time, and have enough room to get a few more of his carefully sourced cheeses on the shelves. He invited some cheese-makers down for the opening and, for some, like Ruth Kirkham, it was their first visit to the big city.

The shop soon got a reputation in and around London for British farmhouse cheeses, and chefs would come in and hand-select cheeses in peak condition for their cheese boards, thus further helping promote our country's fine cheese-makers. Jane left the business in the mid-1990s to move to Fern Verrow Farm in Herefordshire, where she grows organic fruits and vegetables, and rears rare-breed cattle, sheep and poultry. She also is a regular face at Borough Market, and her stall is not to be missed.

Randolph's stock soon outgrew the Shorts Gardens site and he bought another shop in Borough Market in 1998, where he could both mature and sell cheeses. Both shops sell artisan biscuits, chutneys and everything else you could think of to go with cheese.

I've come across many cheese-makers who've been put on the map by Randolph, and it's not always about getting prizes; it's about getting your cheese into the public's homes. If places like Neal's Yard and Patricia Michelson's La Fromagerie in Marylebone didn't exist, we'd all still be buying prepacked cheeses from shops and supermarkets.

Borough Market

If you live in London and enjoy good food, you needn't go anywhere else to shop than Borough Market. There are some who will disagree, and tell you it's overpriced and pretentious, but how else can Londoners access a small-time artisan producer coming all the way from Cumbria, or Co Kerry once a week to compete with the multiples. Markets are very much where food shopping is at now – the biggest change since the revolution of the supermarkets in the 1970s and '80s saw a real shift away from local markets. What's great about Borough, and other farmers' markets, is that you can talk to the producer while he or she wraps up your purchase, and you just can't get that level of service or product information in a supermarket.

Its previous life was as a wholesale fruit and veg market, which took a bit of a downturn with competition from New Covent Garden and Spitalfields. The Market began to take on a new look when Randolph Hodgson opened his second Neal's Yard Dairy there in 1986 and Ken Greig's company, Greig and Stephenson won an architectural competition to renew the old market.

In addition, Henrietta Green brought her Food Lovers' Fair to the market in 1998, with only half a dozen stalls, including Cumbria's Peter Gott (see page 140), who persuaded other traders to join the market. Indeed, many of the successful ones would have initially shared a corner of Peter's stand just to get a foot in the door.

These guys, along with George Nicholson, chairman of the market until 2006, were the driving force behind its success today. Borough has been voted the best food market in the country and, during the time it has taken me to write this book, the market has almost completed the first phase of its upgrade. It now hosts a restaurant, Roast, on the first floor of the reconstructed floral hall, featuring the facade from the original Covent Garden Market, bought for a quid.

Apart from the market stallholders, some of whom travel long distances on a weekly basis, new businesses are moving in, like Ben Wright and Robin Hancock, London's premier oyster sellers (see page 60). When I was in Kerry last summer, I came across Tim and Bronwyn Youard of the Derreensillagh Smokehouse in Caherdaniel (see page 219), good old-fashioned smokers. Then they spent their week smoking salmon and doing the local Kerry markets, so I suggested Borough. I had a call some weeks later from Tim saying that they were on their way over with a van full of salmon. We have it on the menu in the restaurants now and the Wright Brothers oysters, too, and that's how people get into – and should get into – the market.

Tony Booth is one of Boroughs 'characters'. He is one of our suppliers for the restaurants and specializes in wild mushrooms from around the world. At any one time, he'll have at least half a dozen wild varieties, as well as black and white truffles in season. He sources well from British producers, like Clive Ovenden (see page 34) and Peter Ashcroft (see page 132), and gets hop shoots from Kent.

Borough is an important part of London food culture and London life, and helping change the way we shop.

Wild mushrooms in London

For the last twenty years, I've been picking wild mushrooms in London. I first gathered them on Wimbledon Common when I worked at The Dorchester and was tempted by the Italian waiters bringing us baskets of porcini. Then I moved on to Epping Forest, near where I lived for several years. London isn't the obvious place to pick wild mushrooms, but we're surrounded by woods, so why not? Even Hampstead Heath is a good source of ceps and chanterelles, if you know where to look.

Mushroom picking is so unpredictable and the fact that you have picked baskets full of trompettes-de-la-mort one year in a certain spot doesn't mean you'll find one within miles of that same spot the following year. Sometimes it's not even that the Polish or Italian pickers have been out before you, because they will often concentrate on one or two types of mushroom that we may ignore, like honey fungus, which needs blanching in water before cooking to get rid of impurities.

These days you have to be up early to get them because of the increasingly popular pastime of mushroom foraging. If you've read through the rest of the book, you may well think I just go out and seek free food, whatever county I'm in. Well, you're not far from the truth, and why not? If there is food for free to be had, then take advantage of it. We pay over £20 a kilo in the restaurants for good ceps and those from Epping don't cost a penny – they are a gift of nature,

although you do need a licence from the ranger's office, or you may be banned from free food foraging for life.

I introduced a work colleague, Andy Kress and his wife Jane, who was our pastry chef at Le Caprice, to mushroom picking some 12 years or so ago, and they are now fanatics. They go mushrooming more than I do, and occasionally bring me a token of their successful day to remind me that I haven't been and I need to get myself into the woods. Andy did get me hooked on fly fishing in return and I seem to fly fish a little more than him these days.

Once you are confident about what you're picking, then you may well harvest five or six varieties in a day. There are a couple of books I use as 'bibles': *Mushrooms and other Fungi of Great Britain and Europe* by Roger Philips, who also wrote *Wild Food*, an equally inspiring book, and Peter Jordan's *Mushroom Picker's Foolproof Field Guide*. Jordan also sells a set of handy identification cards that you can carry around in your pocket.

There is something relaxing about spending a couple of hours on a crisp morning trying to focus on fungi that are well camouflaged in amongst the woodland leaves. You can get the kids involved and occasionally invite reliable mates along, but be careful, as they are likely to return secretly without you. There is nothing better than fresh forest mushrooms on toast or with scrambled eggs for brunch after a morning's foraging.

Andrew Casson's East End Honey

A jar of honey arrived on my desk one morning from one of my colleagues and fellow mushroom foragers, Andy Kress. He gave me a brief rundown on the contents of the jar of clear honey, labelled East End Honey. I got in touch with its producer, Andrew Casson over in Romford, and the honey quickly got itself on the shelf in the Rivington Deli and on the restaurant menu, drizzled over drop scones with Dorset blueberries.

This may seem an unusual subject to put in the London chapter, but there are actually several people in and around London producing honey these days, and they have been for some time. Andrew got interested 8 or 9 years ago, when he was teaching kids in Newham City Farm what real food is all about, and in the case of something like honey, how it gets into the jar. Andrew found the honey-making process a great part of the education of how food was made from start to finish, and probably easier for the kids to digest than wringing a chicken's neck.

Andrew discovered that his gran, who lived in Cumbria, was a keen beekeeper, so there was certainly some honey in the family blood. He left the farm and joined the Romford Bee Keeping Association, bought some hives and located them in Becontree near Barking and some near Hainault. He says that the surrounding railway tracks are good unspoilt spots for wild flowers and berries, and the bees can collect a wide variety of nectars from fruit trees and flowers in gardens and allotments. Andrew will produce about 40kg of honey per hive during the summer, with up to 50,000 bees living and working in one colony (hive) during the summer.

His honey is light in colour, but changes over the year, depending on what's flowering. Bees really get to work when the temperature gets up to about 10°C, which can occur as early as March these days. It's something you don't really even consider, bees out that early in the year collecting nectar to start the honey-making process.

Berkshire   *Buckinghamshire*   *Hampshire*

Kent   Oxfordshire   Surrey   Sussex

THE
SOUTH

K ENT–'THE GARDEN OF ENGLAND'– probably has the proudest culinary history in the region, with hops having been grown there for centuries. The county is also home to several vineyards and is an important supplier of much of Britain's fruit, particularly apples, pears and soft fruits. The National Fruit Collections are housed at Brogdale Farm, Faversham, and farm shops and pick-your-owns are everywhere. Sheep have grazed on the salty Romney Marshes for centuries and a rich variety of seafood is landed off South East shores, including delicious Dover sole and Whitstable oysters. Hampshire is known for its strawberries, watercress, lavender and fine pigs. The New Forest is an important source of furred and feathered game, as well as wild mushrooms. Regional food is less apparent in the affluent Home Counties, but this area has become home to many thriving English vineyards. Cheese-making in Kent is pretty non-existent, but move further west into East and West Sussex and you will find some excellent goats'-, sheep's- and cows'-milk cheeses.

As well as being such a centre for cultivated fruit and vegetables, the South is also a paradise for those, like me, whose passion is foraging for wild vegetables, herbs and fungi for free. With all that's available here in this respect, and the rich abundance of fine seafood, a man could live like a king on next to nothing, providing, of course, he had enough pennies for the occasional glass of the local beers made from Kentish hops and the ever-improving wines.

Whitstable oysters

Whitstable is one of the most obvious and closest seaside destinations for Londoners, and I make regular visits there, not just for the town's charm but also for its oysters. On the way through the town, you will pass a piece of history, the original Wheelers oyster bar, with its pink façade and an ever-inviting quaintness. It feels like it is run pretty much as it may have been back in the late 1800s.

It was opened in 1856 by Richard 'Leggy' Wheeler, a skipper of a local oyster boat called Bubbles. It was later taken over by the Walsh family, who kept the Wheelers name. Their son, Bernard, who was born in one of the upstairs rooms there, went on to open a London branch in Old Compton Street in 1929. The original in Whitstable is now run by Delia Fitt, a local who reckons she's been opening oysters since she was ten years old.

Like every other oyster fishery around the country, Whitstable has suffered its oyster problems over the years. Many oyster businesses have thrived and then fallen by the wayside. During the early sixties, the Ministry of Agriculture and Fisheries began research on artificial breeding techniques for oysters, using the Pacific oyster. A team of biologists led by John Bayes was employed by the old Seasalter and Ham Oyster Fishery Company to set up a hatchery in Whitstable, and began a restocking programme for both natives and rock oysters. This proved a successful enterprise, resulting in a healthy oyster seed export market. In 1986, John Bayes bought the company, which today is big business, supplying many parts of the world.

John Bayes changed the face of oyster farming in Whitstable and is credited as the man who kept the industry going when everyone else had given up. His ramshackle beachside hatchery, situated under the Reculver Towers eight miles east of Whitstable, has provided millions of rock oyster seedlings around the world. Although these are hardier than the natives and easier to breed, he still perseveres with the natives, although only 5% survive soon after spawning, whereas rock or Pacific oysters have a much higher survival rate and mature two years earlier than the native. Natives in the wild are much more susceptible to climate conditions, as well as predators, and their survival rate is little better than a million to one.

In 1976, the Whitstable Oyster Fishery Company was bought by Barrie Green and John Knight, who had been in business for years and built up 18 DIY shops in the South East. The oyster business wasn't worth anything; in fact, it was in debt to the tune of £40,000 and had no assets apart from the derelict Royal Native Oyster Stores. The duo's only intention was to keep the Whitstable oyster tradition going, albeit just ticking over for the moment. They found boxes of company archives, handwritten manuscripts and sepia-tinted photos. Indeed, the whole history of the Whitstable oyster was just sitting there in dilapidated boxes.

Because they had other business interests, they just kept the company going as it was for a couple of years, buying oysters in from elsewhere and purifying them in the Royal Native Oyster Stores' basement. When Bill Warner, who had been running the business, finally retired, it was time to have a bit of a shake-up. They began by renovating the old fishermen's huts on the beach and renting them out at weekends (well worth a look for a potential weekend break). Barrie's sons, Richard and James then joined the company after leaving school and this was the platform to return the oyster business to its former glory.

Today the Whitstable Oyster Fishery is certainly back on track and the Royal Native Oyster Stores is a full-on fish restaurant, attracting Londoners by the carload, and Whitstable natives are certainly back on the menu. They have even set up the Whitstable Brewery, producing oyster stout and many other local brews. If you're lucky, you may just find a Whitstable Dredgerman's Breakfast, which consists of streaky bacon fried until the fat runs, with shelled oysters placed over the bacon and cooked for 3-4 minutes. The whole lot is served with thick bread and butter, and washed down with strong tea.

If you are a real oyster lover, then you should join in the Whitstable Oyster Festival in July, when there are various celebrations, from 'oyster parades' by local school kids to the 'blessing of the waters'.

Crayfish, crayfish everywhere

The mention of crayfish often throws confusion into the conversation, as most people's perception of a crayfish is the larger saltwater, lobster-like species known by the same name in many other countries and often called 'spiny lobster' or rock lobster'. Our saltwater version of the same lobster species is also called crawfish, similar in name and enough to confuse even the experts.

Small freshwater crayfish rarely reach the table, that is unless you are in the know. It's beyond me why, because they plague our rivers, ponds, lakes and gravel pits, and munch their way through anything in their path, including vegetation and fish eggs.

In the 1970s, the American signal crayfish was introduced to European farmed crayfish stock, as it was immune to a disease devastating stocks at that time. Its abilities to escape, breed and rampage our waters were totally underestimated and they have now wiped out most of our native white-clawed crayfish in the South and Midlands. They travel for miles on land, which is probably why Scotland is still slightly out of their reach, although it's only a matter of time.

As they tend to haunt crevices in the banks of rivers and streams, etc, they are largely invisible to the human eye, although they are often only feet away from us if we are near natural clean freshwater rivers, rather like rats and mice in cities. I rarely see a crayfish when I'm fishing, although most of the time I'm probably almost treading on the damned things.

I remember, when working at the Grosvenor House Hotel many years ago, every Thursday a trolley-load of the things would turn up, live and kicking, just as we were about to finish the shift and go to the pub. We had to cook, gut and shell them before we got away; good tactics on the chef's behalf, as we got them done in no time.

So why aren't we serving them in our restaurants today? Who knows? They're not cheap, although they need culling on a very regular basis to help maintain our freshwater environment. For years I had been trying to get a good reliable source of crayfish and, out of the blue, I got a call from an artist mate of mine who had a friend that had escaped the London rat race to live a quieter life on a boat in Oxfordshire, fishing for crayfish. I met up with Jamie Fawkes, weekly phone contact was made and we got crayfish on the menus in the Rivington and then in J.Sheekey. Customers were contentedly digging into bowls of steaming crayfish cooked in wheat beer from Whitstable, with chopped wild fennel picked by our wild herb guys at Foragers (see page 32).

When Jamie first arrived in Oxfordshire, he did a bit of van driving and got completely bored, and then one day bumped into a friend who had a licence to fish a stretch of the upper Thames. Soon after, he got productive and was pulling kilos of crayfish out of the water for a couple of London restaurants. Rivals smashed his traps up, but he managed to get them banned from the river and now has the 20-mile stretch all to himself.

CRAYFISH COOKED IN BEER WITH WILD FENNEL *serves 4–6*

When I was in Finland a couple of years ago, I was lucky enough to arrive in prime crayfish season. At this time of year, the Finns pay crazy money for crayfish, washed down with strong shots of aquavit. In New Orleans, I also witnessed a crayfish 'broil' up a remote part of the Mississippi, with jazz band and all.

So why shouldn't we celebrate the culling of these tiny delicacies that are overrunning our British waters? Can we convince ourselves that crayfish feasts are the way forward with a clear conscience?

For those concerned about despatching live shellfish in a humane way, the RSPCA recommend first putting them in the freezer briefly, so they go to sleep.

1.2 litres beer

1 tablespoon fennel seeds

1 tablespoon black peppercorns

1 tablespoon sea salt

2kg live crayfish

handful of wild fennel or dill, chopped

Pour the beer into a saucepan with about 600ml water. Add the fennel seeds, peppercorns and salt, bring to the boil and simmer for 10 minutes.

Add the crayfish, bring back to the boil and simmer for 3 minutes. Add the fennel and simmer for another 2 minutes, then drain and serve immediately.

WILD TROUT AND WATERCRESS *serves 4*

Last year I fished on the River Bourne near Stockbridge with chalk stream fishing guide William Daniel. While creeping around the banks, William pointed out wild watercress growing on the banks. Ironically, we were just down stream from the Vitacress factory, but this stuff on the banks was proper small-leaved wild cress and had a delicious peppery aftertaste.

4 trout, each about 250g, gutted and cleaned

salt and freshly ground black pepper

handful of fennel or dill

60g butter, melted

for the sauce

2 shallots, finely chopped

125ml fish stock (or a piece of a good-quality stock cube dissolved in that amount of water)

150g watercress, chopped

1 tablespoon double cream

150g cold butter, diced

Preheat the oven to 200°C/gas 6. Season the trout and lay in a lightly buttered ovenproof dish. Put the fennel, stalks and all, in the trout's cavity, scatter any extra over and pour the butter over the fish. Bake for 20–25 minutes.

Meanwhile, make the sauce, simmer the shallots in the stock until there are 3–4 tablespoons left. Add the watercress and cream, and simmer for a couple more minutes, stirring every so often. Remove from the heat and stir in the butter vigorously so it emulsifies. Season.

Forager

I've always been a lover of foraging for wild food and it all started with mushrooms on Wimbledon Common when I worked at the Dorchester Hotel. The Italian waiters used to bring baskets of ceps in to show us, so we thought we had better have a go.

Miles Irving used to pick mushrooms with his grandfather, who sensibly encouraged the whole family to go with him, and Miles took it one step further. He now has a company appropriately named Forager and they literally pick anything they can find that's edible, at any time of the year.

We met Miles for a coffee at The Goods Shed in Canterbury (see page 40), just next to the station, before we headed into the fields. Miles will forage in the most unexpected places and doesn't really know from one day to the next quite what he's going to find. I've often called Miles and tipped him off to a good rock samphire or sea kale (see opposite) spot when I'm at the seaside.

Our first stop was to check how many rosehips Mile's picker, Ross had collected for Richard Corrigan at Lindsay House. I was surprised they were still around in January, as I had picked some in Scotland several months

ago. They are best picked when they are just going soft, and cold weather and frosts help Miles explained, as it breaks down the fruit slightly, making them less bitter. We drove off to a large field of blackcurrant plants in search of bitter cress, chickweed and sow thistle, all of which you probably have in your gardens. Just in the hedgerow next to the car was wild chervil, which has a larger leaf than normal chervil and a more pungent flavour, but is perfect for salads, soups and chopping into a sauce.

I'd never tasted sow thistle before. It looks rather like a flattened thistle, growing really close to the ground, in clumps. Its taste tells me it is probably a member of the large family that includes chicory and dandelion. It is actually not as bitter as some of those leaves, so a sweetish dressing with a good-quality vinegar would be essential. A combination of young sow thistle, bitter cress and chickweed make a great wild salad that will knock the socks off the flimsy packet stuff in the supermarkets.

One of my favourite vegetables that Miles has introduced me to is alexanders. They are really common in the South near the coast, and you will most certainly have driven past them on the roadsides. They are a really prolific plant resembling wild fennel or angelica, with a rounded celery-like leaf. The Romans apparently introduced them from their native Mediterranean habitat, to flavour their soups and stews. The young stalks can be steamed or boiled and served just like asparagus, or they go really well with a simple grilled or fried fish.

Just as we got back to the car, Miles spotted a few clumps of velvet shank mushrooms on some dead wood. You can't miss them, as they have a bright orange cap and brown velvety stalk, and somehow they are one of the few edible mushrooms that survive the frost and snow.

We headed down to the coast to Faversham and parked in a housing estate. Alexanders lined the roadside and Miles headed for the banks of a stream. Growing just at the edge of the stream was water celery, which is rather like a cross between watercress and celery in taste, but has more of the looks of real wild watercress. Miles grabbed a bunch of wild chervil and another plant that looked almost identical. It was hemlock, which is deadly, and the only real difference was the celery-shaped stalk on the wild chervil.

On the way to the beach, we picked dittander, which is native to this part of the coast and classed as a rare plant. It has the flavour of mustard and could almost be passed off as wasabi. On the beach, we found an abundant supply of sea purslane, which can be used as a salad vegetable or pickled.

This part of the country is Mile's patch. He knows almost every square metre of the beach and countryside, although he's talking with English Nature at the moment to get an agreement to go on to protected land and get agreements with farmers to pick edible plants. As you can imagine, some of the farmers don't like letting such funny folk on their land.

So the day's foraging was a successful one, but when there are so many wild edible plants and fungi out there, it just makes sense to use them – and if you can persuade chefs to get genuine wild produce on their menus then all the better. Many wild plants have higher levels of nutrients than cultivated varieties, and you can work that out from their taste.

We headed back to The Goods Shed for a spot of lunch, including the ingredients we had just foraged, cooked by Rafael, the head chef who had also been out with us.

SAND SOLES WITH BUTTERED ALEXANDERS AND WILD GARLIC *serves* 4

This was the dish prepared for our lunch at The Goods Shed by Rafael. He cooked it perfectly, and the simple marriage of the fish and the alexanders was spot on with the delicate wild garlic. In fact, it was three-cornered garlic, which looks like a long thick blade of grass, with a delicate garlicky flavour.

You can use any type of sole for this dish, or any fish come to that, but I find the sand sole – which is of the Dover sole or common sole family, but generally about half the size of the Dover sole – perfect for it. By the way, the latter is called Dover sole purely because large amounts of the fish used to get landed in Dover, but they were not necessarily from that area. Ask your fishmonger to skin the dark side of the fish and trim the fins.

> 250-300g young alexanders stalks with the leaves removed
>
> salt and freshly ground black pepper
>
> 8 sand soles, each about 160-200g, black skin removed and fins trimmed
>
> 3 tablespoons vegetable oil
>
> 120g butter
>
> handful of three-cornered garlic or wild garlic leaves

Cut the alexanders into 8-9cm pieces and boil in salted water for 5-6 minutes, or until tender, then drain.

While the alexanders are cooking, season the soles. You will probably need to cook them in 2 or 3 batches, and then keep them just warm or reheat them when they are all cooked. Heat some vegetable oil in a (preferably) non-stick frying pan and cook the soles, skin side down first, for 3-4 minutes on each side, adding a knob of butter to the pan towards the end of cooking.

Melt the remaining butter in a pan, tear the garlic leaves into smaller pieces and cook gently in the butter for a minute or so until wilted Add the alexanders, reheat for a minute or so and season. Spoon over the soles and serve.

Clive Ovenden

The mention of Romney Marsh and Dungeness normally makes people think of the famous Derek Jarman Garden around his famous converted fisherman's shed, but food and farming in the area is much less likely to come to mind. At one time, though, the surrounding area was literally landscaped with acre upon acre of asparagus growing and arable farming. I've visited Dungeness quite often over the years to fish for bass off the beach, and very nearly once bought one of the old fisherman's sheds myself. It seemed like a good idea at the time, but close friends persuaded me not to. Reflecting back on it, I shouldn't have taken their advice, as the sheds are now worth a fortune, and it would have been a tidy little investment, even if I didn't take advantage of it as a getaway spot.

One farmer still in the area is Clive Ovenden, who is a grower in Brookland on Romney Marsh and at one time was the biggest pumpkin and squash grower in the country. Tony Booth at Borough Market (see page 21) put me on to him. Clive's family were arable farmers on Old Hall Farm and when Clive took over, he got into supplying supermarkets with what were then unusual vegetables, like courgettes, squashes and broccoli. He soon gave up on supplying the multiples for the same reason as most farmers do: that producers just can't survive on the prices supermarket chains want to pay for well-grown produce.

Clive and Deborah Ovenden are now New-Age farmers, if that's the correct term to use for growers staying ahead of the times and, in their case, sometimes being too far ahead of them. Over the years, they have experimented with small amounts of every vegetable you can imagine, and it seems now that the vegetables that were not in vogue a few years back have taken their turn and are making a comeback. Good old British vegetables like sprouting broccoli, beetroot, salsify and brassicas are back in vogue. Most chefs don't want mini vegetables at extortionate prices any more; they want to cook vegetables that people can taste and not just admire on the plate. For Clive and Deborah, it's difficult to know from year to year just what chefs are going to want, and the same is true of the general public come to that, as chefs tend to set the trends for the public with their writing in food magazines and columns, and TV appearances.

After a two-hour chat in their living room, we really put the world to rights, and I take my hat off to them as they have planted and grown nearly every seed in the

book, so much so that they are now going abroad as far as the USA for their seeds. Music to my ears was when Clive mentioned planting tayberries and loganberries for this year, fruits that everyone else seems to have given up on. He is now taking this bold move one step further and growing the even more obscure joster berries, tummel berries and boysenberries.

When I mentioned what everyone was after these days, they had tried it years ago, and good old sprouting broccoli and Pink Fir Apple potatoes were out of favour with them and would just get dug back into the ground. Clive really didn't believe me when I told him sprout tops were in and I found it hard to believe how much salsify he sold. One of the vegetables we use most from Clive is beetroot, not just the red, but white, golden, elongated and striped, which takes the beetroot into a new era.

'Organic' is not in the Ovenden's vocabulary, but they grow everything with no sprays and rotate the numerous crops annually to avoid disease, and to keep their naturally well-irrigated and fertile marshland in peak condition. A lot of their 200 acres on Romney Marsh is conservation land and they actually only grow on 70 acres of it, which means that the wildlife does the dirty work for them, keeping pests down with the help of an abundance of ladybirds and natural pest predators, like birds and game birds. Crops that are over-the-top, like pumpkins and squashes, just get left so that invites birds on to the land, not just for lunch but to continue the natural ecology cycle. They don't even use irrigation or greenhouses, except to bring on young plants, as the land is a natural source of moisture, which encourages the roots to grow deep into the ground and away from predators and disease.

PUMPKIN SOUP *serves* 4-6

Pumpkins and squashes are underused in the kitchen, perhaps because of their relationship with the 'old-fashioned' marrow, or their unusual shape that can make them seem daunting to tackle. There are hundreds of varieties and butternut squash is probably the most consistent of all; it has a deep orange flesh and is a manageable size for domestic use.

1 small leek, roughly chopped

1 small onion, roughly chopped

30g root ginger, finely chopped

a few sprigs of thyme

a good knob of butter

1 kg ripe yellow pumpkin or butternut squash, peeled, deseeded and roughly chopped

1.5 litres vegetable stock (or a couple of good-quality stock cubes dissolved in that amount of water)

salt and freshly ground black pepper

1 tablespoon chopped parsley

2 tablespoons toasted pumpkin seeds

In a large heavy-based pan, gently cook the leek, onion, ginger and thyme in the butter until soft.

Add the pumpkin and stock, bring to the boil, season with salt and pepper, then simmer for 20 minutes.

Blend in a liquidizer until smooth, then strain through a fine sieve. Add the parsley, reheat and adjust the consistency with a little vegetable stock or water if necessary, and season again with salt and pepper. Serve scattered with the toasted pumpkin seeds.

CLIVE OVENDEN AND CHILDREN, from left to right: Sophie 10, Zoe 13, Ryan 8 and dad. The children set up their own egg selling operation, using a wide range of chicken breeds, at the local farmers' market, which is now a rapidly expanding operation.

Food Fore Thought

Sheep have been farmed on the Kentish Downs since ancient times, but along the coast, the drained Romney Marshes produce very special animals with great eating qualities. These large animals are hardy enough to withstand the cold easterly winds that blow in from the sea and because they graze on the salty marshes, their meat has an unmatchable flavour.

Traditionally, lowland sheep would have had their tails docked, so a lambs' tail pie would have been a traditional Kentish dish, and commonplace on the dinner table. It would have been a seasonal dish, only made at lambing time, because the meat had to be fresh. The tails were skinned and cut like oxtail, and cooked with local root vegetables, then the whole was packed into a pie dish, together with green peas and sliced hard-boiled eggs, and occasionally mint or parsley.

If you visit some of London's farmers' markets, you may well have come across the bubbly Todd Cameron of Food Fore Thought. I suppose a market scenario in a car park in Marylebone hasn't quite got the appeal of Todd and his partner, Mason Palmer's 735 acres of National Trust land in Winchelsea, on the edge of Romney Marsh.

Saltmarsh lamb is always tempting and, when you see Todd's Llwyn/Hampshire cross-breeds peacefully grazing on the marsh, you will realize the appeal of such a natural way of breeding lamb. But the proof is in the eating and, as well as selling Llwyn/ Hampshire Down cross-breed lamb, Blonde d'Aquitaine bull crossed with Aberdeen Angus beef and Berkshire pig meat, you can actually get it cooked for you on the stand as a little taster to convince you before you buy.

Todd and Mason are both from farming backgrounds and met when working for the Country Landowners' Association, immediately hit it off and decided to set up in business. Todd had been involved in a couple of business ventures before which didn't quite work out, so he was hungry to make a go of it and get it right.

They have about 2,000 Llwyn/Hampshire Down crossed lambs, which spend their first three months on the rich marshland, then they go off up to the derelict Greyfriars Monastery in Winchelsea to feed on wild herbs from what was the monks' herb garden. This is what makes the meat really special and, unlike the traditional Romney Marsh lamb, these have a much better meat-to-bone ratio.

Food Fore Thought is Soil Association-registered and their lamb and beef are certified organic. In springtime, I may be persuading Todd to lop a few tails off, so we can get that traditional Kentish dish on the menu.

Gulls' eggs

Most delicacies are of the simplest form, from caviar to foie gras and asparagus, and a boiled lobster with good mayonnaise. The word 'delicacy' is sometimes misused, or misunderstood, and it may take a trained palate to differentiate between delicacy and a luxury food.

Gulls' eggs are one of the rarer and least known of delicacies, and the mention of gulls' eggs as a starter normally puts even discerning diners off, but it turns on those that know the eggs. A boiled egg from a battery chicken, with little or no flavour, never gets a reaction! But a gull's egg or two, well that's just indulgence.

Until the Second World War, eggs of all sorts of wild birds were consumed and considered delicacies. Then protection laws were enforced and these days only the eggs of the black-headed gull are collected, and even licences to gather these are few and far between.

The season lasts only a month, usually during late April and May, and you will see them on very few restaurant menus – mainly in London, and mostly in the Pall Mall Gentleman's clubs at that.

So, what's with eating gulls' eggs then? When I'm down in Dorset, talking to local fishermen at the bar, gulls' eggs and the like will come up in conversation, and I'm sure they think I'm nuts. It is not as easy as nicking ordinary seagulls' eggs, as the blackheaded are not your ordinary gulls and, what's more, by law the gathering of eggs is only permitted until 9.30am on weekdays and 11.30am at weekends. The early eggs are eagerly sought after and can fetch up to £2.50 each in London by the time we get them – twice that for a scallop, for God's sake!

The Solent has the biggest nesting colony on the south coast, home to around 60,000 pairs of birds and, on a good day, collectors will harvest at least 1,000 eggs and get them to London pretty sharpish.

Boiled for about 7–8 minutes, served with some good mayonnaise – made with some English and Dijon mustard – the only other thing they need is some homemade celery salt (see page 168). Generally, they are served on cut cress, or they come in a basket and you just get charged for how many you've eaten.

The Goods Shed

Farmers' markets are popping up all over the country and a small percentage of the public are going back to buying from local markets and supporting our growers and farmers instead of boosting supermarket profits.

The advantage of a supermarket is that you can get anything at any time of the day, and virtually all the year round. What you gain in convenience and uniformity in size you completely loose in flavour. Fair enough, but do you really want to buy melons and tomatoes that have been imported for pennies and which then sat in a warehouse for months on end waiting to ripen so that huge mark-ups could be charged when they are in demand? The answer is, of course, no. We would prefer to support our own growers and farmers, and put tasty produce from a good source in our baskets. We would also like to know that the farmer will get back a good percentage of the final selling price.

Selling local produce with a conscience is what Susanna Atkins is doing at The Goods Shed, Canterbury. Her father is a local farmer who was after a more effective way to sell farm produce. They thought that a permanent local farmers' market would be the answer, so went after the disused Victorian goods shed next to the station, which had been empty for 20 years. Susanna reckons there's one in every town, just waiting for this to happen.

In mid-2002, The Goods Shed opened as a farmers' market and it has developed from housing individual traders to what is now a mixture of permanent traders and a large central fruit and vegetable table. Local growers (including Miles Irving's foraged wild food, see page 32) bring in their produce and what is sold is tallied up at the end of the day, or bought and used in The Goods Shed restaurant. Susanna explains that this way the growers get back 80p in the pound, so everyone wins.

Just to put customers' minds at ease that they are getting a good deal, there is a price comparison chart with high street supermarkets and when I was there only one item came out as a couple of pence more per kilo.

In The Goods Shed you will find local traders like fishmongers Standard Quay Fisheries from Faversham and a great cheesemonger Tom Vandenbergh. He only sells British unpasteurized cheeses that he himself selects. He knows everything there is to know on the subject and has almost all the cheeses that James Aldridge was involved in developing (see opposite) and that are made by Hurst Farm in Crockham Hill, Kent, including Tom's favourite Crockhamdale.

Tom arrived in England from Holland in 1991 and had an interest in cheese from a young age. He set up a market stall in Canterbury Market in the late 1990s and then took the space in The Goods Shed. He's built up a great local reputation and people come from miles around to buy his cheeses and listen to his cheese stories. There's an art to selling cheese and Tom certainly has it.

The Goods Shed also has its own restaurant, serving the very produce for sale in the indoor market, plus other locally sourced ingredients. After our morning's foraging (see page 32), Rafael the chef cooked us several courses that included the ingredients we had picked. We started off with delicious brawn served with toast and a selection of leaves, like bitter cress and chickweed. Next, we had scrambled eggs with velvet shank mushrooms and then sand sole with buttered alexanders and 3-cornered garlic. Braised oxtail was next, with yet more mushrooms and a side dish of perfectly roasted new potatoes tossed with sea purslane.

This was all washed down with a couple of glasses of Forager's elderflower cordial. Sadly, I had to get back to London and skip dessert, but the whole experience was a real treat. I'll be back.

The cheeses of the South

Eastside Cheese Company Years ago, when I worked at the Candlewick restaurant at Mr Pontacs bar and restaurant in the city, the cheesemonger brought me a piece of a cheese called Tornegus. British cheeses were not at the top of shopping lists then, and the story of it being a Caerphilly with a washed rind seemed absurd at the time. What I didn't know then was what its creator was up to.

James Aldridge worked in the building trade and his partner, Pat worked in a shop near Southampton, selling run-of-the-mill ham, provisions and cheeses. Due to an injury, James had to think of a new career, so they arrived at the idea of a cheese shop. They found a site in Beckenham and started selling the usual blocks of good-value Cheddar, along with unpasteurized farmhouse cheeses, which he selected and personally collected himself from worthy cheese-makers.

He bought up as many cheeses as he could from each dairy, even if they weren't ripe, and matured them himself, so that he could offer his customers cheeses at different stages of maturity. This maturing process enabled James to understand just how cheeses reacted in a different environment and how maturing changed their characteristics. Some cheeses need their natural environment to develop and James's fascination with his cheeses got him experimenting with washing the rinds of some of his favourites and continuing to mature them. His favourite of all was Ducket's Caerphilly, which he transformed by washing in Kentish wine, flavoured with lemon verbena and mint, and it became the very Tornegus that I was wary of so many years ago.

He became a unique authority in creating and giving cheeses a different natural identity and, naturally, the shop soon got a reputation, with people travelling for miles to pick James's brain, taste his latest experiments and take cheese away. James became completely obsessed with cheese and decided to sell up the shop to work from home, rind washing and maturing, and even experimenting and making his own cheeses.

Over the years, his reputation for experimentation and inventing new cheeses got out into the world of cheese-makers and James became the 'cheese doctor' that makers would go to with their problems, generally leaving with them solved and occasionally a newly created cheese. James gave good advice for nothing and the love of it, and would happily travel to cheese-makers to help them develop new cheeses and not even charge for expenses.

Many of the great cheese-makers of today had some form of advice from James, and some still make cheeses with his recipes, like the Blunts with their Flower Marie in East Sussex. Although I never met James before he died, some seven years ago, I know lots of people who became his good friends. I really haven't enough space in this book to give you even some of their stories. All I'll say is that James was hugely responsible for the revival of British cheeses and made cheese-makers aware there was more to cheese-making than hard-pressed cheeses.

In his memory, there is the James Aldridge Memorial Trophy, donated by HRH Prince of Wales for the best raw milk British cheese. The Blunts, who had worked closely with James developing the Flower Marie, won the trophy the first year for their Golden Cross goats' cheese.

Two Hoots Cheese It's unusual to find a cheese-maker making three types of blue cheese; it seems like competing with yourself. Sandy Rose started making cheese just two years ago and has since won several awards for her first two cheeses, Barkham Blue and Barkham Chase. Sandy was brought up on her father's dairy farm in Sherlock Row in Berkshire. Sandy and her husband then bought a smallholding in Hook and raised dairy goats and rare-breed cattle, including Red Polls.

They experimented with simple soft goats' cheeses for their own use and then got into the idea of cheese-making and made a decision to explore producing on a larger scale. Sandy's cousin, Anne Wigmore is an established cheese-maker and makes Waterloo, Wigmore and Spenwood at Riseley near Reading.

So Anne was the first port of call for a bit of work experience and inside information. Sandy went to work for Anne, doing a bit of cleaning and just generally helping out, to get a bit of an insight into what was involved in the real cheese-making world.

Sandy and her husband then bought a farm in Barkham, Wokingham, and made their first cheese, Barkham Blue using a mix of Jersey and Guernsey milk from a farm in Gloucestershire. In their first year, 2003, it won the best new cheese at the World Cheese Awards.

Their next cheese was Barkham Chase, which has similarities to the first but a slightly more piquant flavour and distinctive character. Their newest cheese is a blue made with ewes' milk, Loddon Blewe – if its siblings are anything to go by, I reckon this one is going to be a big hit.

Brogdale

Kent is often referred to as 'the garden of England', and apples in the region's orchards are considered the best in the world. The Cox's Orange Pippin and the Bramley's Seedling were originally propagated here. We do get slightly blinkered by the poor choice of apple varieties offered in most shops and supermarkets these days, and we forget what a massive heritage of varieties of apples and other fruits we actually have, or have had.

Thankfully, though, we have institutions like the Brogdale Horticultural Trust, hosting our treasured national fruit collections, to remind us of what was once commonplace in England. This living museum of fruit trees in 150 acres of land just outside Faversham hosts over 2,000 apple varieties – if you could ever imagine there were that many – with names like Pig's Nose Pippin and Scotch Dumpling, and many more.

The thing to do is to get a guide for the day, otherwise you just won't know what's what. The trees are laid out and meticulously documented in a grid system like I've never seen before, with what I could gather was a couple of trees of each variety. The whole collection of apples, pears, plums, quinces and fruit bushes is just an enormous fruit bowl that's been organized like a filing cabinet.

There is nothing organic about this lot, though, and the main point is the preservation of the varieties that has been going on since the early 1800s, when the collection was originally held at Chiswick. The reason for the non-organic orchard is that pests and disease have to be dealt with effectively and speedily to preserve the plants for the future, and each day someone will patrol the rows attending to those needing any such care.

There is lots going on at Brogdale and it is actually quite difficult to take it all in, with all the varieties – few of which are even vaguely familiar. So, after your guided tour, you may need to visit their shop to recap on things and take a few home, but make sure they are labelled.

So, what has happened to all those forgotten varieties? Well, it's obvious … supermarkets – and, in turn, us – demanding perfect specimens in uniform sizes, which has forced many fruit farmers to pack it in. Farmers around the country are fighting back, though, and charities like Common Ground, are doing their bit to promote the cause and support orchards by setting up Apple Day in October each year, where you will see growers selling their old varieties of fruits on the roadsides and in the local markets.

Kent hops

Hops were introduced to England by the Romans, and not for beer-making. They were originally seen as a luxurious vegetable, the young shoots used in salads or lightly cooked like asparagus and served with butter. We learnt a lot about vegetables from the Romans, but, sadly, left some delicacies like hops behind. Their history in cooking is not that consistent and they didn't really appear again in the kitchen until the fifteenth century. A century later, they were farmed in Kent by Flemish settlers to preserve and clarify beer. Their use in beer-making continued, but culinary use again evaporated. Around 30,000 acres of Kent used to be dedicated to hops, but it is nothing near that now, as a lot gets imported. I can feel a culinary renaissance for hop shoots coming on. I was sent a jar of pickled hop shoots a few years ago by a PR company, with a note referring to them as the most expensive vegetable in the world, although if we want to get more people eating hops again, their prices will have to be in line with, say, asparagus. The Italians still use them, as do the Dutch, who treat them like green beans, and it's time we did.

For years now, I've asked our suppliers to source hop shoots and the answer has always been 'no can do'. Come on, Kent is full of them; well, it used to be anyway. I had almost given up the hop trail when another PR company, sent me some bumf on hops, informing me that Booths supermarkets in the North were going to be stocking them. I found it slightly bizarre that something native to Kent was being marketed in the North. I got straight on to the supplier and had them on the menu within a week.

My source was a company in Kent called Norman Collett, who mainly specialize in apple and pears, but thought they'd have a punt at hops. There was nothing to it really, after speaking to Ashley and Andrew at Collets, as a lot of their growers had hops growing wild in among fruit trees.

Hops could be the new asparagus, or samphire more like, as I reckon asparagus is going to get cult status again, and the farmers charge proper money for it. Hop shoots are picked in April and May, and are delicate, with none-too-long a shelf life. They are well suited to accompany fish or simple dishes – the Italians do a flat omelette with hops scattered over it.

Chegworth Valley

Bearing in mind it may be some time before we come round to the fact that not all apples are round and shiny, there are a new breed of growers that have the value-added product in mind, taking full advantage of the flavours for which fruits were grown and not their looks.

David and Linda Deme bought Water Lane Farm in 1983, which was then a dairy farm and owned by Leeds Castle. Over the next ten years, they planted 30,000 apple and pear trees, including some rare varieties, and in 1990 added raspberries and strawberries, and other soft fruits.

Their good business intentions were geared to the demands of the supermarkets and major wholesalers, with the usual uniformity. Pressures on colour and price kicked in and the most important factor, taste, was not even taken into consideration. Fortunately, farmers' markets were emerging and these were the obvious places to showcase their fruit directly to the customer.

Being in the markets, a natural next step was to start selling the obvious value-added product, the juices of the fruits. So David and Linda bought a small traditional press and started filling bottles for the markets and giving samples to the punters. Because they were farming lots of different fruits and soft fruits, the juice sideline became fun and viable, and who wouldn't want to take a bottle of quality juice home along with a few apples?

Dealing directly with their customers, as opposed to conglomerate buyers, also made them realize that many people were concerned about the use of chemicals, both on the fruit and in the juices. So they converted some of the farm into organic production, and now a large part of the farm is certified organic, which adds even more clout to that delicious juice in the bottle, now marketed under the name Chegworth Valley.

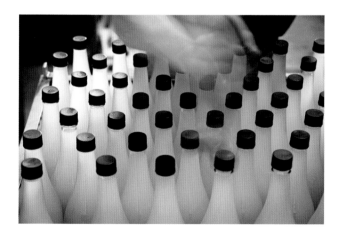

APPLE AND BLACKBERRY JELLY *serves* 4

I've got a thing about jellies, which I think goes back to my discovering that jelly was not the packeted rubbery stuff you buy in shops and dissolve in hot water. Grown-up jellies are great and you can have really great easy fun creating different versions throughout the year. Summer is easy, with elderflower and various summer fruits, but by late autumn, we are only really left with those blackberries that are just dying to be picked.

You can buy various apple juices in the shops, from the highly pasteurized stuff in the shops that doesn't really resemble apples, to the quality stuff, like those produced by Chegworth Valley. Ideally, a clear juice is more suitable than a really cloudy one, so you can see the blackberries suspended in the jelly, but flavour is what we are really after here.

500ml clear apple juice

100g caster sugar (or less if the juice is sweet)

4 sheets of leaf gelatine

120g blackberries

Bring 100ml of the apple juice to the boil. Add the sugar and stir until dissolved.

Meanwhile, soak the gelatine leaves in a shallow bowl of cold water for a minute or so until soft. Squeeze out the water, add the gelatine to the hot apple juice and stir until dissolved. Add the rest of juice, stir well and put the jelly somewhere cool, but do not let it set.

Fill individual jelly moulds or glasses, or one large mould, with half the berries, then pour in half of the cooled jelly. Put in the fridge for an hour or so to set, then top up with the rest of the berries and unset jelly. This allows the berries to stay suspended and not float to the top. Return to the fridge.

To serve, turn out and offer thick Jersey cream to go with the jelly.

QUINCE CHEESE *makes about 1.5kg*

The poor old quince, although once very popular in our fruit pies and sauces, doesn't get used much in British cuisine these days, but it again is coming back – believe me. This dish is not exactly a cheese in our terms, but a fruit preserve that goes particularly well with most hard and blue cheese. In Spain, this paste, known there as *membrillo*, is extremely common.

    1kg preserving sugar
    1.2kg quince, peeled, cored and grated or
    finely chopped

Dissolve the sugar in 750ml water and bring to the boil. Continue to boil for about 5 minutes to make a light syrup.

Stir the quince into the syrup, bring back to the boil and simmer very gently, stirring every so often, for about 45 minutes, until the mixture turns into a thick grainy paste. Alternatively, you could cook it in a covered pan in the oven preheated to 160°C/gas 3. It is ready when a spoon dragged across the bottom of the pan separates the paste, showing the clean bottom of the pan. This can take up to an hour or more, depending on the quince.

Spread the paste into lightly greased shallow dishes or trays and place in the lowest possible oven for 3-4 hours to harden further. Remove from the oven and leave to cool.

Once cool, wrap in greaseproof paper and store in the fridge in sealed containers. It will keep for up to a year. You can make this into a much lighter paste, almost like a jam, by removing it from the heat when the quince has broken down and putting it into jars.

Kentish cherries

Wild cherries are native to Britain and, once again, the Romans were probably responsible for the hybrid varieties we know and love today. Our commercial orchards are diminishing and scarcely cover 500 hectares in Kent today. Sadly, the big cherry buyers tend to go abroad for their cherries, because of the unpredictable cropping here and they are probably cheaper abroad.

Morellos and the sweet dessert cherries are the most common types cultivated here today, and probably most English cherries bought in markets and from roadside stalls in Kent are devoured before they even get home.

Cherries are important in Kentish cuisine and are traditionally used in cherry batter pudding, cherry brandy and cherry huffkins. Brogdale Horticultural Trust also houses 220 varieties of cherry, of which only 12 or so are grown commercially. Henry Bryant at The Bounds in Faversham also grows several types of cherry, including some of the older varieties traditionally associated with Kent, such as Bradbourne Blacks or Noir de Gubon, and you are probably not likely to find these varieties for sale in shops as they are generally sold as just 'cherries'. But, who knows, as with apples, some of those old varieties may just make a comeback and we may even be able to name the variety of cherry we are using on our menus.

CHERRY BATTER PUDDING *serves* 4

If you know your international puddings, then you may just recognize this one from across the water in France: yes, it's a kind of *clafoutis* – in fact, it is *clafoutis* and, inevitably, the old question is raised, who originated it? Well, this one is definitely Kentish and a simple dessert to use up just some of those excess summer cherries.

    25g melted butter, plus more for greasing

    50g plain flour

    50g caster sugar

    2 eggs, beaten

    250ml single cream, warmed

    1 tablespoon cherry brandy

    a few drops of vanilla essence

    450g ripe red or black cherries, stoned

    icing sugar, for dusting

    thick cream, to serve

Preheat the oven to 200°C/gas 6 and grease a round ovenproof dish or tart tin or, better still, a non-stick one.

Sieve the flour into a bowl and stir in the sugar. Mix in the eggs and slowly whisk in the cream to form a light batter. Stir in the cherry brandy, vanilla essence and melted butter.

Scatter the cherries over the prepared dish or tin and pour in the batter. Bake for 20 minutes, then turn the oven down to 190°C/gas 5 and cook for a further 20 minutes, or until the batter has risen and is golden, but still creamy inside.

Dust with icing sugar and serve hot or warm from the dish, with thick cream.

Bristol   *Cornwall*   *Devon*   *Dorset*

Gloucestershire   *Somerset*   *Wiltshire*

THE
SOUTH WEST

ABOVE Fisherman Jack Woolmington on his trawler, unloading his catch from his nets (see page 56).

FISH AND FISHING ARE A BIG PART OF West Country life. All along the beautiful coastline, and in the many fishing ports, you will still see a way of life that has been handed down for generations. Although these days fish is in short supply and, sadly, with depleting stocks and restricted fishing, local fishermen struggle to survive, that relationship with the sea still continues in some form or another. There are even divers now scouring the seabeds to hand-pick scallops, primarily to keep chefs happy with their enormous saucer-sized specimens, but secondly – and perhaps unintentionally – to save the sea bed from being devastated by trawlers.

Although the South West is pretty synonymous with fish, dairy products are also a strong feature, and the famous clotted cream and farmhouse cheeses are testimony to serious dairy farming. When I was young, we always only had Stilton in the house, so I didn't really get to appreciate the famous cheeses of my own region, although I was aware of the local gossip about the mysterious Blue Vinney.

Fish has, however, always been close to my heart. Growing up in Dorset, just yards away from the sea, it's difficult not to have a passion for it. As a kid, I would fish for anything in the summer, from small mackerel to heavier stuff like skate and pollack from the wrecks offshore. After school and at the weekends in the summer, we would sit on the end of the pier with light trout rods and have great sport, normally ending up with a good feast. Holidaymakers alongside would be casting half a dozen feathers

There was a local culture of friendly trading that left its mark on me, whether it was exchanging some fish for a brace of pheasants or a few rabbits, or doing a bit of handiwork in return for wild food. In London that just doesn't happen – well, not often. I'm glad I experienced that and many other memorable aspects of growing up in that part of the world.

I was extremely fortunate having all this wonderful produce right there on my doorstep and quite often it would literally appear there, quietly deposited by some friends of the family. Most of the people I knew had a second form of income, whether it was fishing in the summer and helping to build houses in the winter or part-time fishing in between making bespoke nets for exactly that purpose.

with heavy lead weights and catch 3 or 4 fish at a time, but we would be quite content pulling them in with a bit of a struggle, one by one, on a tiny float and single hook. The onlookers probably thought we were just mad young kids having a bit of a laugh, and they were right. In contrast, winter would consist of cold nights on beaches with a tilly lamp in hope of a cod, and prawning with baited nets from the end of the pier in West Bay.

I suppose half the problem these days is getting people's taste buds in tune with those delicate flavours of the sea. It would be unthinkable to me not to like that stuff, but still people are quite squeamish at the thought of getting stuck into a lobster or crab. I had no choice in the matter and luckily just ate it all with relish.

Although the meat products of the region are also top-notch and highly regarded throughout the country – if not the world – there are not that many traditional West Country recipes for meat, as roasting ovens were only introduced to this part of the country at the beginning of the twentieth century. Before that, spits were generally used for cooking meat, poultry and fish over wood or peat fires. I suppose this is a difficult method of cooking to record, unless you have a special marinade or stuffing up the sleeve of your fisherman's smock. However, names like Dorset Horn or Gloucestershire Old Spot still excite the palate of any meat eater.

STARGAZY PIE *serves* 4

You don't often see this on restaurant menus, and you are possibly not likely to ... Imagine putting a pie in front of a guest with fish heads staring back up at him. The logic of the highly eccentric arrangement of the fish in this dish lies in preserving as much of the essential oils in the pilchards as possible; to this end, the heads are kept and the fish arranged so that their oils run back into the pie filling as it cooks.

In Mousehole (pronounced 'mowzol'), near Penzance, a famous local tradition is that of Tom Bawcock's Eve, celebrated the night before Christmas Eve. The story goes that, one winter in the distant past, the sea was too stormy for any of the fishing boats to go out, and the people of the village faced starvation, let alone a bleak Christmas. Brave Tom ventured out and caught sufficient fish to feed the village, some of which was made into the first Stargazy Pie.

1 onion, finely chopped

3 rashers of rindless streaky bacon, chopped into rough 5mm dice

good knob of butter

½ tablespoon flour, plus more for dusting

3 tablespoons dry white wine

250ml fish stock (or a corner of a good-quality fish stock cube dissolved in that amount of hot water)

300ml double cream

2 tablespoons chopped parsley

2 hard-boiled eggs, shelled and chopped

salt and freshly ground black pepper

6 pilchards, herrings or small mackerel, filleted, any residual bones removed and heads reserved

200g puff pastry, rolled out to a thickness of about 3mm

1 egg, beaten

Gently cook the onion and bacon in the butter until soft. Add the flour and stir well, then slowly add the wine and fish stock, stirring well to prevent lumps forming. Bring to the boil and simmer for 10 minutes.

Add the cream, bring back to the boil and simmer until reduced by half and thickened. Remove from the heat; add the parsley and chopped egg, season and leave to cool.

Preheat the oven to 200°C/gas 6. Cut the fillets of fish in half and lay them in a shallow pie or flan dish, then lightly season. Pour the sauce over them, then lay the pastry over the dish and trim it to size. Make 6 small slits in the pastry and push the reserved fish heads through them, then brush the top with the beaten egg.

Bake for 40-45 minutes. Serve with greens in autumn and winter, or a selection of spring vegetables.

Bring back pilchards, I say...

Well, in fact, they are back, it's just that it would seem that no one wants to buy them any more – although they will buy the posher version, sardines. Well I've got news for you, the pilchard is actually a grown-up sardine. In fact, a sardine reaches pilchardism when it's over 11cm long. Supermarkets are also trying to rehabilitate pilchards by calling them 'Cornish sardines'.

The European pilchard, *Sardina pilchardus*, is a migratory fish, like its cousin the herring, and there was a prolific pilchard fishery off the Cornish coast in the Middle Ages. By the nineteenth century, the fish had become the centre of a vital and profitable trade in the West Country. Most of the pilchards caught were salted, packed into barrels, and exported to Europe . Nothing from the curing process would be wasted and even the oil that drained from the barrels would be sold to the leather tanners for their lamps. The skimmings from the water in which the fish were washed was bought by soap boilers, and any damaged fish went for manure.

Because the West Country was a poor area, excess fish were used to pay part of the fishermen's wages. They would eat the fresh fish as a dish called 'dippy', where the fish was simmered with potatoes and local cream, but most would be preserved by smoking, salting or sousing in vinegar. Fresh, pilchards can be cooked in exactly the same way as sardines or mackerel - grilled or fried.

A similar fish, the sprat, also used to be very common off the West Country coast. I remember, my father and some other locals would wait close to the beach in small rowing boats with seine nets for the massive shoals to arrive just offshore. They would make several trips back to the beach with full nets and then I think they just sold them to the local fish wholesaler in exchange for beer money.

Although the trade in pilchards has now largely died away and been replaced mostly by mackerel fishing, the Pilchard Works in Newlyn, Penzance, has been producing traditional Cornish salt pilchards since 1905. Now a unique award-winning working museum, it still uses the traditional old screw presses and packs the fish in old wooden barrels. Much of their product has long been exported to Italy, where they are known as '*salacche inglesi*' and said to be more valued than their own local anchovies.

PILCHARDS ON TOAST *serves* 4

This dish does bear an obvious resemblance to those rather grim canned pilchards in tomato sauce, but the combination is a good one, and the acidity of the tomato just cuts that oiliness of the fish to produce a snack or supper dish that is both satisfying and healthy.

> 2 shallots, finely chopped
>
> 6 tablespoons extra-virgin rapeseed or olive oil, plus more for brushing
>
> 3 ripe tomatoes, skinned, deseeded and cut into rough 1cm dice
>
> 1 tablespoon chopped flat-leaf parsley
>
> salt and freshly ground black pepper
>
> 2 teaspoons white wine vinegar
>
> 8 pilchards, scaled, filleted and any residual small bones removed
>
> 4 slices of bread, about 1cm thick

Gently cook the shallots in the oil for 2–3 minutes without allowing them to colour. Add the tomatoes, vinegar and parsley, season and simmer for another couple of minutes. Take off the heat and set aside.

Meanwhile, preheat the grill to its hottest temperature. Make a couple of diagonal slashes across the skin side of each fillet, then brush them with olive oil, season with some sea salt and freshly ground black pepper, and grill for about 3–4 minutes with the skin side up.

Carefully put the fillets in a tray or on a plate and spoon the tomato mixture over them

Toast the bread, then arrange the pilchards on top of the toast and spoon the tomato mixture over.

CORNISH RED MULLET SOUP *serves 8-10*

Cornish red mullet has a particularly fine flavour and, simply fried, the fillets make a delicious main course, leaving you the bones for a soup made in the tradition of Mediterranean fish soups as here. Fresh mullet is always preferable, but this recipe is just as successful with the frozen fish that can be bought at a reasonable price. This recipe is enough for about 8-10, because it freezes well, and it seems a rather pointless exercise just making a small batch for four people.

2 tablespoons vegetable oil

1 kg whole red mullet, fresh or frozen, roughly chopped

1 onion, roughly chopped

1 leek, roughly chopped and washed

1 small fennel bulb, trimmed and roughly chopped

1 red pepper, deseeded and roughly chopped

1 potato, roughly chopped

6 garlic cloves, chopped

good pinch of saffron strands

1 teaspoon black peppercorns

3 juniper berries

1 bay leaf

a few sprigs of thyme

1 tablespoon tomato paste

230g tin of chopped tomatoes

glass of red wine

4 litres fish stock (or 4 good-quality fish stock cubes dissolved in that amount of hot water)

salt and pepper

In a large heavy pan, heat the oil and gently fry the mullet, vegetables, garlic, spices and herbs for about 10 minutes.

Add the tomato paste, chopped tomatoes, red wine and fish stock. Bring to the boil, season with salt and pepper and simmer gently for 50 minutes.

Blend about one-third of the soup in a liquidizer, bones and all, and return it to the pot. Simmer gently for another 20 minutes.

Strain the soup through a sieve or conical strainer and adjust the seasoning if necessary.

SOUSED MACKEREL *serves* 4

As I mentioned earlier, I had lots of fun as a kid, catching loads of mackerel off the end of the pier in West Bay. Gran would cook up the first batch the following day, when they no longer had rigor mortis. She would cut them like kippers, flour them and fry them. Mackerel really need to be eaten within a couple of days of being caught to appreciate fully their delicate oily flesh. The rest of our catch would get soused, an old-fashioned way of preserving fish, then eaten with brown bread and homegrown tomatoes for the next few days. If you can get samphire, it makes a great addition, simply blanched in boiling water for 20 seconds and added when you serve the fish.

> 8 medium-sized mackerel fillets, cut from 250-350g fish, trimmed and any residual small bones removed
>
> 2 small onions, or 2 large shallots, cut into thin rings

> 1 medium carrot, thinly sliced at an angle
>
> 1 bay leaf
>
> 8 white peppercorns
>
> ½ teaspoon salt
>
> 150ml cider vinegar or white wine vinegar

Preheat the oven to 180°C/gas 4. Roll up the mackerel fillets, skin sides out, and secure each roll with a cocktail stick. Arrange them, not too close together, in an ovenproof dish just large enough to hold them.

Put the rest of the ingredients in a pan with just enough water to allow you to the cover fillets with the mixture. Bring to the boil and pour over the mackerel.

Cover the dish with a lid or foil and cook in the oven for 25 minutes. Leave to cool in the dish.

Serve with brown bread and butter.

Scallop divers

Darren Brown is a local Dorset lad who dives for scallops from his locally moored rib. Why dive for scallops, you may wonder? Well several reasons, both ecological and culinary. Firstly, dredging scallops damages the seabed, which doesn't happen with scallops hand-selected by divers. The eating quality of the latter is also generally better, as they haven't been tossed around in the nets at speed, becoming waterlogged. Chefs pay a big premium for dived scallops, as the result is generally larger meat. It's rather like bespoke fishing in that they pick the best and leave the smaller ones undisturbed – certainly not the case with trawlers. This way of fishing scallops has its downside – the weather – but the upside is the ready market and better price, and enterprising Darren, once a chef himself, knows exactly where his market is – London restaurants. 'Why mess around down here when I can get top price from London chefs?' says Darren. You'll also see him in London's Borough Market on Fridays and Saturdays, cooking his catch and serving it back in the shells. He brings local fish up with him as well – great Dover soles from local fisherman Jack Woolmington (see page 50) and delicious local prawns in season. I have fond (and bloody cold) memories of catching those little prawns off the end of the pier in the middle of the night.

LEFT Darren Brown (in the centre with the hat) with his catch on the quay.

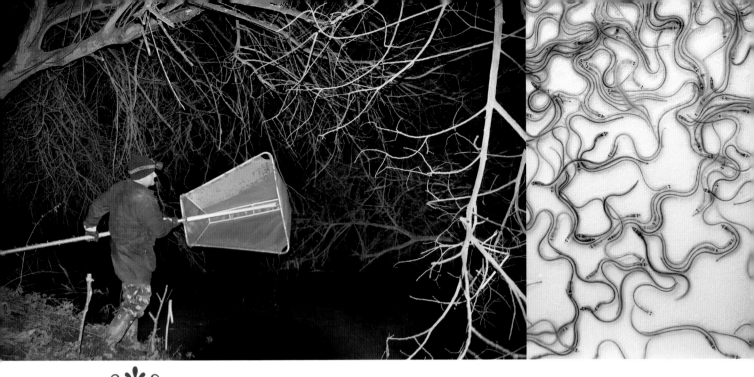

Elvers in crisis

You may well have heard of the elver-eating competitions in and around Frampton in Gloucestershire, but sadly those celebrations have long since died away, as the tiny elvers, or glass eels (so called because they are almost translucent), have become an increasingly rare commodity. The life story of the eel is a mysterious one, and completely opposite to that of the salmon. The eel begins its life as larvae in the Sargasso Sea – a lens of warmer water on the surface of the Atlantic off the American coast – and then makes a long (up to 3 years') journey piggy-backing on the Gulf Stream to our rivers.

There it matures and then heads back across the ocean to spawn and begin the cycle all over again. After their astounding transatlantic journey, the baby elvers, still only about the length of a matchstick, arrive in the rivers like the Severn around May to June each year.

Richard Cook and his father Horace have been in the elver business for some years now and from their stories, it's been a cut-throat one too. On our visit to Westbury on Severn, the season was just under way and the elvers were few and far between. For two evenings, we joined Dave, a hardened elverman, on his fire-lit tump (his patch) on the

banks of the Severn during one of the highest spring tides of the year. We waited until full high tide, about 9.30pm. Elvers have to be caught at night because they are negatively phototactic, meaning that only the lack of light will bring them to the surface and close to the banks, where they are easier to catch.

Dave had a good fire ablaze, made from a couple of old wooden pallets, to keep us warm, and he had a few tins of cider for his expected guests. In a couple of hours, he had caught about 30 elvers, which amounts to about 100g. Because they're now so scarce, the price is high and the guys on the bank could get as much as £300 per kilo for their catch. In the height of the season, a good fishermen can weigh in a few kilos, which makes a pretty good living for part-time fishing.

In case you are worrying about such fishing when the elvers are in such desperate decline, it is all well controlled and the majority of the catch from here goes live for breeding in China, Japan and parts of Europe, including Lough Neagh in Northern Ireland, where Father Kennedy runs a cooperative, restocking the loughs with the Cooks' elvers. Richard then buys them back at their adult stage for smoking at the Severn and Wye Smokery. This final stage completes the eels' life cycle. Isn't it mad to think that you'll pay up to £300 for a kilo of elvers, yet you can go and buy the smoked eel at a mere fraction of the price!

The elver station that Horace has set up in Chaxhill is crucial to the future of the eel. He has about 12 tanks in which the elvers are housed once they have been weighed in and sold. In fact, the demand for the tiny eels was so high a few years ago that they bought an aeroplane to transport the things to their destination. I could write another book on the elver stories and, sadly – or perhaps thankfully, in the circumstances – the demand for eating them, at least here, is ever-diminishing. At that price, what do you expect?

We have always served them in the restaurants simply with olive oil, garlic and a hint of chilli, but Horace showed me the local way, which I've since got rather hooked on. I did add a little something to the local recipe, though, that Horace welcomed, especially when I told him how much we pay for it in London. That little addition was some wild garlic leaves, the season had just started, and Horace and Richard drove us up to the local woods in search of these fragrant leaves before we could have our elver feast.

The first thing you need is some good fatty bacon, and Gloucester Old Spot pigs produce just that. I cut it into thin strips, leaving all the fat on, and gently cooked it in a frying pan for a few minutes to release the fat. I then turned the heat up, dropped the elvers in with some torn wild garlic leaves, seasoned them well, then added a couple of beaten eggs. You just stir in the egg and that lightly coats the eels and bacon. I dished this up for Horace with a glass of local Weston's cider, and the old boy was in heaven.

BELOW The Severn Estuary has the second highest tidal range in the world, producing the Severn Bore, a rush of water that starts at Avonmouth and travels inland as far as Gloucester, attracting surfers from all over the world.

The Severn and Wye Smokery

Richard Cook has the right idea and is sending his elvers to Lough Neagh, a serious eel fishery just outside Belfast. He then buys them back when they're grown, to smoke them at his successful Severn and Wye Smokery, situated in Gloucestershire on the edge of the Royal Forest of Dean, between two of England's most celebrated salmon rivers. So he doesn't just smoke eels; his smoked wild salmon appears on many restaurant menus.

Duchy of Cornwall Oysters

A few years back we were offered Duchy of Cornwall natives by our new-found oyster suppliers, the Wright Brothers. I knew very little about them and hadn't even tasted this particular type of oyster, so the thought of a new oyster on the menu was quite exciting. I had previously met Ben Wright and Robin Hancock, the founders of the Wright Brothers, at the wedding of photographer, Jason Lowe in Provence. They turned up there with a thousand or so oysters, which they had collected in Mornac-sur Seudre on the French Atlantic coast, for the wedding breakfast, just to ensure the day started in style.

Ben Wright and Robin Hancock's earlier careers had little to do with the fish business, except for their passion for oysters. Ben was a City lawyer for one of the top five international law firms and Robin was a music producer for some big names in the music business. Apart from sourcing the best oysters from around the world, the most exciting project for them has been the leasing of the oyster beds on the Helford River from the Duchy of Cornwall.

I had a vision of what to expect as Ben and Robin had been banging on about it for months, showing us archive pictures of the old-style oyster dredgers on the creek, which still operate today in the local area. The famous Frenchman's Creek of Daphne du Maurier's novel is a side creek of the Helford. Ben explained that the Helford Creek had seen better days and many of the oysters are dredged by sail ships on the nearby Fal, and then re-laid on the Duchy beds on the Helford.

On our visit to the beds, we made it through the mist and got close to the river at Port Navas Creek, where the Duchy oysterage joins the river. Oysters have been grown on the Helford for a few centuries now and the evidence of oyster fishing dates back to the second and third centuries, when the Celts first settled there and built coastal forts during the Roman invasions. The Duchy is one of the very few private oyster fisheries left in the UK.

While the Helford was once the source of a good majority of the oysters in the UK, like a lot of other oyster fisheries around the British coast, its stocks have been sadly depleted over the years through neglect and fuel pollution. However, the river is now a marine conservation area and, with voluntary help from the local community and using traditional oyster-farming methods, the oysters should make a comeback.

The Helford hasn't been stocked properly for the last 20 years, so the boys will now have the task of raking the river beds, rather like taking over an overgrown piece of farmland. The existing oysters will be dredged up to assess the stock, then re-laid on the cleaned-up river bed, and Ben will camp out in Cornwall to nurse their new project through its tender renaissance.

The Helford also has a sea bass nursery and mussels grow wild in the Creek, where the fish can breed undisturbed by fishermen and hopefully get fish stocks up again. Ben and Robin also have romantic plans to build a café on the oysterage, where you can sample the Duchy of Cornwall natives while looking over the Creek.

So once again we will be seeing Duchy of Cornwall natives on restaurant menus across the country; or, if you're in London, you can visit the Wright Brothers yourself and enjoy their fare at their new oyster bar in Borough Market's Stoney Street.

Portland Shellfish

Nick Assarati, his father Martyn and their dog Ralph moved to Portland in 1997 to set up a family shellfish business. Nick had previously worked for a few major fish suppliers in London and on the Essex coast, and knew the market to tap in to. Now they are the only fish business on Portland. Ironically, Nick's main business is with London restaurants, hotels and serious food shops, with a few select drops en route, like Chewton Glen. His local business is tiny, but he serves notable fish restaurants like The Riverside in West Bay. Of course, the local fishermen need someone like Nick, as he shifts a lot of shellfish each week, so much so that he also sources products like langoustines and scallops from Scotland. Nick likes to refer to their business as a 'passive' fishery in the eco-friendly sense and expresses the opinion that the locals are all very aware of sustainability and the implications for their future livelihoods, for example always making a point of returning any undersized fish to the sea in a state that ensures they will survive.

Picking crabmeat by hand is a tricky business, but Nick strives for quality picked white crabmeat and doesn't diminish its quality by pasteurizing it. However, this choice necessitates quick production and prompt delivery, which is what he is very good at.

BAKED LYME BAY SPIDER CRAB

serves 4 as a starter

We used to catch spider crabs by the dozen when we were kids, and we regarded them as pests in our prawn nets – quite apart from the fact that they were pretty scary-looking things. I used to love brown crab, but in Dorset, no one encouraged us to eat the spider crabs. We were told they were taken to Spain and made into soup, but I don't think people really knew their fate and were just guessing at what the resourceful Spanish really did with our unwanted delicacies. If you can't find spider crabs, and they've all gone to Spain, use normal crabs.

1 large (1½ – 2kg) cooked spider crab or brown crab

½ onion, finely chopped

1 garlic clove, crushed

100g butter

2 teaspoons English mustard

3 tablespoons sherry

3 tablespoons fish stock (or a corner of a good-quality stock cube dissolved in that amount of hot water)

100–200g prepared brown crab meat (depending on how much there is in the spider crab)

50g fresh white breadcrumbs

juice of ½ lemon

salt and freshly ground black pepper

2 tablespoons grated Cheddar cheese

thin slices of toast, to serve

To get the meat out of the crab, twist off the legs and claws, then crack them open and remove the white meat. Now turn the main body on its back and twist off the pointed flap. Push the tip of a table knife between the main shell and the bit to which the legs were attached and twist the blade to separate the two, then push it up and remove. Scoop out the brown meat in the well of the shell and put with the rest of the meat.

On the other part of the body, remove the dead man's fingers (the feathery grey gills attached to the body) and discard them. Split the body in half with a heavy knife. Now you need to be quite patient and pick out the white meat from the little cavities in the body. Add this to the rest of the meat.

Preheat a hot oven or grill. Gently cook the onion and garlic in half the butter until they are soft. Add the mustard, sherry, fish stock and brown crab meat (to bulk up the quantity). Stir well, then add two-thirds of the breadcrumbs (reserving a few to scatter on top) with half the lemon juice. Season to taste and simmer for 15 minutes, stirring occasionally.

Blend one-third of the mixture with the rest of the butter in a blender, then stir it back into the mixture together with the spider-crab meat. Add more lemon juice and seasoning if necessary.

Spoon the mixture back into the shells or an ovenproof serving dish. Mix the remaining breadcrumbs with the Cheddar and scatter over the top. Lightly brown under the grill or in the oven. Serve with thin slices of toast.

Cider and scrumpy

The word 'cider' derives from the Latin *sicera*, meaning strong drink, and if you've experienced the real West Country scrumpy – farmhouse cider, the name comes from the dialect 'scrump', meaning a small or withered apple – you will know it certainly is that. Its smell alone will send your head spinning.

Cider-making was introduced to this country from France in the twelfth century, when it was produced in the fertile valleys of Kent and Sussex. The idea of making alcohol from apples soon caught on, and today we tend to associate cider production with the West Country and the West of England.

Originally, there were no orchards in the South West and the apples were crab apples and hedge-apples, grown along the divides of fields. The cider they produced was as strong as hell, and had to be smoothed with honey, and quite often spiced.

Seventeenth-century cider lover, Lord Scudamore experimented with various varieties of apple until most of his estate was converted to apple orchards. By grafting and crossing varieties, he eventually came up with the ultimate cider apple, Scudamore's Crab.

Cider apples have a sweet juice and acidic pulp, which is essential for cider-making. Early cider apples had wonderful evocative names like Slack my Girdle and French Longtail. These fruits have more or less disappeared now, as those large old trees, with their tangled branches, took up too much room and the apples were difficult to harvest. They have been replaced by squat, bush-like trees that are easier to manage.

The exact method of cider production changes from region to region. The traditional way in the West Country was to crush the apples between horse-driven stone wheels. The pulp was then spread on straw mats or wooden racks and cloths, and a large 'sandwich' made by laying these on top of each other. This was then set in a wooden press and the juice squeezed out.

In the seventeenth and eighteenth centuries, cider-making seemed to have been at its peak, with much of the product making its way to London, where some was held in almost as great esteem as the best French wines. A little of this tradition survives here and there, but most of the cider business is now dominated by large commercial brewers. However, some new small producers are again striving to produce ciders that could rival these products of a golden age, like Bollhayes Bottle Fermented Devon Cider made by Alex Hill in Clayhidon using the *mèthode champenoise*.

POT ROAST GLOUCESTERSHIRE OLD SPOT PORK LOIN WITH SCRUMPY *serves* 4

A well-sourced piece of pork really needs very little doing to it, and a good layer of fat should not put you off, because that's where a lot of the flavour lies. The fat melts away during slow cooking, so you can drain off excess as the cooking progresses and use it another time.

If you wish, you can make a gravy by adding half a tablespoon of flour to the vegetables in the roasting pan and then stirring in some chicken stock and simmering for 15 minutes or so. With a cut like this, though, I prefer to keep it natural, as the meat is quite moist and the celeriac and apple mash really does the job of a sauce.

1 piece of pork loin, boned, weighing about 1.5-2kg (boned weight)

salt and freshly ground black pepper

1 onion, roughly chopped

1 carrot, roughly chopped

1 celery stalk, roughly chopped

a few sprigs of thyme

300ml scrumpy or dry cider

for the celeriac and apple mash

1 celeriac, peeled and roughly chopped

60g butter

3 cooking apples, peeled, cored and roughly chopped

1 tablespoon brown sugar

Preheat the oven to 220°C/gas 7. Remove the pork rind with a sharp knife and cut it into strips to cook separately. Score the fat in a criss-cross with the knife, season and cook the pork in a roasting tray for 30 minutes, turning halfway. Lower the oven to 160°C/gas 3, add the vegetables and thyme and return to the oven. Spoon some cider over the meat every so often until it's all used, and drain away any excess fat into a container during cooking. Cook fat side up for the last 45 minutes.

Towards the end of that time, make the celeriac and apple mash: cook the celeriac in boiling salted water for 10–12 minutes until tender. Drain and coarsely mash.

While the celeriac is cooking, melt the butter in a pan, add the apples and sugar, cover and cook for 10–12 minutes, stirring occasionally, until the apples are falling apart. If the mixture is wet, remove the lid and cook for a few minutes more over a low heat until it dries a little. Mix with the celeriac mash and season to taste.

Cut the pork into thick slices and serve with the mash.

CORNISH PASTIES *makes 6–8*

I do believe the good old Cornish pasty is making a comeback. Not that it has ever *quite* gone away, but there are, thank goodness, a couple of serious pasty companies setting themselves up as rivals to those high-street, fast-food joints. At last, proper fast food on our streets and in our railway stations – and from the West Country.

Cornwall's most famous food was, in fact, originally a sort of 'fast food' for miners, fishermen, farmers and children to take to work or school. The pastry forms a perfect insulation, keeping the filling hot or warm until lunchtime. The fillings would vary, depending on the wealth of the household. Some would contain only vegetables – swede, onion and potato, with the addition of leek – or perhaps also some off-cuts of a home-boiled ham. You still occasionally come across examples of the Cornish habit of initialling the corner of pasties to help identify their owner. You can even find variations on the pasty in all corners of the world where Cornish miners have travelled to find work. I've seen versions in places like the Caribbean and Africa, with brightly coloured yellow pastry and spicy fillings.

My dad used to buy great Cornish pasties for my school lunchbox and perhaps it was because we were in the West Country that they tasted so good. They were so good I would take an extra one or two to school to sell to mates for money to play cards or pitch-and-toss. Nowadays, I recommend the award-winning pasties from the Chough Bakery in Padstow and Proper Cornish in Bodmin, as well as those from the West Cornwall Pasty Company and Oggy Oggy. Ann Muller's famous Lizard Pasty Shop in Helston is also well worth a visit; she makes her pastry with lard and uses best beef skirt.

for the filling

200g swede, peeled and cut into rough 1½cm pieces

1 large baking potato, peeled and cut into rough 1½cm pieces

salt and freshly ground black pepper

2 tablespoons vegetable oil

2 onions, finely chopped

500g rump or rib steak, trimmed of fat and chopped into 5mm pieces

250ml beef stock (or ½ good-quality beef stock cube dissolved in that amount of hot water)

1 tablespoon Worcestershire sauce

for the pastry

500g plain flour

2 teaspoons salt

125g butter, chilled and cut in small pieces

125g lard, chilled and cut in small pieces

a little milk, to mix

1 egg, beaten, to seal and glaze

To make the filling: heat half the oil in a large heavy frying pan and gently cook the onions for 2–3 minutes until soft. Remove from the pan and put to one side. Heat the pan again over a high heat, add the rest of the oil, season and add the meat. Cook over a high heat for 3–4 minutes, turning, until evenly browned. Remove the meat from the pan and add to the onions.

Add the stock to the pan together with the Worcestershire sauce, and boil rapidly until you have only 2–3 tablespoons of liquid left. Then add the meat and onions back to the pan and simmer until the sauce has reduced until it is just coating the meat.

While the sauce is reducing, cook the potatoes and swede in separate pans of boiling salted water until just tender, then drain and mix into the meat.

To make the pastry: mix the flour and salt together, then rub the butter and lard into the flour with your fingers, or mix it in a food processor, until it has the texture of fine breadcrumbs. Mix in some milk, a tablespoon or two at a time, until a smooth rollable dough forms that leaves the sides of the bowl clean.

Roll out the pastry on a lightly floured board to a thickness of about 3mm and, using a plate or bowl as a template, cut out 6 circles about 18cm in diameter. Spoon the filling evenly in the centre of the 6 discs of pastry. Brush around the edges with the beaten egg and bring the edges of the pastry up around the filling, then crimp the edges together with your fingers, or roll the edges back over and then crimp them. Brush the tops with the remaining egg mixture and cut a small slit in the top for steam to escape. Chill for about 30 minutes.

Preheat the oven to 200°C/gas 6. Bake the pasties for 20 minutes, then turn the oven down to 180°C/gas 4 and cook them for another 20 minutes or so until golden. If the pasties are browning too fast, cover them with foil or greaseproof paper (if they are going to be reheated, finish cooking them while they are still quite pale brown).

JUGGED HARE *serves 4–6*

I wasn't much of a hare fan when I was young and probably only ate it a couple of times. It must have been something to do with the way they would just appear from nowhere, hanging in my grandparents' porch. Hare were plentiful in Dorset and probably difficult to get rid of, so often ended up as dog food instead of in a traditional West Country dish. Game would often just turn up as a kind of favour, I suppose . . . a bit of local trading for a few pounds of Granddad's tomatoes or a some heads of his fine, prize-winning chrysanthemums. The sink full of blood probably didn't help persuade my appetite either. These days, though, I'm a big fan of hare's unique flavour, whether it be simply braised or in a rich sauce with pasta.

A freshly caught and skinned hare will yield a good half-litre of blood, which is traditionally used to thicken the sauce. You will certainly need a good game supplier or a friendly poacher to supply you firstly with a hare and secondly the blood. If the latter is too difficult, then don't worry, as hare has such a good gamy flavour anyway, and, combined with the marinating and slow cooking, you should end up with a memorable feast as here.

I've suggested using the legs, as it's a shame to braise the whole saddle, as the fillets, when removed or roasted on the bone, are very tender and make a substantial meal with a quite different flavour and texture.

8 hare back legs

500ml red wine

4 juniper berries, chopped

1 bay leaf

a few sprigs of thyme

salt and freshly ground black pepper

1 tablespoon flour, plus extra for dusting

vegetable oil, for frying

1 onion, finely chopped

50g butter

½ tablespoon tomato paste

3 litres beef stock (or 3 good-quality stock cubes dissolved in that amount of hot water)

Cut the hare legs in half at the joint and then cut them once more through the middle of the thigh, so you end up with 3 pieces from each leg. Put the pieces into a non-reactive bowl or dish, together with the red wine, juniper, bay leaf and thyme. Cover with clingfilm and refrigerate for 24–48 hours.

Drain the hare in a colander over a bowl and pat the pieces dry with some kitchen paper. Season the pieces of hare and lightly flour them, dusting off any excess. Heat the vegetable oil in a heavy frying pan and fry the pieces, a few at a time, until well coloured, then put to one side on a plate.

Meanwhile, in a heavy-based saucepan, gently cook the onion in the butter for 3–4 minutes until soft. Add the tablespoon of flour and stir well over a medium heat until it begins to turn a sandy colour. Add the tomato paste, then slowly add the red wine and herbs from the marinade, stirring well to avoid lumps forming. Bring to the boil and simmer over a medium heat until the liquid has reduced to half the volume.

Add the beef stock and hare, bring back to the boil, cover and simmer gently for 1 hour (you can cook this in the oven preheated to 160°C/gas 3). Remove a piece of meat to check if it's tender; if not, continue cooking for another 30 minutes or so.

Once the meat is tender, remove the pieces of meat from the sauce and simmer the sauce until it has thickened to a gravy-like consistency, then return the pieces of meat to warm through and serve. Adjust the seasoning, if necessary. Serve with mashed or roasted root vegetables – beetroot is particularly good with it.

Leakers bakery

There was a sort of snobbery among shoppers in my home town as to which of the three local bakers – all of which were pretty good – they bought their bread from. My father used to buy from Leakers, although Gran bought from down the road. The Leaker family sold to Caroline Parkins and her husband Paul in 2001. Caroline, who'd been working in a restaurant in Avebury, had been looking out for a place of her own. Her love of Bridport took her there often, and one day she stumbled on Leakers, fresh on the market. Nothing has since changed in the look of the shop – it is just as I remember from childhood – but Caroline's passion for baking and using purely local produce is very evident. It's interesting how things change and now the bakery that used to be the most traditional in the town has been taken up a notch or three. People are once more coming into the old market town from surrounding villages to buy their bread, instead of settling for the mass-produced stuff from the supermarket.

As well as the various types of bread, all made with flour from Stoate and Sons at Cann Mills in Shaftesbury, Caroline's team make pasties, pound cakes, cider breads and soft buns. I munched on delicious cheese scones and flourless flapjacks, while Caroline packed a goodie bag for my daughters, which unfortunately had only one chocolate brownie in it by the time they got it!

Not surprisingly, at first the locals thought that the unusual loaves sounded a bit off-the-wall, and some probably still do, although my father is now buying from there, so the new artisan baker's reputation must be hot gossip in the local pubs.

WILTSHIRE LARDY CAKE *makes about* 12 *squares*

This cake is just what its name suggests – lardy, but not as bad and fatty as it may sound. It's sort of based on a puff pastry-type recipe, layering the dough with fat and then folding and rolling. These days you don't get many recipes recommending the use of lard, but here it makes the cake deliciously gooey. It is rather filling, though, so you don't need too much. Lardy cake is traditionally from Wiltshire, although you find it in bakeries throughout the South West, and I remember eating it as a kid just out of the oven at Leakers and other local bakers.

200g lard, softened, plus more for greasing

50g butter, softened

200g mixed dried fruit

75g mixed candied peel

200g granulated sugar

for the bread dough

650g strong white bread flour

2 teaspoons salt

1 teaspoon caster sugar, plus more to sprinkle

7g sachet of easy-bake yeast

400ml warm water

First make the bread dough: in a warm bowl, mix the flour, salt, sugar and yeast. Add the warm water and mix to a soft dough. Knead by stretching it and folding it for about 10 minutes on a lightly floured surface.

Mix the lard, butter, fruit, peel and granulated sugar together and divide the mixture into 3 equal parts.

On a lightly floured surface, roll out the bread dough to a rectangular shape roughly three times as long as it is wide, and spread two-thirds of its length with one-third of the lard mixture, then fold both long ends of the dough into the centre and firmly press the edges with your fingers or the rolling pin. Repeat this process twice more, using up the remaining lard mixture, then roll it out to its original size.

Turn the dough over and place it in a shallow baking tin lined with lightly oiled greaseproof or silicone paper, with enough room for it to rise again. Leave to prove in a warm place for about 30 minutes, or until it has almost doubled in volume.

Meanwhile, preheat the oven to 190°C/gas 5. Bake the cake for about 45 minutes. Turn it out upside down on to another tray or large dish and leave to cool a little. Sprinkle the cake generously with caster sugar.

The lardy cake is best served warm, just as it is.

Cheeses of the South West

As well as having a long tradition of making some of the nation's favourite cheeses, the rich heritage of dairy farming in the South West has also lately spawned some of the most exciting new cheese-makers, whose expertise and innovation now regularly help them sweep the board at the Annual Cheese Awards in all categories.

Cheddar is, of course, our most famous cheese and the one widely copied worldwide. I'm always amazed when I go travelling, as there seems to be Cheddar of some description on the shelves wherever I go. From what I've tasted, though, the basic recipe and method must get pretty abused, and the results are fit only for basic cooking.

The original cheese may well have started its life in the village of Cheddar on the southern edge of the Mendips, but history tells us that it was widely made throughout Somerset and surrounding counties since the fifteenth century. In the seventeenth century, the communal pooling of milk to make very large wheels of Cheddar was well documented. Generally, milk was contributed from surrounding farms to a common dairy, or 'Cheddar Club', to make large cheeses for maturing. These days, Cheddar is made in all sizes, the smaller cylinders, known as truckles and weighing from about half a kilo, are probably the best size to keep at home, as you can cut off what you need and keep the rest wrapped in its natural cloth to mature to exactly the state you prefer. Many cheese-makers make their cheeses much larger, up to about 30kg, which tend to get cut into chunks for supermarket retail.

The flavour of Cheddar does change considerably with exact manufacturing methods and degree of maturity. It should be a pleasing yellow in colour, with a smooth waxy texture and distinctly nutty flavour. A good farmhouse Cheddar from a small producer, such as Somerset's glorious Keen's and Montgomery's or Denhay Farm (see page 76), will give you best results.

Generally, a 'mild' Cheddar has been matured for only 3-5 months, a 'mature' Cheddar over 6 months and a good 'farmhouse' over 9 months. If you are only used to run-of-the-mill, vacuum-packed rindless supermarket Cheddar, then a farmhouse version may at first actually be offensive to you, but it's worth persisting – eventually you'll realize what your taste buds have been missing.

Double Gloucester and, the now much less familiar, *Single Gloucester* cheeses are obviously strongly associated with their county of origin. Both cheeses evolved in the late eighteenth century and were originally made with milk from Gloucester cattle, which apparently lends itself well to cheese-making. Single Gloucester uses skimmed milk from the evening milking mixed with whole milk from the morning, whereas Double Gloucester is made from whole milk from both evening and morning milkings. This is one of the possible reasons for it being called 'double', but some argue that it is simply because single is made in thinner wheels.

Double Gloucester is much more highly coloured than Single as it is traditionally dyed – at one time with carrot juice or saffron but nowadays with the vegetable dye annatto. It is matured in flat 30cm wheels, which have led to fascinating folk customs in the area, notably the cheese rolling on Whit Monday at Coopers Hill between Gloucester and Cheltenham, where four cheeses were rolled down the hill, chased by the assembled crowd – an event recently discontinued for reasons of public safety.

Usually matured for around 3 or 4 months, Double Gloucester has a smooth, buttery texture and a clean creamy, mellow flavour. Single Gloucester is generally ivory in colour and, has a more delicate, milder flavour that generally doesn't lend itself to lengthy ageing. Look out for cheeses from Smart's Traditional Gloucester Cheese in Birdwood, one of the few farms currently making farmhouse versions of both cheeses. Charles Martell, of Stinking Bishop fame (see opposite and page 75), also makes an award-winning Single Gloucester.

When I was very young, I remember hearing strange tales about a rare – almost mythical – Dorset cheese known as *Blue Vinney*. I also remember reading Richard Mabey's book, *In Search of Food*, in which he ended up in Bridport in search of the fabled cheese, but eventually even he had to leave empty-handed.

The history of the real Blue Vinney is actually much less of a secret. In the 1800s, Blue Vinney (from 'vinew' an Old English word for mould) could be found in nearly every farmhouse in Dorset. Farmers' wives would make it using leftover milk after the cream had been skimmed off for butter-making. The resulting cheese had a very low fat content, which tended to discourage the necessary blueing. As a result, cheese-makers were reputed to have resorted to all sorts of inventive measures to encourage the mould to develop – maturing the cheese on damp barn floors, in harness rooms, next to old boots, etc. Sadly, perhaps as a result of increasingly stringent hygiene legislation, production of this cheese gradually diminished over time, completely disappearing in the 1970s. That was exactly the time, when I was about 9 or 10, that the cheesey gossip began to circulate – mostly to

ABOVE LEFT Charles Martell, cheesemaker, fruit grower and creator of the celebrated Stinking Bishop (see left and page 75).

do with the tales of the arcane methods of production.

One of a tiny handful of Blue Vinney producers left today is Mike Davies, owner of Woodbridge Farm, near Sturminster Newton, who revived the old recipe for Dorset Blue Vinny back in 1982. (Mike has always spelt his cheese without the 'e' as he reckons he had a licence to do so because he 'resurrected it'. Why not?) Mike had taken a cheese-making course when he was a student at the Canning College of Agriculture in Somerset, and when it came time for him to diversify his farming, he had stored up quite a passion to make a great cheese, and knew Blue Vinny was the one – but one made without reverting to any of the old dodgy maturation tricks.

He managed to dig up a few old recipes from the Ministry of Agriculture, Fisheries and Food's offices in nearby Dorchester and started experimenting in his garage on Saturdays, using cut-off bits of drainpipe as moulds. He uses unpasteurized milk from his own herd of Friesians, which graze on grass in the Blackmore Vale fields. Mike insists on controlling every aspect of production and his head cheese-maker, Priscilla Vinning – who has been working for him for 25 years and looks after the daily process – is like part of the family. Mike's daughter Emily, brother Richard and Emily's husband Iain have taken over the day-to-day running of the dairy. However, Dad is still there – as he was the day I turned up – pulling cheeses apart at random and checking the quality and individual character of each batch.

Mike tells me the only difference between his and the original recipe is the use of vegetarian rennet and, of course, the strange goings-on to get blue mould in the cheese. The Blue Vinny ageing process takes 5 months, after which the interior of the cheese gets quite dark and develops a sharp flavour that has a long finish.

As an example of clever modern family farming, Emily – after returning from trips to local farmers' markets a couple of years ago - found that they needed an outlet for off-cuts of their Blue Vinny. So, she started making various soups featuring their cheese and taking them to market. They were a great hit, especially in the winter months, Emily tells me, and they now make and sell 2,000 pots a week, using their own milk and cream, together with vegetables from local farmers, who are glad to get rid of odd-shaped and -sized specimens.

Beenleigh Blue is one of my favourite blue cheeses. It is

probably the best known of the several cheeses from the Ticklemore Cheese Company, founded by Robin Congdon, that are among the most inspirational and exciting cheeses we have in this country. He has been farming on the Sharpham Estate overlooking the Dart Estuary since the 1970s. While working on the farm, Robin spent some time milking ewes and this inspired him to make yoghurt with some of their milk. He soon got into cheese-making, became fascinated by the workings of cheese-making bacteria, and has become an expert on these helpful microbes. 'The interactions of these invisible workhorses are critical to every aspect of making a great cheese,' he says.

Beenleigh Blue was his first creation with partner Sarie Cooper in the late 1970s, and I remember using it when I was at the Dorchester. Its taste certainly reflects a well-made ewes'-milk cheese with that slight saltiness of, say, Roquefort, developing into a sweet aftertaste. It was, in fact, the first blue sheep's-milk cheese to be made in the area for many years and, perhaps as a result, there are a couple more now being made in Britain – a sure sign that British cheese-makers will soon be giving the French a run for their money. Beenleigh Blue is made from January to July and matured for about 7 months, so has seasonal availability from September to February.

Devon Blue was created by Robin in the mid 1980s rather more conventionally, in really more of a French style, using cows' milk and *Penicillium roquefortii* to

Dorset knobs

I have fond memories of the famous Dorset Knob biscuit. My gran used to leave a packet out on the kitchen table with some butter and Stilton for when I got in from a night out with the boys. Without a good layer of butter and some cheese, they can be rather bland, but either one or both fats really bring out their delicate yeasty flavour. The problem with these rather brittle objects is that there is a distinct art to cutting and eating them. It is rather like opening an oyster — you insert the point of a knife into them and twist . . . with luck you end up with two halves, not a shattering of crumbs.

My great-grandfather had the right idea: he used to eat only the brown variety, which they still make in small amounts today, and he'd dunk them in the cup of tea he had just before he went to bed. His problem, though, was that the bits used to sink to the bottom of the tea instead of shattering all over the room.

The home of the Dorset knob is a small Victorian bakery in Morcomelake, 4 miles west of Bridport. The biscuits as we now know them were originally made from leftover dough to which butter and sugar were added. This was then rolled and cut into small button shapes, which were baked in the dying heat of the oven until they were dry, like rusks. The name came from hand-sewn Dorset knob buttons, which were still being made in the last revival of the once-thriving cottage industry of Dorset buttonry in the eighteenth century.

The biscuits originally formed the traditional meal of local farm workers at the start of the day, and the Moores Company have been making them since 1850. Apparently, they were a favourite food of Thomas Hardy, who had them at suppertime with some Blue Vinney. Still made in the traditional way, and only from January to March, each biscuit is moulded by hand and has three separate bakings, lasting a total of four hours.

This unique example of traditional craft baking is one of the many reasons why the biscuits need to be appreciated, and I have spent much of my adult life convincing and educating people on their eating qualities. I have even managed to turn the opinions of fellow food writers who had already slated the poor little things in the press. The lovely old bakery is soon to move to new premises in Bridport, but on my last visit, things were as normal, except that the Dorset knob season had just started and they were struggling to keep up with demand.

develop the veining. Unlike most cheeses, the curds are moulded without draining and then wrapped in gold foil after 3-4 weeks of maturing, when enough blue has developed. They are then matured in the foil for a further 6-8 months. Devon Blue has a surprisingly creamy mellow taste for a blue cheese, with a rather sophisticated flavour.

Harbourne Blue is the newest addition to Ticklemore's blue cheese portfolio, this time using goats' milk – another example of their pushing cheese-making boundaries. This has consistently won accolades over the years at the British Cheese Awards. The goats' milk gives it a unique character, with a very white, crumbly texture and a more powerful flavour than most cows'-milk cheeses. It is made all year round, using local milk, although its potency can vary throughout the year. I have often served all three of Robin's blue cheeses together, as it is just so unusual for a cheese-maker to make three blues from the milk of three different animals.

His *Ticklemore* is a hard goats'-milk cheese with a character rather like its passionate creator. It is one of only a handful of hard goats'-milk cheeses made in this country and its delicate flavour and cleverly created rind, with the markings of the basket in which it is matured, make it a very classy cheese indeed. I have also used it in cooking and crumbled it into salads.

If you are a fan of perry – alcoholic pear juice, in case you didn't know – then the name *Stinking Bishop* may ring a bell. It's a variety of pear used for making perry, and Charles Martell, another of the region's cheese-makers, has cleverly developed a cheese made in the style of a Reblochon, the French washed rind cheese. His version, with a girdle made of apple wood, is washed in Stinking Bishop perry to create a much-talked-about cheese. The perry activates bacteria in the cheese to create a delicious smelly cheese with a rich, creamy, oozing interior.

I found Stinking Bishop to be one of the best cheeses I have ever come across. It has the silkiness of a Vacherin and the some of the subtle aggression of a Munster. The Gloucester cattle he keeps for their milk are as calm and cool as Charles and his farm. He has renovated a barn made entirely of wood, even down to the feeding stocks, which he says 'keeps the old buggers calm and happy'.

Charles makes his cheeses, including a revived, neglected traditional unwashed Single Gloucester recipe, at Laurel Farm near Dymock. The Stinking Bishop story goes thus. Charles was talking to a neighbour called Bishop one day – over a glass of perry I presume – who confessed that the famous pear variety was named after his great-grandfather, who had grafted the original tree at Colwell near Malvern. He was apparently such an unpleasant old man that locals called him 'stinking Bishop'. The pear tree inherited the name and consequently so did the perry – and now Charles's cheese.

Apart from making cheese, Charles also grows apples and pears, specializing in reintroducing forgotten varieties of cider apple and perry pears. He currently has 100 varieties of apple and 50 of pear under cultivation. An active member of the Three Counties Cider and Perry Association, he releases cuttings to the local authority, who now have an identical orchard for public viewing.

I spotted Birdwood *Blue Heaven* on the cheese counter at the Severn and Wye Smokery's deli. I was intrigued, as there aren't that many British creamy blue cheeses around. It had the texture of Gorgonzola – in fact, in a blind tasting I would readily have mistaken it for just that. As I was admiring the cheese, Melissa Raven, the cheese-maker, strolled into the deli to have a chat with Cookie (Richard Cook), and we ended up organizing a trip to Birdwood House Farm, where she makes the cheese.

At the time, Melissa was moving house and dairy, and having a barn sale for a good old clear out, so cheese production was low. She did have some cheese left for tasting, though, and I was hooked on it. She explained that, as production was currently so slow, Randolph at Neal's Yard wasn't even stocking it and sales were thus mainly local. It's a real shame that such a great cheese is not more widely available. It is made organically with milk from her Friesian and Dairy Shorthorn cattle, which feed naturally on her land. The cheeses mature for 4–6 or 8-12 weeks maximum in her own cellars.

When I first came across *Cornish Yarg* 20 years ago, I thought it a bit gimmicky, not knowing then that wrapping cheese in edible leaves had a long history. Based on an old recipe, Cornish Yarg was developed in the 1970s by Welsh cheese-makers Alan and Jenny Gray (Yarg is Gray backwards). The current makers, Michael and Margaret Horrell, bought the recipe and have been making cheese on Netherton Farm at Upton Cross on the Duchy of Cornwall Estate since 1980.

Its production is quite unconventional, as the cheese is made by hand in open round vats, then goes on to be pressed and brined, before being wrapped in nettle leaves. The leaves, from neighbouring hedgerows and frozen for use throughout the year, are carefully brushed on to the cheese, where they attract a wonderful natural mould. The cheese is aged for about 2 months and, as it ripens, the leaves impart a delicate honey-mushroom flavour.

The Devon cream tea

A noteworthy part of West Country life is, undoubtedly, the cream tea. Although it's not something that locals tend to go for, it still exists in a big way as a tourist pleaser. The principal element is, of course, the beautifully unctuous local clotted cream. The term 'clotted' comes from 'clout', meaning 'a patch', and refers to the way the thick crust is formed on top of the cream as it is cooked. Surprisingly, clotted cream is said only to be made in Devon and Cornwall – and Phoenicia (modern-day Lebanon). The art of making the cream of Cornwall was possibly exchanged with the Phoenicians when they came to Britain to trade tin in 500 BC.

The idea of clotted cream had a practical purpose – before the advent of refrigeration it would make sense to preserve the excess dairy milk and cream. The milk would separate from the cream and the cream would get transferred into big pans, which were then floated in trays of constantly boiling water, in a process known as scalding. The cream would then become much thicker, develop that rich golden crust and 'clot', to give it that rich buttery texture. Today's method is a little more mechanical and sophisticated, but since 1998 Cornish clotted cream has been protected under EU law, which does not allow it to be made outside of its region of origin.

SCONES *makes 8*

Scones are made across the country, but are essential for an authentic Devon cream tea. Recipes vary slightly and, down West, very similar cakes can be referred to as Chudleighs, Cornish splits or Devonshire tetti cakes. You can adapt the recipe to suit by adding dried fruit or using buttermilk instead of milk for a richer texture.

225g plain flour, plus more for dusting

2 teaspoons baking powder

50g butter, cut into small pieces

pinch of salt

1 teaspoon caster sugar

about 150ml milk

1 small egg, beaten

Preheat the oven to 220ºC/gas 7. Sieve the flour and baking powder into a mixing bowl, then rub in the butter until the texture of breadcrumbs. Add the salt and sugar, then slowly mix in just enough milk to form a stiff dough.

Roll out the dough on a floured surface to about 1.5-2cm thick and cut out rounds 6-7cm across, re-rolling the trimmings as necessary. Arrange the rounds well apart on a baking tray. Brush the tops with the beaten egg to glaze.

Bake for 10-15 minutes, until lightly coloured.

Serve warm, with clotted cream and jam.

Denhay Farm

When I left Dorset in 1980 to face the big city, I wasn't even aware Denhay Farm existed. It's strange that you can grow up just a couple of miles from a great producer and not really know of their existence – or taste their produce – until you're grown-up, 15 years on. Back in my youthful Dorset days, Denhay only produced Cheddar and it wasn't until 1989 that they developed their celebrated air-dried ham, the nearest thing to the famous European prosciutto and Serrano hams to be made in Britain.

Denhay Cheddar has the EU's protected designation of origin (PDO) mark, which guarantees its authenticity, rather like the *appellation contrôllée* for French wines and cheeses, etc. It is normally matured for 6–9 months, producing a delicious medium-strength creamy Cheddar and is made in various sizes, one of which – Dorset Drum – is matured in a smaller 2kg cloth-wrapped truckle. Without knowing it, I had probably enjoyed this cheese in my sandwiches with Granddad's tomatoes on fishing trips.

The farm has been making Cheddar since 1958, and to help use up the whey they kept pigs. Amanda Streatfeild, one of the current generation at the farm, explained that the ham was created in 1989 using an old Dorset recipe given to them by a friend. They aimed to produce a ham that could be eaten like prosciutto, but not seen as an imitation. The whole legs are cured in Bramley apple juice, Dorset honey, curing salts and local herbs. Then, first lightly smoked over beech wood – local, of course – they are air-dried for up to 1 year.

The Dorset blueberry

I first came across the Dorset Blueberry Company through Tony Booth, our specialist greengrocer in Borough Market, where the DBC also have a stand. We are so used to buying imported blueberries, which are generally quite tasteless, that discovering a new UK source – and in the West Country – was a complete breath of fresh air and serious seasonal menu material.

The Dorset Blueberry Company is the largest producer of blueberries in the UK and this family business has a history dating back to 1949, when the present owner's grandfather planted the very first blueberries in the UK, after responding to a post-war article in *The Grower*, offering readers 100 free blueberry plants from Lulu Island, British Columbia. They flourished on his free-draining, acidic Dorset soil and the decision was taken to plant commercially, so he ordered 1,000 plants, which arrived on the *Queen Mary* in 1959.

The eventual 8 acres of planting lasted until 1998, when the present owners, Jennifer and David Trehane, took over 5 acres of the original plantation. They immediately put into action a plan for growth, including adding a few more acres of cultivation and installing a packing facility up to supermarket standards, to get the most out of their seasonal July to September crop.

In 2000, a freak hailstorm damaged the nearly ripe crop, reducing the quality of most of their fruit. Determined not to make a loss, they sold the fruit at local farmers' markets, and people bought it for jam and pies. The Trehanes very soon realized that there was an opportunity to add value to their crop, and quickly developed a range of prepared products, including juices, jams, sauces and baked goods.

BLUEBERRY PIE *serves* 4

Although this may seem like an American dish, wild berries like bilberries, whortleberries and blueberries – depending on what part of the country you are in – have been used in pie-making for centuries, and the blueberry is purely the name given to the cultivated version of these wild cousins. So, thanks to Mr Trehane, we don't have to go out in bushes in search of these rare berries. My preference would be clotted cream to go with these, although a ball of vanilla ice cream wouldn't go amiss.

600g blueberries (fresh or frozen)

120g plus 1 tablespoon, caster sugar

1 teaspoon arrowroot or cornflour

1 egg white

icing sugar, for dusting

for the pastry

50g butter, cut into small pieces, plus more for greasing

50g lard, cut into small pieces

200g plain flour, plus more for dusting

30g caster sugar

1 egg, separated

1–2 tablespoon(s) milk

To make the pastry, rub the butter and lard into the flour with your fingers until breadcrumb-like. Add the sugar, egg yolk and enough milk to form a smooth rollable dough. Divide the dough into two balls.

Roll out one of the balls of pastry on a floured surface to about 3mm thick and cut out 4 discs large enough to line four 10cm diameter by 3 cm deep individual tart tins, leaving about 5mm overhang. Roll out the other ball in the same way and cut 4 more discs to fit the tops.

Lightly grease the tins with butter and then line with the larger pastry discs to just above the top of the tin. Leave to rest, with the lids, for 30 minutes in a cool place (not the fridge or the pastry gets too hard to work).

Meanwhile, put the berries in a pan with the 120g sugar and 1 tablespoon water. Bring to a simmer and cook for 2 minutes, stirring occasionally. Mix the arrowroot with a little water, add to the berries and simmer for 2–3 minutes more, stirring occasionally. Transfer to a bowl and let cool.

Preheat the oven to 200°C/gas 6. Spoon the berry mixture into the pie shells, with not too much liquid. Brush the edges of the tops with the egg white beaten with the remaining sugar, lay on the tops and seal the edges by pinching with your fingers. Brush the top with more egg and make a small slit in the centre.

Bake the pies on a baking tray in the oven for 20–25 minutes until golden. Turn the oven down a little or cover the pies with foil if they begin to colour too rapidly. Take from the oven and leave to rest for about 15 minutes before turning them out of the moulds.

Derbyshire   *Herefordshire*   *Leicestershire*

Rutland   *Shropshire*   *Staffordshire*

Northamptonshire   Nottinghamshire

Warwickshire West Midlands Worcestershire

THE
MIDLANDS

ALONGSIDE THE GREAT HEARTLANDS of the Industrial Revolution paradoxically lies some of the most fertile agricultural countryside in Britain. The high level of milk production makes the Midlands a major cheese-making region, giving us Stilton, Derby cheese, Shropshire Blue and Leicester among others. What's more, I've found two new major cheese producers who have revived an old tradition and, by the time this book is published, will be well and truly on the map. Fruit and vegetables grow in abundance across the region: the Vale of Evesham goes green with asparagus in May, and its plums are some of England's finest. Plums are also a favourite in Lincolnshire, where they make plum bread. Pears feature on the coat of arms for Worcester; and the region's cider and perry are celebrated. On the livestock front, the Tamworth pig is the breed of choice for most of the pork products, which include Lincolnshire and Newmarket sausages, pork scratchings, and traditional dishes based on offal, such as faggots. Perhaps the most British of all meat dishes comes from the Midlands – the legendary Melton Mowbray pork pie. The region is also home to many other totemic British-manufactured food products, like Worcestershire Sauce and Marmite.

I was always a bit confused about where the Midlands ended and the North began, but after doing this book, I now know the Midlands right up to its boundaries. It is certainly not the food desert that some people led me to expect.

Within this proud beating heart of England there is a wealth of good produce, from good old pork pies to top-notch goats' cheeses.

ABOVE AND OPPOSITE The dairy herd at Quenby Hall (page 92) at rest and during milking, for the production of Stilton cheese.

Huntsman Farm

Huntsman Farm in the Wye valley is overlooked by Charlie Westhead, who I had just visited at Neal's Yard Creamery (page 90). Good food deserves good surroundings and, on my arrival, I had literally to drive over the River Wye, just downriver from where I had caught a couple of salmon earlier in the year.

Rosamund, Richard Vaughan's wife greeted me and, what do you know, she comes from Lyme Regis, just 6 miles down the coast from West Bay, so we had a bit of a natter, including some local chit chat, and reminisced about Lyme Bay and Chesil Beach before we even got our wellies on to tour the farm.

Richard Vaughan's rare-breed meat has been appearing on a few selected menus in and around London over the years, and more so in people's homes, through his many private mail order clients. Richard cleverly doesn't sell just the best joints, but encourages his customers to buy a box of the various cuts that make up the animal. This puts serious cooks to the test and ensures his rare breeds go to a good home and his customers get the best out of the beast.

Richard, the youngest son, took over the farm the family had been running for over 500 years and made a small profit running it as a mixed farm. His farm was a model farm and all the supermarket buyers that visited were suitably impressed for years, never questioning his farming methods or the meat. After 6 years or so, he discovered by accident that all the beef he was sending to the abattoir was just going into the mix with other farmers, and his efforts, care and attention to detail with his farming methods were just being lost and a total waste of time.

Richard rethought his strategy a little, let out his arable land to a neighbour and decided to concentrate on the top end of the meat market – where flavour was appreciated – and cut out the middleman. Since 1996, Richard has sold his rare-breed Middle White pigs, Longhorn beef and Ryeland sheep directly to the end-user, which has given him a sense of satisfaction and confidence that his meat is going to a good home with a sense of identity.

Sadly, we have got used to beef looking lean with no marbling and a small proportion of fat around it. The same is true of pork; most of us probably wouldn't buy a piece of pork with a couple of centimetres of fat on it, but would complain if it were tasteless. It's all gone to pot, because we are buying with our eyes instead of pursuing good taste and relying on the producer. I know

it's not always possible to buy direct, but Richard Vaughan gives you that opportunity, whether you are a restaurateur or a home cook.

I suppose Richard is best known for his Middle White pigs and he is the largest breeder in the country. Other pig farmers around the country, like Peter Gott, all speak highly of Richard Vaughan's Middle Whites, which are the white pigs with squashed-up noses, if you haven't seen them. Richard has 53 of the 300 Middle White sows in the country. They live up to 6 years and produce 8–9 piglets on the first litter, rising to up to 14 on the second, so these sows need to be carefully selected to ensure they have enough teats to feed these large litters.

All of Richard's pigs are in good condition, with tails and teeth intact, unlike those on some commercial pigs that often get removed to prevent them mauling each other. No chance of that here; instead, there is a sense of tranquillity about the farm and everyone's happy.

The Middle White was the specialist pork pig back in the 1930s and more than likely originated from crossbreeding of the now-extinct Small White and an imported Chinese pig, which accounts for its snubby nose and short body. It was an important porking pig, with a good generous covering of fat, which meant good flavour in the meat. Sadly, the invasion of Danish bacon hit our shelves and farmers began breeding larger leaner pigs as our tastes changed, and flavour went out of the window.

We are used to seeing pork named by breed these days on restaurant menus and, hopefully, we are becoming aware that it is a meat worthy of such definition. With a bit of luck, shops and supermarkets will soon follow suit, so we will all be a lot happier.

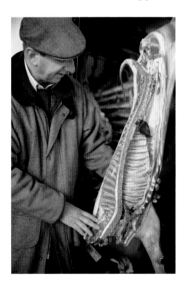

Mrs King's pork pies

Thanks to Borough Market in London, I now have a decent source of pork pies without travelling north of Watford. A good pork pie is pretty hard to come by these days, and everyone has got used to the bog-standard pies you buy in shops and supermarkets, which can be OK, but are pretty far removed from the real artisan product.

I decided to pay the Hartland brothers a visit in Cotgrave, just outside of Nottingham and, on arrival, found the boys hard at it, making pies by hand. It was just as I'd imagined it would be, as Ian, who works at Borough Market, had briefly explained to me over a few beers one night. The fascinating thing is that there is no real mystery or secret to good pie-making, just simply good ingredients and, as I discovered, good technique.

Ian Hartland let me into some of his little trade secrets, and a lot of the skill is really in the pastry-making, and in how its rolled and formed around the meat. The Hartland boys used to use German lard as fat in the pastry, and, in their constant process of development, have now moved on to Italian lard, which gives the pastry a crisper finish and texture.

The history of their pies goes back to Elizabeth King, who started a shop in her name selling pies and baked goods in Nottingham in 1883. Over the years, she developed a reputation for making special pies for special occasions. You see, the pork pie was once a festive food, Ian tells me, and people would order a pie of a size to suit the family or guests, not a bit like popping down to the supermarket and loading cocktail pies in your basket.

Ian's grandfather, who owned the pie business Pork Farms, heard that the famed Nottingham shop was for sale and bought it as a showcase for traditionally made pies, and continued in Mrs King's footsteps for handmade quality pies. The Hartland boys now run the business and still make very traditional pies out of their up-to-the-minute unit in Manvers Business Park, using uncured meat (for natural colour) and no added flavourings or herbs.

They sell small individual pies or larger party pies, and will also knock up a bespoke pie to suit your party. It almost felt like we were talking birthday cakes, but I suppose the celebratory feel of the Melton Mowbray has got a little lost these days, as every shop corner and supermarket stocks them. Incidentally, pie-makers in the area are in the process of getting the EU to declare the Melton Mowbray pork pie a protected geographical indication, so that only pies made within a 24-mile radius of the town can use the name.

The brothers don't skimp on their produce for the pies. Pure pork shoulder is used, with no added flavouring, apart from sea salt and pepper, unlike lots of other pie recipes that use a quantity of cured pork and spices to keep the meat pink. While the brothers are skilfully moulding the pies, a pot at the back of the small factory boils away with a good gelatinous stock made with trotters, to pour into the pies once they are cooked. You can even buy the pies uncooked, with a little pot of the jelly to take home and finish off the process yourself.

PORK PIE *makes 6–8*

Homemade pork pies are nothing like the ones you buy. The pastry is easy to make and if you haven't got a mincer at home on your mixing machine, you can just chop the meat up very finely by hand. Also, a helpful butcher might mince the filling for you. You can use various types of moulds for this, including individual open-bottomed soufflé rings, or raise them by hand like the Hartland boys do, but I'm not going to let you into their little secret method. All you do is take a large disc of pastry and shape it round the filling into a bulgy-sided pie, then join it to a smaller circle of pastry at the top by pinching round the edge. You could use the recipe opposite to make 2 big pies or even one very large one.

I prefer to eat these pies warm rather than cold, as that brings out the flavour and the pastry tends to be crisper. You can also add seasonings like anchovy essence, mace or allspice and a bit of sage to suit your taste – it's entirely up to you. I haven't given you details of the long tedious task of making a jellied stock here, as once the pies are cooked they probably won't be hanging around long enough to get filled with jelly.

for the filling
1 kg boned shoulder of pork, including
20–30 per cent fat
sea salt and freshly ground black pepper

for the hot-water crust pastry
500g plain flour
½ teaspoon salt
175g lard
1 egg, beaten

First prepare the filling: chop some of the best bits of pork into rough 1cm dice and mince or finely chop the rest. Season it well and mix in the diced meat. Take a small teaspoonful of the mixture and fry it to check the seasoning, then adjust it if necessary. Preheat the oven to 200°C/gas 6.

Make the pastry: mix the flour and salt in a bowl and make a well in the centre. Bring 200ml water and the lard to the boil, then stir it into the flour with a wooden spoon to form a smooth dough. Leave the dough covered for about 15 minutes or so, until it can be handled.

Divide the dough into 6-8 equal pieces. Take one of the balls of dough and divide it into 2 balls, one twice the size of the other. Roll the larger piece on a lightly floured table to about 12–14cm in diameter. Use the smaller piece to make another circle about half the size for the top. Put some of the filling in the centre of the larger circle, lay the smaller circle on top and raise the sides of the larger one up, then pinch the lid and the top of the sides together with your fingers. If it looks a bit of a mess, you can reshape it, as the pastry is quite pliable. Repeat with the rest of the pastry and filling.

Brush the pies all over with the beaten egg and cook them for 35–40 minutes. If they are colouring too much, cover them with foil and turn the oven down.

Serve them warm or cold, preferably with homemade piccalilli.

Goodman's geese

I was looking forward to meeting Judy Goodman, who had promised us lunch, but we were running very late, as I had somewhat misjudged the time. The girls and I were starving after a three-hour trek across country and up the M5 from Sturminster Newton in North Dorset. Luckily, Judy had prepared cold roast goose with apple sauce and local organic salad leaves. Just the job. We even got some Worcester raspberries for pud that Judy had frozen at the end of the season and just lightly defrosted on the Aga and dusted with caster sugar. They were delicious, and a great alternative to them fresh or cooked into a compote.

Walsgrove Farm was once a dairy farm and, as with lots of farming stories across the country, they had to rethink their business strategy. The Goodmans always eat goose at Christmas and, in 1981, when her father-in-law failed to find a goose anywhere, Judy promised to raise a few for the following year just to be sure.

The following year, milk quotas arrived and prices dropped, so Judy decided to buy a few more geese. By 1985, Judy had 300 geese and was starting to get a bit of media coverage. Much success and demand followed, including being named Worcestershire Woman of the Year. Judy puts it down to the presentation of the birds, which she sends out in a well-designed, goose-sized cardboard box with

fresh herbs and the livers, giblets and hearts, cleaned and packed separately, together with some extra fat for roasting the potatoes. Of course, once you get past the trimmings, the quality of the bird is the determining factor and this is down to their grain, wheat and maize feed, and, of course, their free-range roaming.

Judy hasn't got that much competition and goose is the only kind of poultry left that is actually seasonal and festive. As well as on Christmas Day, goose was traditionally eaten on Michaelmas Day (29 September) and St Martins Day (11 November). Michaelmas Day was a regular holy day of the old church calendar and has long been celebrated as the festival day of St Michael the Archangel, when goose is traditionally eaten, before it gets its winter coat.

ROAST MICHAELMAS GOOSE WITH APPLE SAUCE

Judy recommends getting your bird to room temperature before cooking it, which should apply to most meats, but poultry tends to go straight in the oven from the fridge in most cases, which means the exterior will cook quicker and dry out as the heat struggles to penetrate into the chilled centre. With goose and duck, however, this method means the heat can immediately start rendering the fat, giving the skin a crisp and delicious finish, instead of being flabby and indigestible.

So how big should your goose be? Well, a goose

weighing about 4–5kg should be enough for 5–6 people, and I would suggest getting a couple of birds, if your oven can take them, for more than 8–10.

The secret in rendering down the fat is to begin the cooking with the breasts down in the pan, so the skin fries in the hot fat that's released from under the skin. This is the mistake that a lot of people make with goose, by just bunging it in the oven for hours on end and hoping for the best, and you just end up with a dry fatty bird.

Judy also covers the legs with foil after seasoning them and smearing goose fat over them, then roasts the bird for an hour on its back, turning it over on to the breasts to finish the crisping process for another 45 minutes or so, then back breast up for the final 15–20 minutes.

I've tried lots of different ways with goose over the years and found that, unlike duck, the legs need extra slow and longer cooking, so the breasts can get just cooked to medium and you end up with slow-cooked crisp legs. You also need to get enough fat rendered down from them to get your roast potatoes started. If your goose doesn't come with giblets, to make stock for a good pan gravy, in place of its liver use about 100g chicken livers.

1 oven-ready goose, preferably with giblets

salt and freshly ground black pepper

for the stuffing
2 onions, finely chopped
1 tablespoon chopped fresh sage
80g butter
100g fresh white breadcrumbs
1 tablespoon chopped parsley

for the apple sauce
1kg cooking apples, peeled, cored and roughly chopped
2 tablespoons caster sugar
50g butter

Preheat the oven to 160°C/gas 3.

To make the stuffing, gently cook the onions and sage in 60g of butter for 2–3 minutes without allowing them to colour. Remove from the heat and stir in the breadcrumbs.

Meanwhile, season and fry the goose livers in the remaining butter in a hot frying pan for a couple of minutes on each side, remove from the heat and let cool a little. Chop the livers into rough smallish pieces and mix into the stuffing with the parsley, then season to taste.

Remove the legs from the goose by pulling them away from the bone and cutting at the joint. Remove any fat and skin from underneath the goose on the backbone and put the legs in a snug-fitting oven tray. Season the legs and cook for 2½ hours, basting every so often. Drain off the fat and use to roast the potatoes. Keep the legs warm until required, or put them back in the oven for the last 15 minutes of the rest of the goose's cooking time.

Increase the oven setting to 220°C/gas 7. Spoon the stuffing into the cavity of the bird and season the breasts, spoon over a little of the fat that the legs have been cooking in and put them in a roasting tray with the breasts facing down and cook for 50 minutes, draining off surplus fat from time to time.

Turn the oven down 200°C/gas 6, then turn the bird back up on its back and cook for a further 30 minutes. This will produce a bird that is pink, allow longer for medium. Leave to rest for 20–30 minutes.

Remove the breasts from the bone with a sharp knife and slice thinly across, skin side down. The leg meat can just be carved off the bone, or cut into chunks.

While the bird is resting, put the apples in a pan with the sugar and butter, cover and cook gently, stirring every so often, for 15–20 minutes, until the apples start to disintegrate. You can keep the sauce chunky and natural, or blend it. Check the sweetness and add more sugar if necessary, although it shouldn't be too sweet.

MAKING GOOSE (OR ANY POULTRY) GRAVY

It's always a good idea to get ahead of a big meal like Christmas (or Michaelmas) Day with a good batch of gravy that has been carefully made and looked after, rather than scrabbling around after all the meat is cooked, waiting for the liquid in the roasting tin to take on some flavour. In fact, it's a good idea all the year round to have a good stock of gravy in the freezer for roasts and quick sauces.

With goose, or any poultry come to that, you are only going to get a certain amount of giblets and a neck to flavour a gravy, so I strongly recommend getting some extra chicken bits from your butcher, like wings, necks and bones – and make the gravy a couple of days ahead.

This recipe should make enough for Christmas day, so scale up the quantities for large batches to freeze.

500g chicken or duck bones, or a mixture, chopped into small pieces

1 large onion, roughly chopped

2 medium carrots, peeled and roughly chopped

1 celery stalk, roughly chopped

1 leek, trimmed, roughly chopped and well rinsed

2-3 garlic cloves, chopped

1 teaspoon tomato paste

1 tablespoon flour

2 litres chicken stock (2 good-quality stock cubes dissolved in that amount of water will do)

6 black peppercorns

a few sprigs of thyme

1 bay leaf

Preheat the oven to 200°C/gas 6. Roast the bones, giblets, vegetables and garlic for about 15–20 minutes until lightly coloured, giving them a good stir every so often. When they're a nice golden-brown colour, add the tomato paste, followed by the flour and stir well. Return the pan to the oven for another 10 minutes.

Remove the roasting tray from the oven, add a little of the stock and give it a good stir over a low heat. This will remove any residue from the tray and begin the thickening process. Transfer everything to a large pan, cover with the remaining stock and some cold water if this doesn't cover the bones. Add the peppercorns, thyme and bay leaf. Bring to the boil, skim off any scum and simmer for 2 hours. It may need occasional topping up with water. Skim occasionally as required.

Strain through a sieve and remove any fat with a ladle. Check its strength and reduce if necessary. If not thick enough, stir in some cornflour mixed with a little water.

Worcestershire Sauce

Worcestershire Sauce is our version of fish sauce or soy sauce – the one we keep next to the Colman's mustard. Few of us turn the bottle to reveal the 'Vinegar, molasses, sugar, salt, anchovies, tamarinds, onions, garlic, spices and other flavourings' listed in the ingredients, never questioning the contents of the stuff that perks up our usual hangover remedy, a Bloody Mary. Considering that Lea and Perrins have been knocking out the sauce for over 170 years, it contains a scarily modern list of ingredients, the kind of which you'd gather to knock up a rather contrived 'East meets West' sauce. Quite how those flavours first became married in the bottle is down to Messrs John Wheeley Lea and Mr William Henry Perrins. The two were partners in a chemists' shop in Broad Street, Worcester, and they got their lucky break one day back in 1835 when folklore has it that Marcus, Lord Sandys called in on his return from a stint as Governor of Bengal. He asked them to make him up a batch of sauce using a recipe he'd brought back from India. Messrs Lea and Perrins got to work on it, but when the end-product was tasted, it was ghastly, to say the least. They sent the bottles on to his lordship despite the shocking taste and kept back a few samples, being chemists, just in case something remarkable happened in the bottle. The story goes that these jars of sauce did end up doing remarkable things in the bottle after two years' maturation in the cellars, and the sauce had improved beyond all recognition. By 1837, Lea & Perrins Original and Genuine Worcestershire Sauce was in commercial production, and by 1843 they were selling 14,500 bottles a year.

Today, Worcestershire Sauce's reputation still relies on a fairly secret recipe, so no one really know quite how much it has changed over the years, except it's now matured in stainless steel, not wooden barrels.

In 1930, Lea & Perrins merged with nearby Birmingham sauce manufacturer HP foods, makers of the famous HP Sauce, now owned by French firm BSN.

Cheeses of the Midlands

Red Leicester For some reason, I've always shied away from Red Leicester, perhaps it was the colour. That bright orange and slightly artificial look about it has never turned me on. Red Leicester in its unpasteurized form hasn't been made in the district of Leicester for some years, and the more you try to research this the less information you get. So, what happened to it? Did it go out of vogue? I wonder, or did it just get forgotten about and the commercially made Red Leicester took its glory?

Well, those cloth-wrapped, unpasteurized Red Leicester flats have just about made a comeback at Sparkenhoe Farm in Upton, near Market Bosworth. Jo and David Clarke ran a mixed arable, grain and dairy farm, with a few sheep and a B&B, but this wasn't really making them a good enough living. One evening, David was chatting with friends in the pub, and the subject of Red Leicester cheese came up. Over a few pints, they bemoaned how sad it was that it just didn't exist in the area – well, not the proper stuff anyway.

They did some research and found that, in the 1850s, a Mr Chapman made the cheese and ended up selling his herd of pedigree Longhorn along with a bull called Sparkenhoe. The remarkable fit between that and the name of their farm made them think they'd better set about making cheese – except they didn't know where to start. They both went on a cheese-making course at Rease Heath College in Nantwich, under the tutorship of Chris Ashby, a cheese expert who has put many successful cheese-makers through the training process.

It was going to cost a fair bit of money to set up, especially if they wanted to go unpasteurized, but they were successful in getting a grant from DEFRA for 50% of the start-up costs and started building in May 2005.

Their first cheese production day was on 2 November 2005, when they made just 30kg. The following day they were a bit more ambitious and made 300kg, and, sadly, everything went wrong, the machinery broke down, the lot. Fortunately, things have settled down a bit since.

They have 150 Holstein Friesians, which David looks after, then hands the milk over to Jo. The cheeses are made in the traditional way, except they use annatto these days and not carotene to colour it. The cheeses are cloth-bound and left to mature for 5 months.

At the time, I wrote this, the plan was to sell in local

markets and delis, as well as to Paxton and Whitfield and Neal's Yard in London. I promised to get it on the menu in the restaurants as soon as enough cheese was mature.

Neal's Yard Creamery It felt like the winding road up to Dorstone, towards Arthurstone, was never going to end, and I was a bit conscious that Charlie at the Neal's Yard Creamery might well have already packed up for the day. Luckily, when we got there, they were still at it and just wheeling the freshly moulded cheeses into the fridge.

Ragstone goats' cheese is one of the most used cheeses on our restaurant menus, appearing in salads, crumbled on to mixed beets, or on the individual cheese boards, together with a couple of other selected cheeses from the region.

Back in the 1980s, Charlie Westhead had been curious as to what was going on through the window of London's new cheese shop, Neal's Yard Dairy in Covent Garden, which had just been opened by Randolph Hodgson. His interest must have shown, as they offered Charlie a job behind the counter, working among artists and 'resting' actors. He served a kind of apprenticeship in the shop and ended up driving around the country collecting cheeses from farms for Randolph.

Working daily with the best cheeses in the country, Charlie really got a taste for the cheese business and quite fancied making cheese himself. A small dairy on Ragstone Ridge, Ide Hill in Kent, had been making the dairy items that Neal's Yard had once made in the shop and had to expand off site when business grew. It had been run by Perry James and Beatrice Garroche, who made a soft cheese called Perroche, from their names.

The creamery also produced Greek-style yoghurt, the first made in the UK, and crème fraîche, as well as a couple of soft cheeses. Charlie moved to a creamery in picturesque Dorstone, overlooking the Wye Valley and Black Mountains in 1990, and continued making the same cheeses, crème fraîche and yoghurt that were made in Kent and supplying them to Randolph at Neal's Yard.

When Charlie first arrived there, he bought his goats' milk for his Perroche, Dorstone and Ragstone from a small farm close by, but they turned out to be unreliable, so Charlie encouraged another local farmer, Richard Barter at Lime Kilns Farm near Ross-on-Wye, to start goat farming and supply milk for his cheeses and goats' curd.

His later cheeses, made from cows' milk from the September Organic Dairy at Almeley are Finn, an Irish name meaning 'White Ancient One', as this is the only cheese he makes and matures there. The other, Wealdon Round, is organic and has a light semi-soft texture to complement the Finn.

Charlie produces the finest selection of soft cheeses I've ever come across and they would all stand up to any French soft cheeses that dare rival them.

Stilton, a brief history The king of British cheeses started life in the tiny roadside town of Stilton, in the region known as Huntingdonshire, now a part of Cambridgeshire. Stilton consisted of literally just a few buildings on either side of the Great North Road that was the stopping-off point for business travellers and farmers taking livestock to markets, sometimes as far afield as Smithfield in London.

The town's residents would be kept busy by travellers all the year round, and its blacksmiths, as you could imagine, had a steady source of income shoeing horses and dipping the feet of geese in tar, for their long trek to the market. Judy Goodman has it easy now up in Walsgrove Farm: she just pops them in a box with the trimmings and off they go with the postman.

The other great source of income was supplying the travellers with ale, and simple local cheese. Cheese was the most common way of preserving excess milk from both cows and sheep, and inns would offer anything from freshly made soft cheese to the mature versions, some of which would form natural blue veins.

One of the first local documented cheese-makers of quality in the early eighteen hundreds was Mrs Frances Pawlett of Wymondham. It was not necessarily the blue-veined cheese she was responsible for making, but she applied the cheese-making standards of the era and instituted the shape and size of the modern-day cheese. Mrs Pawlett and her husband became the leading forces, supplying the town of Stilton with cheese, but didn't have exclusive rights, as almost every local farm made a cheese of some description. What they also did, though, apart from making their own cheese, was collect quality cheeses from other dairies within the area of Rutland and Leicestershire, maintaining standards for the cheese that was becoming such a popular commodity with travellers.

The Bell, The Angel, The Talbot and The Woolpack were all competing for the retail Stilton market as thousands of cheeses were being sold every week, many to London, which was only 70 miles away and merely a comfortable day's travel by stagecoach at that time.

With the arrival of the railways in the 1840s, the coaching and posting business collapsed, and with it went the Stilton cheese market. The advent of the railways altered the Stilton cheese industry almost immediately, and its success as an internationally recognized cheese relied purely on its availability in London. On the other hand, the railway allowed more of the London aristocracy to visit Melton Mowbray in support of the local hunts, and the cheese was again promoted to such an enormous extent that railway wagons would get filled with cheeses on a weekly basis, with special deliveries even being made to the Houses of Parliament.

Up to the end of the nineteenth century, hundreds of farmers' wives were making Stilton in and around the Melton Mowbray area, some only producing a couple of cheeses a day, which would go to local markets and fairs in the town. At this time, specialist dairies were built to make the cheese, and cooperatives were formed. Some farming families become extremely wealthy, like Henry Morris of Saxelby, who owned seven dairies by 1910. Several specialist dairies were built before the First World War, several of which are still making cheese today.

BELOW large drums of Quenby Hall Stilton in the maturing room

Quenby Hall Stilton I heard a whisper in the cheese making world during the early summer months that there was a new Stilton cheese-maker out there who was about to kick up a bit of a storm, with his first batch ready just before the 2005 Christmas market. I left it until I got well stuck into the middle England research to check it out, then went to Randolph Hodgson to find out exactly who was responsible for the newest take on this world-renowned cheese.

Freddie de Lisle was the man I should see, said Randolph, and off I headed north to Leicestershire. I don't remember ever visiting Leicester before, although I must have done so at some stage of my life, and driving away from the station it just didn't feel at all like I was in Stilton country.

The minute Randolph Hodgson mentioned Freddie de Lisle, I just had to meet him. With a name like that, it sounded as if I was off to visit one of the Krays' boys, who had fled north to go under cover as a cheese-maker. I've also never headed up the long driveway of an impeccable Jacobean manor to visit a cheese-maker and may well never again, but I guess it was never going to be a scruffy old farm track, with Freddie de Lisle at the end of it.

I had about an hour tops with Freddie, as he had a high-level meeting in Leicester to attend, and my train was delayed from London, so we were all rushing around a bit on my arrival, and Freddie's PA managed to fall down the stairs leading me to Freddie's office in the cellars of the house. We quickly exchanged signed books, mine my fish book and Freddie's, *The History of Stilton*

Cheese by Trevor Hickman.

Sitting in 1,200 acres of land, Quenby Hall was built by George Ashby between 1615 and 1620. Freddie took me down to the large building predating the house that would have once been the dairy. It is now used for grand dinners and hired out for private parties, but still retains some of the relics of its cheese-making days.

The Ashbys were a self-supporting farming family and cheese would have been made just for their own use and that of friends. In the last part of the seventeenth century, cheese production there increased because of the park being enclosed, allowing better grazing control and thus a higher yield of milk. Around this time, a drum-shaped cheese was made at Quenby called Lady Beaumont's, which had a great reputation in the area and was sold in local markets and inns.

Mary Beaumont was the daughter of Sir Erasmus de la Fontaine of Kirby Bellars. She married Thomas Beaumont of Cole Orton and was related to the Ashbys. She gave her recipe to Elizabeth Scarborough, the cheese-maker at Quenby Hall dairy and her cheeses were produced in large quantities in the late seventeenth and early eighteenth century. The cheese was a pressed cheese coloured with marsh marigold flowers and the petals would be boiled with alum to produce a yellow dye that was added to the milk. The curd was crumbled, wrapped in linen and pressed with a 57lb weight. Like all farmhouse cheeses produced on farms in those days, however, the cheese was made so it would produce a blue mould under the crust while in storage.

From about 1715, Quenby Hall began to fall into

disrepair, as the Ashby family concentrated their energy on other estates. Elizabeth Scarborough married one of the Orton family of Little Dalby and began making Quenby cheese elsewhere, which developed into a recognized Stilton.

Freddie's family bought the Hall in 1972 and, in 2004, Freddie went about building a new dairy to reinstate Quenby Stilton in the marketplace. Freddie's mother's artist's studio was temporarily turned into a dairy to test and make the first cheeses, while the new cheese making room was being built, and he used an old kebab knife that he bought in Istanbul to cut the first curds.

He employed Sarah Strong, a local cheese-maker, and brought John Lambert out of retirement as head cheese-maker. At the time I visited, the 2005 batch wasn't quite ready for sampling, so I had a couple of months' wait until December to give it a go.

Sure enough a half-Stilton arrived in my office as promised, just in time for the Christmas festivities, and I still have some now, which I save for special house guests.

MULLED PORT JELLY *makes about 600ml*

Everyone has the odd bottle of port knocking around at Christmas time, and a great way to use it up is a jelly to go with obligatory lump of Stilton that goes on and off the dinner table.

3 gelatine leaves
600ml port
1 clove
½ cinnamon stick
65g sugar

Soak the gelatine leaves in cold water. Meanwhile, in a saucepan, bring half the port to the boil, together with the clove, cinnamon and sugar.

Squeeze out any excess water from the gelatine leaves and dissolve them in the hot liquid. Add the rest of the port, pass through a fine sieve, allow to cool, then store in a sealed jar in the fridge.

AUTUMN FRUIT CRUMBLE

In and around the Peak District, there is more to a rambler's country walk than meets the eye. Who picks wild blackberries, elderberries and wild blueberries these days? Sadly, most of us just walk past the things and don't realize their potential. I remember as a kid, walking along the old disused railway track, picking blackberries from the hedgerow for Gran to make into a pie or crumble, and that was my contribution to supper. Nowadays, I ensure an autumn Sunday morning country walk with my girls can become the source of great teatime pie material. I'd really like Ellie and Lydia to grow up with the thought that not all berries come from the supermarket in plastic punnets, and that it is acceptable to go out and pick food for free.

good knob of butter

3 large Bramley apples, peeled, cored and roughly chopped

75g caster sugar

150g blackberries and/or any other wild berries, like blueberries or elderberries

thick or clotted cream, or custard, to serve

for the crumble topping

40g cold unsalted butter, cut into small pieces

30g ground almonds

60g caster sugar

80g plain flour

Preheat the oven to 190°C/gas 5.

First make the filling: melt the butter in a pan, add the apples and sugar, and cook for 6-7 minutes, stirring occasionally until they are beginning to break down but are not too soft. Remove from the heat and stir in the blackberries and other berries. Put in a suitable ovenproof pie dish or individual pie dishes.

Mix all the topping ingredients in a food processor or mixer, or rub between your fingers until they look like breadcrumbs.

Sprinkle the crumble topping over the top of the filling and bake in the preheated oven for 30-40 minutes, until the top is golden brown.

Serve with thick or clotted cream, or custard.

Bakewell and its famous pudding

My journey last year to Bakewell managed to kill two birds with one stone, as I managed to catch some nice wild brown trout while we were there. A semi-culinary party were invited by Lord Edward Manners to stay in the delightful Haddon Hall for the weekend above the old original fourteenth-century kitchens and to fish the Wye. As you've probably noticed, most of my research trips involve a spot of fishing, and when there is a highly sought-after river involved, why not?

We returned most of our catch between us, except for a couple of nice fish on the last day, which fellow chef Raymond Blanc and I cooked with some locally gathered wild herbs like sorrel and wild garlic. Raymond knocked up a classic truite au bleu in the fishing hut with nice-sized fish straight out of the water, which is the whole idea of the dish. I had only ever eaten truite au bleu a couple of times, and that was with farmed fish, so it was a treat to have the dish caught by me and cooked by Raymond.

After everyone left Haddon Hall to return south, we went in search of the famous Bakewell pudding, even checking into the Rutland Arms Hotel, once the White Horse, where supposedly the pudding was first created.

The story goes that the Bakewell Pudding was first made by accident in the White Horse in 1860. Although, strangely enough, a book I have on my bookshelf by Eliza Acton, dated 1845, has a recipe for Bakewell Pudding and describes it as being a popular dish throughout the North, not only in Derbyshire, so the story may well be a bit of a myth. Whoever devised it, the recipe became so popular that, in 1860, Mrs Wilson, wife of a tallow chandler, set up a business making these puddings in her home, which is now the Original Bakewell Pudding Shop.

Although we think we found the original Bakewell Pudding Shop in the square, there were also a couple more also claiming to be the original. I bought a pudding from each and they all seemed to have modest traces of almond essence, although all were quite tasty.

One thing is clear, that the early recipes do not mention almonds. Acton uses citrus peel but no pastry, whereas our modern-day Bakewell Puddings do, and that suggests that the recipe has been altered over the years with ingredients that were possibly then in short supply or simply not available at all. However, the Bakewell Tart, which seems the popular variation outside of Bakewell, is quite far removed from the pudding, and is more of a French frangipane tart, unlike the pudding, which is more of a clafoutis cum custard tart.

makes one 20cm pudding

- 150g puff pastry
- 250g butter, melted
- 1 egg, beaten, plus 7 extra egg yolks
- 250g caster sugar
- 1 tablespoon ground almonds
- 3 tablespoon raspberry jam

Preheat the oven to 190°C/gas 5. Roll the pastry out to a thickness of about ⅓cm and prick it all over with a fork to prevent it rising, then use to line a 20 x 3cm deep, preferably sloping-sided, tart tin (I use an ovenproof non-stick frying pan, as this seems to be as close to the original as you can get). Leave to rest for 1 hour in the fridge.

Meanwhile, in a mixing bowl, mix the butter, egg and extra yolks with the sugar and almonds, and stir over a pan of simmering water for 3–4 minutes until it reaches a honey-like consistency.

Spoon the raspberry jam evenly over the bottom of the chilled pastry case, then pour the almond filling into the pastry case and bake the pudding for 45 minutes, or until the top is golden and the filling just set. If it's browning too much, turn the oven down halfway through.

Serve the pudding warm or at room temperature, with or without some cream.

ELDERFLOWER CORDIAL

This is another hedgerow treat that can be gathered and stored in bottles for the winter months. It's a posh kind of cordial, and a real treat just mixed with some sparkling water or made into a cocktail. Elderflowers have no real association with this part of the world, or any other come to that. However, it's just too easy these days for kids to grab a bottle of a commercial cordial from the cupboard and dilute it with more chemicals, and, in fact, these days, old-fashioned cordials seem to be left on the shelves in favour of expensive fizzy drinks.

Making your own drinks can be fun and, if you are using elderflowers, you are really just paying for the sugar and a bit of your own time in the country air. Elderflowers normally start appearing in mid-June, depending on the part of the country in which you live. If you want to make cordial that's going to keep, then you will need to put a fair amount of sugar in to preserve it. Once it's made, you can then dilute it for drinks or it makes delicious jellies with seasonal fruits.

    1 carrier bag of elderflowers (about
    800g–1 kg, or 20 or so heads)
    1kg unrefined or granulated sugar
    2 lemons, halved

Remove any leaves and stems from the elderflowers and shake out any insects. Place in a non-reactive pan with the sugar, squeeze the lemon juice in and put the lemon halves in the pan. Add 4 litres of water, bring to the boil and simmer for a minute. Remove from the heat and leave to infuse (covered) for 24 hours, stirring every so often.

Next day, strain through muslin and store in sterilized bottles. If you wish to keep it longer than a few days, then immerse the filled bottles in a pan of water, bring to the boil and simmer gently for 15 minutes, then leave to cool in the water and store in a cool place.

BOOZY BAKED WORCESTER APPLES *serves* 4

These are a rather grown-up version of baked apples. The booze and filling is cleverly contained in the pastry, which also makes them easier to transport. The ideal apple for this would be Worcester Pearmain, but they are not always available so I would go for a dessert apple, like Cox's, Pink Lady or Braeburn.

An appropriate alcohol for these apples would be cider brandy, if you can find it, which is our version of Calvados. It is marketed down in Somerset as Somerset Royal and pretty good it is too, or you may like to add a drop of homemade sloe gin to this recipe, or a mixture of the two. If you have neither, then Cognac, Calvados, sherry or rum work well, and will give a good aroma when you break through the crust.

    4 medium-sized dessert apples (see above)
    1 small egg, beaten
    thick custard or double cream, to serve

    for the pastry
    250g plain flour
    pinch of salt
    ½ tablespoon caster sugar
    60g lard
    25g unsalted butter

    for the filling
    30g walnuts, chopped
    30g nibbed almonds
    1 tablespoon ground almonds
    6 dates, chopped
    1 tablespoon raisins
    2 tablespoons brown sugar
    3 tablespoons apple brandy
    good pinch of mixed spice

Preheat the oven to 200C/gas 6. First make the pastry: mix the flour, salt and sugar in a bowl and make a well in the centre. Heat 100ml water with the lard and butter in a pan until they come to the boil, then pour on to the flour and stir in with a wooden spoon to form a smooth dough. Leave the dough covered for about 15 minutes or so, until it can be handled.

Divide the dough into 4 balls and roll each of them on a lightly floured table to about 14–16 cm in diameter and cut into circles large enough to cover the apples.

Cut the stalk end off the apple and remove the core, making a hole about 1.5 cm wide – enough to pour filling into. Mix the ingredients for the filling together and stuff into the apples. If any is left over, just spoon it on top.

Put an apple in the centre of each piece of pastry and bring the pastry up the sides of the apple, gathering it up and pinching it together, leaving the top of the apple and filling exposed. Place on a baking tray, brush with the beaten egg and bake for 45 minutes, or until the pastry is golden. If the pastry starts browning too much, cover with foil. Serve with thick custard or double cream.

Bedfordshire   *Cambridgeshire*   *Hertfordshire*   *Essex*

Hertfordshire   Lincolnshire   Norfolk   Suffolk

THE
EAST

THIS REGION IS KNOWN FOR ITS FLAT expanses and open skies, as well as its lengthy coastline. The vast fertile fields of Lincolnshire are said to produce one-fifth of the nation's homegrown food, and Grimsby and Great Yarmouth are still England's main fishing ports. Each coastal village or town has developed its own specialities: Cromer its small, weighty crabs; Stiffkey and Leigh-on-Sea have the best cockles in Britain; Wells-next-the-Sea specializes in whelks; and Southend is famous for whitebait. The oyster beds of Colchester have been exploited since Roman times, and sea salt is still gathered at Maldon. Abundant herring at Great Yarmouth led to numerous smokehouses and the tradition of the fish smoked as bloaters. Samphire, the succulent marsh plant, is also harvested all along the coast. The grain fields, coastal marshes and flat fens shelter a profusion of partridge, quail, woodcock, wild duck and pheasant. East Anglia is well known for soft fruit farming, especially around areas like Tiptree and Elsenham, both associated with jam making. Ham and bacon curing is another traditional industry and Norfolk is known for its Norfolk Black turkeys. Hot English mustard, produced from seed grown in brilliant yellow fields surrounding Norwich, is another world-renowned product.

The East Anglian coast is the nearest stretch of inspiring seashore to London for me and somewhat closer than my home town of West Bay. I tend to visit West Mersea Island quite often,

From the beaches of Suffolk up to the Norfolk Broads I had a good old forage all along my way for interesting sea vegetables and wild garlic plants, much to the surprise of many of my dinner guests afterwards. I even found a new oil to drizzle on my lovely new findings and to add to the array of salad dressing accoutrements on my kitchen cupboard shelves.

Fresh and tasty crabs, oysters, cockles and whelks, together with delicious vibrant rock samphire, are abundant all along the coastline of the East. A drive across the causeway to West Mersea is a must for all seafood lovers, but don't forget to take your own bread and wine if you are off to my favourite, The Company Shed. Otherwise, at Cookie's crab shop (opposite) you can eat outside overlooking the salt marshes.

mainly for a visit to one of my favourite eateries, The Company Shed. It is in my 'top ten' recommendations for a proper and simple fish-eating experience – if you're into fish and seafood that is, but I doubt if you would be on West Mersea Island if you weren't. The Island still seems relatively unknown, not a bad thing that, as it would be a shame if The Company Shed suddenly got jammed with sightseers.

The Company Shed is literally that, a shed, next to the yacht club. Run by Richard and Heather Haward, it sells locally caught fish and seafood to take away and cook at home or to eat in. Be warned, though; if you're eating in there, you do need to bring literally everything to accompany your fish, including bread and butter and wine.

If you're leaving London for the coast after work, make sure you get to your hotel before 9pm, as most restaurants stop serving food then, and you'll be lucky to get a prawn sandwich. Pathetic, I know, but that seems to be our eating culture when you get out of London. The safest bet for a lateish dinner is the Lighthouse in Aldeburgh – last orders at 10.00 p.m. One night we showed up there at 9.45pm and the place was full, but we were still fed. I think some other establishments should take their example and feed hungry travellers late. The food is always good there, with local offerings like asparagus in season, and the young staff are very friendly.

Cromer crab

Whether you've been there or not, the mention of Cromer brings to mind the seaside town's renowned crabs. Cromer, unfortunately marketed as the 'jewel of Norfolk', is your standard English seaside town and could readily disappoint the non-crab-eaters, with its skyline view of white caravans on the cliff tops.

Being a purist when it comes to shellfish, I prefer having a whole boiled crab in front of me, so that I know it has been boiled only recently. Unfortunately, the pre-prepared crabs dressed back in the shell are abundant here, so you need to know what to look for in a fresh crab. There is generally a feeling of dryness about them and the brown meat can be like reconstituted sawdust, so the things just scream for mayonnaise. This kind of misses the point for me, and that's exactly why I'd rather tackle the shells and claws for the moist white meat. The other thing that bugs me is that fishmongers in a town famed for its crabs and seafood – and this is the case not just in Cromer – display crab sticks next to the real thing … why, I really don't know.

While staying with my friend Ivor Barka at the Gate House, Gunton Park, I offered to cook one evening as we had James Ellis the gamekeeper coming for dinner and he was bringing the fillets from a recently caught fallow deer. Crab seemed like the obvious candidate for a starter, as Cromer was just a few miles away, and I just managed to grab a couple of freshly cooked ones from Brian and Julie Davies's crab shop (see below) before they closed for the day.

I had gathered some sea spinach and sea peas from Dunwich beach earlier in the day, and asparagus from Suffolk where I found the rapeseed oil (see page 120) and I supplemented these wild delights with some Suffolk mustard and local cider vinegar from Groveland Fruit Farm Shop, along with some peas and broad beans. I just love the whole thing of creating dishes from nothing and, before I left Southwold, I had no idea what I was going to serve for dinner, that's what cooking local and seasonal is all about.

The great thing with a crab, or most crustaceans come to that, is that the shells need not go to waste and I incorporated a soup made using the shell into the dinner and a crab dip from the brown meat, served with some chicory leaves. A whole crab may seem a rather expensive investment for a dinner, but not if you can get three separate dishes out of it.

Cookie's crab shop

On my travels I've come across very few places you can literally stop the car and jump out for a lobster or crab salad and eat it outside, while overlooking the salt marshes. You need to be at Cookie's at the right moment, though, when the local shellfish is just in, otherwise you may have to settle for frozen imports and slightly impolite service, but when you're hungry that becomes slightly irrelevant when there are no other fruits of the sea on offer for miles. Located in Salthouse on the north Norfolk coast, their menu also features delights like kipper and tomato soup, crevette and garlic anchovy salad, and buckling salad. If you want a nice glass of white wine to accompany any of these, you do have to take your own. In season, they also have bunches of marsh samphire stacked up outside to take home and cook.

CRAB AND SAMPHIRE SALAD *serves* 4

This salad literally got created en route from Suffolk up to Norfolk, by means of a bit of foraging for the pea shoots and sea spinach, and spontaneous farm shopping – even the dressing and right down to the Suffolk mustard. I favour the purist approach to crab, but when you are faced with lots of delicious seasonal and free ingredients in your basket, a bit of concocting doesn't do any harm. Small leaves like pea shoots are ideal and sea pea shoots even better.

40g (podded weight) peas

salt and freshly ground black pepper

handful of samphire, trimmed

60g (podded weight) broad beans

handful (50-60g) of small salad leaves, like pea shoots, land cress or harvested sea vegetables

200-250g freshly picked white crab meat

for the dressing

1 tablespoon cider vinegar

1 teaspoon Suffolk mustard

4 tablespoons rapeseed oil

Cook the peas in boiling salted water with a pinch of sugar for 3–4 minutes until tender, drain and leave to cool. Blanch the samphire briefly in boiling salted water, then drain and leave to cool. Cook the broad beans in boiling salted water for 3–4 minutes until tender, drain and leave to cool. If the broad beans are large, then remove the outer skins.

Make the dressing by mixing all of the ingredients together and seasoning lightly.

To serve, toss the vegetables and salad leaves in the dressing, season and arrange on plates, then scatter the crab meat over the salad.

Samphire

Samphire like most other wild sea vegetables is irresistible to me as I walk past it on the seashore and the marshes around the coast. Once I start gathering samphire, it almost seems a shame to stop, because it's free and a delicacy to most food lovers; but it's totally alien to others.

There are two main edible forms of samphire in Britain: the first and original is rock samphire, which is only really good for cooking and pickling; the second is marsh samphire, known as glasswort, so called because it was used as a source of soda for glassmaking. In Ireland, it is known as Peter's Cress and up north in the Morecambe Bay area, samphie. Traditionally, rock samphire was highly esteemed and glasswort was seen as food for the poor. The leaves of the plants before they flower in July and August can be cooked like French beans or pickled, as was very popular in Victorian times.

The revival of the fish trade, supplying commercial kitchens in the South East, has led to samphire enjoying renewed popularity, but it is mainly glasswort that is seen these days. Rock samphire is still seen on restaurant menus, but no one gathers enough of it to pickle, except the really serious foragers. It goes as well with lamb as it does with fish. Rock samphire is in season in high summer and is found growing on rocks and sands around the sea coast, together with sea spinach or sea beet and sea purslane. Glasswort, or marsh samphire, is found on the edges of tidal creeks.

In East Anglia, glasswort was accepted as samphire, and folk were very happy to pickle this as they would rock samphire. The old way was to pack it into jars with vinegar and store it in the bread ovens overnight – quite simple to do yourself for greens for the winter months.

Dorothy Hartley, the great scholarly food writer, refers to a recipe in her *Food in England* for samphire hash, in which it is mixed with pickled cucumbers and capers, and bound with an egg.

The oysters of Colchester

It's not much of a gastronomic centre now, but Colchester – or Camulodunum, as it was known in AD 47 (after Camulos, the Celtic name for their god of war), was the capital of Roman Britain – and of oyster cultivation. The Italians have been knocking British food since then: the Roman historian Pliny commented that the only good thing about Britain was its oysters. The Romans were pretty knowledgeable about such delicacies and taught us a thing or two about the eating qualities of shellfish, as opposed to seeing it as a substitute for meat and fish when they were in short supply.

The Romans became traders of the oysters that grew in the creeks surrounding Camulodunum and, not only did they transport them around the country, but they took them across the Channel, keeping them alive in roped sacks towed behind their ships. Evidence of this love of our native oysters was later found in excavations, and oyster shells and other shellfish remains form historic records in the ruins of the ancient city.

When the Romans left Britain in the early fifth century AD, the luxury status of the oyster fell away and they became a cheap alternative to meat, even being pickled to feed the poor. Up to the mid-nineteenth century, there was still a thriving oyster industry in the Blackwater and other estuaries along the Essex coast. Oyster boats sailed round the coast and up the Thames, mooring at Billingsgate, where their catch fetched low prices, before being sold cheaply in East End streets and ale houses. When trains became an alternative – and quicker – means of transportation, demand for oysters grew inland, and subsequent over-fishing diminished stocks. If you want to read more about the history of oysters, I'd recommend *The French, The English and The Oyster* by Robert Neild (Quiller Press).

Clean water is essential for oysters, as they feed by filtering it. Towards the end of the nineteenth century, as coastal cities grew in size and more waste was dumped in the sea, it meant big problems for the oyster. Attempts to make it illegal to sell oysters from polluted beds failed, and they were blamed for outbreaks of diseases such as typhoid. By the start of the First World War, the oyster trade in England had dropped by 75 per cent.

Since then they haven't been seen as everyday food, and most of us are so out of the habit of eating them we have no idea how to open them, and may even have an irrational fear of oysters. There's nothing to be afraid of: they are reared in clean, government-tested water before they reach wholesalers, and should come with a health

certificate indicating their source. Perhaps oysters take the rap for our other excesses. My first such experience was in college days when we went on an annual wine tour to France. We found ourselves sitting in a café in Marseilles knocking back Muscadet and oysters like they were going out of fashion. I suffered for days afterwards, but in all honesty, I couldn't really blame the seafood.

Our native season officially starts in September and goes on through the following months with an 'r' in them (though September can still be a bit hit and miss). Until the water is colder, oysters are still broody, releasing the larvae, which makes them milky and – in my experience, though not everyone agrees – can be unpleasant to eat. But, for those that can't wait, there are rock oysters, which were introduced after the outbreak of disease from countries such as Portugal, because the rocks were more hardy and used to the warmer waters.

Maldon is most famous for the sea salt marshes and a historic battle, but on a chilly morning a few years back I went there in search of the oysters that are the reminder of the area's busy past. Oysters aren't reared there now, but those that escaped from captivity, as it were, have since bred. While we waited for the tide to go out, between hot coffee and sausage sandwiches, we picked young, tender wild sea spinach leaves on the banks. We then waded into the silty estuary and gathered native and

rock oysters camouflaged in the grey wet sand. We were totally alone in the few miles of the peaceful tidal estuary, gathering food for free. If this had been France, we wouldn't have been alone, I can assure you.

There are still a few serious oyster gatherers in West Mersea, like Richard Haward, who continues the tradition of getting his oysters up to London and selling them along with lots of other local seafood at The Company Shed, next to the yacht club in West Mersea run by Richard's wife Heather (see page 102). You will also catch him on Fridays and Saturdays at London's Borough Market. Richard is one of eight growers who applied to the European Union to give protected geographical indication to native Colchester oysters. The aim is that this unique oyster, the only oyster to be grown in Essex from Roman times to 1926, will be given recognition as a regional speciality.

Another successful local trader, The Colchester Oyster Fishery, run by Christopher Kerrison, grows oysters in the upper part of the Pyfleet Creek and recently started marketing Colchester Piccolos, which are half-size versions of the rock oyster and grow to about 40 grams, rather like a cocktail oyster I once come across in New York's Grand Central Oyster Bar, called the Kumamoto. Christopher knows his shellfish and, as well as his local oysters, sells crab, clams and lobster.

The other well-known oysterman is Mike Dawson who has been oystering since he left school in 1981, when he went to work for veteran oyster fisherman Peter French. He subsequently retired and set up the West Mersea Oyster Company in 1990. He sells about 70 tonnes of natives a year and has beds on the Blackwater and surrounding creeks.

Mike says that natives can be really temperamental and, when we have really extreme conditions, like hot winters and cold icy summers, they don't hold up. There are certain wider parts of the creeks that are deeper and not so good for the oysters, as it is too cold, whereas in the shallower, narrower parts, it tends to be a bit warmer. The movement of the water and the spongy marshes either side of the creeks that run into the Blackwater act rather like a radiator, so when the tide comes in, it is warm and it feeds the creek with nutrients like plankton.

Mike, like the others, deals in a certain percentage of rock oysters, which are much sturdier in these extreme conditions and grow quicker; he also grows a smaller species, which he has called the Mersea Pearl.

Like Richard Haward, Mike has also set up an oyster bar, where you can buy all the local delicacies and good old lobster and chips and deep-fried fish. With guys like this, West Mersea is becoming one of the best places on the coast to eat really simple local fish and seafood.

BAKED SEA SNAILS WITH GARLIC
SHOOTS *serves* 4

Sea snails, or whelks, are associated with the seaside or East End seafood stalls, where they are sold in little tubs with malt vinegar, and are generally as edible as rubber bands. However, I find whelks much tastier than their landlubber snail cousins, and this dish is like a marine version of that bistro staple, *escargots à l'ail*. Along the Essex and Suffolk coastline, you will find many fishermen landing cockles and whelks. Sadly, though, I just don't think the demand is there now from the general public, just the old diehards.

Fishmongers may be able to order live whelks for you, or you could use large mussels or queen scallops in the shell. This recipe makes good use of garlic shoots – they look like spring onions and are the part of the plant that grows above the ground. They're hard to find, but my friends at L. Booths in London's Borough Market sell them. If you grow garlic, you could harvest your own, or use garlic chives or finely chopped wild garlic.

2kg small-to-medium-sized live whelks

about 500g sea salt

6-8 pieces of garlic shoots or chopped wild garlic leaves or garlic chives, trimmed and finely chopped

150g butter, softened

juice of ½ lemon

salt and freshly ground black pepper

crusty bread, to serve

for the cooking liquid

1 onion, roughly chopped

12 white peppercorns

1 teaspoon fennel seeds

a few sprigs of thyme

1 bay leaf

½ lemon

1 glass of white wine

Wash the whelks well in cold water, then drain them and put them into a bowl with the 300g of the sea salt. Leave for 2 hours, then leave them to wash under a trickle of running water for 30 minutes, giving them a good stir every so often.

Drain them well and then put them in a pan with the cooking liquid ingredients. Cover them with water and add a tablespoon of salt. Bring to the boil and then lower the heat and simmer gently for 45 minutes. Remove the pan from the heat and leave the whelks to cool in the liquid for about an hour or so.

When the whelks are cool enough to handle, remove them from the shell with a small skewer or lobster pick and discard the small disc-like piece of shell attached to the body, as well as the dark grey sac. Rinse and dry the shells on some kitchen paper.

Chop each piece of meat into 3 or 4 pieces and put them in a bowl with the garlic shoots, butter and lemon juice. Season with salt and freshly ground black pepper. Mix everything well and then push the mixture back into the shells.

Preheat the oven to 200°C/gas 6. Scatter the remaining sea salt about 1cm deep on one large, or 4 individual, ovenproof serving dish(es) – Le Creuset works well – and embed the whelks in the salt (you may need more salt, depending on the size of your dishes) so they don't fall over during cooking and most of the butter stays in the shells.

Bake for 12–15 minutes and serve immediately with crusty bread.

English mustard

I remember my grandfather telling me at meal times how Colman's had made their money from what we left on our plates. I used always to try and disguise any excess or hide it under remains of food on my plate, as I felt guilty for helping their seemingly unwarranted success.

Mustard is made from the ground seeds of the mustard plant, which is a member of the cabbage family and a variety of this is used in Asian cooking, the mustard leaf. Mustard has been used in England since Roman times and possibly before. Until the eighteenth century, though, it was only really used in the home, ground at the table like pepper.

Although we instantly recognize the name Colman for mustard, the art of mustard making on a commercial basis was pioneered in London in Garlick Hill by the Keen family – hence the saying 'keen as mustard'. Keen's were eventually swallowed up by Colman's in 1903.

Jeremiah Colman was originally a flour miller, owning several mills in the Norfolk area and one of the first employers in the country to offer staff benefits like a meal service, schools for employees' children, lodgings for working girls and a clothing club. In 1814, Jeremiah took over Stoke Holy Cross Mill near Norwich and started milling mustard seed, which was traditionally – and still is – grown in the fens of Cambridgeshire, Lincolnshire and Norfolk.

The Colman's mustard recipe uses two types of mustard seeds, white and brown, which gives the mustard its distinctive potent flavour. Back in the 1800s, farmers growing mustard crops would take their seed samples to market in small canvas bags to the Colman's agent, where the samples would be inspected and a price offered for the bulk. The Colman's factory is now in Carrow and the brand owned by Unilever, but there is a mustard shop, where you will find a little history of Jeremiah Colman's old mill.

Herrings on the East Coast

There is a classic synergy between herrings and mustard, not only because the hot spicy mustard cuts the subtle oiliness of the fish, but because the herring was once landed in large numbers off the East Coast in fairly close proximity to mustard-making country, and many old-fashioned herring recipes will incorporate mustard in some form or another.

Before the 1950s, many fishermen moved to Great Yarmouth to chase the herrings that moved up and down the coast in large numbers to feed during the autumn months, when the sea got colder. Herring traders followed, who would set up shop to sell the preserved herrings – salted, pickled and smoked – to the rest of Europe.

The 'silver darlings', as they were referred to by Mike Smylie who wrote a book on the history of herrings he actually called *Herring, a History of the Silver Darlings*, did begin to get a bit of a bad reputation, especially after the Second World War, when dye was put into kippers to speed up the smoking process. Tastes for oily fish were changing and herrings in whatever form were considered bony, unpalatable and as food for the poor. At the same time, white fish was becoming much more popular, a development that led to the advent of the dreaded fish finger, developed in Great Yarmouth in 1955.

This was not the only reason for the decline: the herring stocks were also gradually diminishing, which was partly due to overfishing but more due to the fact that the real herring trade in the area had always been the curing and smoking of herrings. When the herrings were landed, they would be graded for size and fat content, and put aside for curing and long slow smoking into what are known as red herrings and, with a lighter smoke, the famous Yarmouth bloaters. Occasionally, you will also find buckling at smokeries like the Cley smokehouse, which is herring cured and smoked with the roe in.

These traditional methods of curing fish are now difficult to find along the coast, as there are no herring boats left, except for one called *The Eva May*. This old wreck, seems to have been disowned and just left as a kind of memory of the wealth that Lowestoft once had when the harbour was jam-packed full of herring boats.

If you do come across one of the old traditional curers, they will more than likely be curing and smoking fish that's been imported from somewhere like Norway or Iceland, but nevertheless there are a few still keeping up the local tradition, even if the herring boats have all gone. The inshore lifeboat crew also do their bit and hold a herring festival in Hemsby in September, in which a thousand bloaters are prepared in the traditional way just to show that nothing has been forgotten.

HERRINGS WITH MUSTARD SAUCE *serves* 4

vegetable oil, for frying

salt and freshly ground white pepper

8 small herring fillets, each about 60g or 4 larger ones

a good knob of butter

for the sauce

2 shallots, finely chopped

3 tablespoons white wine

1 tablespoon cider vinegar

100ml fish stock

2 teaspoons English mustard, or more if you wish

150ml double cream

1 tablespoon chopped parsley

First make the sauce: simmer the shallots in the white wine and vinegar until the wine has evaporated, then add the fish stock and mustard, and simmer until you have a couple of tablespoons of liquid left. Add the cream and simmer until the sauce has reduced by about half and thickened. Add the parsley, season and simmer gently for another minute.

Meanwhile, heat a little vegetable oil in, preferably, a non-stick pan, season the herring fillets and fry them, skin side down first, for 2–3 minutes on each side, adding the knob of butter towards the end of cooking.

Spoon the sauce on to warmed plates and arrange the herring fillets on top.

A day's foraging, fishing and wild-fowling for supper

The estuaries along the coast attract wild fowl like teal and wild duck, and are a great source of marsh samphire and other seashore goodies, like sea kale and sea beet. If, like me, you are a hunter-gatherer, then you could really live the good life here.

A few years back I met up with my ultimate foraging match, Jonathan Young, editor of *The Field* magazine and a serious hunter-gatherer. The purpose of the day was to forage, hunt and fish for our supper, so, in order to fit that lot in, we had to be up way before the crack of dawn. We started the early September day by wild fowling at 3am and lay in our waders and Barbours in the Blackwater marshes, waiting for the sun to come up and the opportunity of bagging a passing wild duck. As it got lighter, I realized we'd been literally lying in beds of samphire, which went on for acres and acres in the creeks off the estuary. After Jonathan and his son had shot a couple of mallard, I was not quite into shooting yet, so we picked enough samphire for supper and some small sea beet leaves from alongside the estuary for a salad. I wasn't sure what type of salad, as we only had three ingredients for dinner so far.

We walked a couple of miles along the black water, which is tough going in heavy chest waders, with guns and bags of wild food. Jonathan had promised wild oysters once the tide had gone out and, when we found our spot, we waded into the estuary, where the old oyster flats would have been hundreds of years ago. There was evidence of oyster history – old wrecked boats and dilapidated jetties. Immediately we got on to the muddy flats, our eyes tuned into oyster shells sitting on the mud and weed. We filled a couple of carrier bags and I was conscious this was yet more weight to get back to the car.

Back on dry land, we picked elderberries, which were the missing link to the wild duck salad for starters. The fish course was to be pike and I had a great recipe up my sleeve, if one was good enough to give itself up. We tried hard with a fly and lures, and eventually hooked one with a baby pike imitation lure.

The great thing with autumn is the ingredients, and we finished off the day with a few handfuls of vibrant yellow girolles, the earthy match for the pike, with a light red wine sauce. Dessert was blackberries in a crumble with apples from the garden and thick local cream.

ROAST MALLARD WITH ELDERBERRIES

serves 4

Wild duck and elderberries are a perfect seasonal marriage, and the tartness of the little berries makes a delicious sauce. There are several types of wild duck that could be used for this dish – teal, widgeon and mallard, the most popular probably being the mallard. Most people wouldn't give elderberries the time of day, but they are well worth the effort and, in the autumn, I always freeze them to use in a dressing for salads, or to drop into a sauce for game birds or venison.

2 plump wild ducks

1 small onion, roughly chopped

1 carrot, roughly chopped

2 celery stalks, roughly chopped

a few sprigs of thyme

a little butter

salt and freshly ground black pepper

½ tablespoon flour

1 glass of red wine

½ teaspoon redcurrant jelly

500ml chicken stock (a good-quality stock cube dissolved in that amount of hot water will do)

80–100g elderberries, stems removed

Preheat the oven to 230°C/gas 8. Put the ducks in a roasting tray with the vegetables and thyme, brush with a little butter and season with salt and pepper. Roast the birds for 30 minutes, then remove from the roasting tray and leave on a plate to rest and catch the juices.

Add the flour to the roasting tray and stir well over a medium heat for a minute or so. Pour in the wine and stir well. Add the redcurrant jelly and gradually add the stock. Simmer for 10 minutes until the sauce has reduced by half and thickened. Strain through a fine-meshed sieve into a saucepan, add the elderberries and any juices from the duck, bring back to the boil (boil for a little longer if it needs thickening) and remove from the heat.

To serve the duck, either chop each in half with a heavy kitchen knife and serve them on the bone, or remove the legs and then cut the breasts away from the bone and slice them into about 6 pieces. Serve with the elderberry sauce and accompany with some buttered autumn cabbage or mashed parsnip.

Roger Human's Tavern Tasty Meats

About thirteen years ago, Roger Human bought an old pub with an acre or so of land and fancied living off that land, so he bought some orphan sheep and goats, and started growing fruit and vegetables for consumption by his own family and his customers. Roger developed quite a reputation for his simple fine food – and what's more, he was enjoying this way of life.

He thought he could do a bit more business with the locals and decided to buy a retail unit, and built a kind of open butcher's shop where the general public could view his day-to-day preparation of rare-breed, locally sourced meats and his sausage making – after all, every good butcher needs to do something with off-cuts. He also brought a young pig farmer, Andrew Hudson, into the business, so they had plenty of resources and experience for their increasingly popular local business.

Pies had to be next, and a team of local girls were brought in to start hand-making pork pies as well as other traditional pies, like steak and ale, chicken and ham, etc, which I happily munched on while Roger showed me around. The pork pies are a big hit with other local retail outlets, including the gift shop at Sandringham, which is famous in its own right for Roger's pies.

If it's a rare-breed cut of meat you're after, then Roger's your man. You can take home cuts from British Lop, Saddleback and Old Spot pigs, along with a few sausages for breakfast. Roger has also selected local rare breeds of beef and lamb, especially for the shop and his loyal customers.

Good-quality, home-cooked and smoked ham is a rare find, and Roger smokes one of the best I've come across, from Old Spot pigs. He explains that for flavour he selects older pigs that have developed good-size hams. He brines them and then cold-smokes them over oak in his smoker at the back of the shop, then boils them. You can buy ready-boned hams, or on-the-bone hams for special occasions.

Roger is constantly playing with ingredients, and has developed a great meaty natural sausage with no preservatives, together with Norfolk Farmhouse, Cumberland and Olde English sausages, all made with rare-breed pork. The good amount of back fat on these animals really gives a great taste and natural moistness to the sausages, without adding large quantities of rusk as a lot of other sausage makers do. They must be good, as he's knocking out between 15,000 and 20,000 a week.

You can also find Tavern Tasty produce at farmers' markets in Aylsham every first Saturday of the month, at Dereham every second Saturday and at Fakenham every fourth. He also delivers free on all orders over £25.00.

Paul Rackham Ltd

It's always interesting to visit a larger quality outfit that totally cares about the welfare of the animals, with the end product in mind. Philip Dale, farm manager at Paul Rackham's beef finishing unit just outside Norwich, met my friend Drew Barwick and myself and we slipped on our boots and headed towards the cattle, who seemed as if they were swanning around in a kind of holiday resort.

Manor Farm is a high-tech finishing unit for quality cattle purchased from all over England and Wales, to provide high-quality beef. They spend about 100 days in luxurious surroundings (for cattle). It has capacity to finish 2,500 cattle at a time, and currently 6,000 go through annually, mainly Herefords and Aberdeen Angus.

The vegetables for their feed could pass muster on any market stall. The animals get fed twice daily on potatoes, carrots and parsnips, which are even chopped up for them. They also get brewers' grains and oats shipped over from the Quaker Oats factory in Ireland.

Philip took us to their unique handling system, which is American in design. On arrival, they're led through this maze-like system with blacked-out sides, which encourages them to move forward without any stress into their partially open pens. Every other day, they're bedded with new straw and walked through on a daily basis to spot sick cattle and also to calm the excitable ones.

Philip took us to another farm afterwards to show us the cream of their cattle, the Suffolk Red Pole. They have about 100 of these ginger rare-breed cows, which live outdoors all year. They started with a pair just 20 years ago, and they're now part of the Rare Breeds Survival Trust. It took me months to get my hands on some of the meat to try, and it was well worth waiting for.

Dan Phipps, the 'contract shepherd'

To the uninitiated, the farming of sheep would seem to be a doddle, the creatures generally looking after themselves, and the scene of sheep happily grazing in fields by the roadside is so common, that any thought about who, if anyone, actually looks after the animals certainly doesn't cross our minds. Even the image of a shepherd holding a crook must surely be a thing of the past? However, my friend Drew (opposite) promised me a meeting with a 'contract shepherd'. I didn't realize such a person even existed and what's

more, I don't think I've ever even come across a proper shepherd either. Rob Gaze, a local producer of herbs, vegetables and Bronze turkeys introduced me to Dan Phipps, who is basically employed by the famous racehorse owners, the Maktoum family. He operates on the many stud farms they own in the Breckland area, where the sheep finish off the grazing once the racehorses have had their fill. The horses move from paddock to paddock, grazing on the best grass, then on to the next, before the sheep move in.

Apart from managing the feeding patterns of the sheep, Dan also functions as a marketing agent and he selects animals according to various carcass specifications and requirements for abattoirs.
I was still intrigued by the 'contract shepherd' bit and, after looking round the stud farm, we drove together to the Stanford Army Battle area, owned by the MOD, where his sheep are finished off on natural grass and wild stuff for a couple of months before eventually going to the abattoir.

Peter Jordan, mushroom aficionado

Mushroom picking, like fishing, is one of those relaxing ways to get away from day-to-day life and go and explore nature. I had been awaiting Peter's call for a few weeks, as I was anxious to go and forage the first English mushroom of the year, the St George's, which appears around St George's Day. Peter also promised the opportunity of another little gem, the morel. These are quite rare in England but, as we discovered, they do exist.

Jason and I arrived in Southwold in the early hours, to be greeted by Peter in his plus fours and bright red socks. He likes to dress for the occasion, and the first time I met him, at the Abergavenny Food Festival, he was wearing a waistcoat embroidered with mushrooms.

Peter took us just up the road and, almost immediately, we came across a ring of the mushrooms and a couple of rare morels. We also gathered wild garlic leaves, which are the perfect accompaniment to mushrooms.

We headed down to the beach and gathered a good amount of wild sea spinach. I just don't understand why no one else picks the stuff; it's got much more flavour than the limp supermarket leaves and it's free.

There are lots of varieties of delicious vegetable that grow by the sea and are great as stand-alone vegetables or

as accompaniments to fish. My favourite is sea kale, which is far removed from the expensive white cultivated stuff. It's got the looks of sprouting broccoli and the intensity of sea beet. For me, it would certainly stand its own against a plate of asparagus, when simply seasoned with sea salt, freshly ground pepper and melted butter.

We cooked our harvest on the beach, cooking the sea kale in seawater, which saves on the salt – although you do have to strain out the sand before you cook with it. I cooked the St George's simply in olive oil and butter and threw in some wild garlic leaves and hop shoots, which we had gathered from a nearby neighbour's garden.

Peter also pointed out sea peas in their infant shoot stage, just showing on the dunes, which I promptly ate and thought what a great addition to a seaside salad they'd make with some cockles and mussels. Peter organizes mushroom forays and can be contacted on info@tastymushroompartnership.co.uk

ST GEORGE'S MUSHROOMS ON TOAST
serves 4

Mushrooms on toast is one of the simplest of luxuries and, if you can get your hands on wild mushrooms like St George's, the treat will be most welcomed by any house guest. Try to avoid washing wild mushrooms, unless it is absolutely necessary, as they tend to soak up the water like a sponge and you will end up with a pan full of water when you try to sauté them. Instead, brush or wipe off any soil, grit, etc.

  2 tablespoons rapeseed or vegetable oil

  400-500g St George's, or other wild mushrooms, cleaned

  salt and freshly ground black pepper

  2 garlic cloves, crushed, or a handful of wild garlic leaves, roughly chopped

  60-70g butter

  2 tablespoons chopped parsley

  4 thick (about 1.5 cm) slices from a bloomer or similar-style loaf

Heat the oil in a large heavy-based frying pan and cook the mushrooms over a medium heat for 3-4 minutes, seasoning them and adding the garlic halfway through cooking, and stirring them every so often. You may need to do this in 2 large pans, or in 2 batches.

Add the butter and parsley to the pan(s) and cook for another minute, stirring well.

Toast the bread on both sides and serve with the mushrooms and cooking juices spooned over the toast.

Asparagus

It is a matter of great debate exactly where the best asparagus is grown, but I have to admit that the stuff that grows near the coast has that slight edge for me on the inland crop, rather in the same way as saltmarsh lamb and sea vegetables.

You will find asparagus for sale all over East Anglia, on the roadsides and in farm shops, during late April and May – and possibly the beginning of June, if we are lucky with the weather. I've been puzzled over the last few years as to why asparagus growers undersell their produce, I may be speaking out of turn here, but British asparagus is such a great product and yet you can buy half a kilo on the roadside – or in a supermarket come to that – for a couple of quid. It is still seen as a luxury food in most people's eyes, yet it's cheaper than green beans that are nowhere near as tasty and certainly not as sexy as tender stems of asparagus. Just how many other vegetables have such appeal? Well, artichokes may come a close second – but nothing else really rivals them. What other vegetable can give you such pleasure when dipped into velvety Hollandaise sauce?

While driving through Suffolk, I decided to pull over randomly at an asparagus grower, which just happened to be Wrentham Vegetables Ltd in Wrentham, Beccles. Standing in a field of asparagus, it really did strike me how undervalued the vegetable is. It's actually a real bargain, especially when you buy direct from farm shops. It is tricky to grow and, if you've ever tried experimenting at home with growing it, you will know exactly what I'm on about. Once its been graded and the runts of the crop sold off for next to nothing, there must be very little for the farmer to play with. So, next time you're buying English asparagus, just appreciate the effort that has gone into growing it for such a short (six-week) season and what good value you are getting.

Anya potatoes

For years I've been buying Anya potatoes from Sainsbury's and wondering why we couldn't get them in the restaurants. Then I was introduced to Clare Harrison, who works for MBM Potatoes, who basically grow and source the best potatoes for the marketplace for mashing, chipping, roasting, etc. Clare will give you the low-down on most spuds, including the queen of spuds, the Anya.

The Anya potato is basically a cross between the Pink Fir Apple potato and the Red Desiree, and can be the most delicious salad potato, although nearing the end of its season it does tend to get a bit dry and floury. MBM developed them in collaboration with Sainsbury's and they have since won the 'Fresh Produce' Q Award at the 2003 Quality Food & Drink Awards.

Arthur McCorquodale at the Scottish Crop Research Institute outside Dundee started experimenting with the Anya – well PFA3, as it was known in its early days – back in the mid-1980s, when Sainsbury's asked his company MBM to try growing Charlottes for them. The Charlotte was so successful that Arthur was determined to find the next queen of salad potatoes. The PFA3 got into the gardens of Lord Sainsbury, and his gardener admired the pink-skinned potato so much that he suggested it be called Anya, after Lady Sainsbury. Arthur thought the suggestion appropriate and loved the way it just rolled off the tongue.

Not only is the Anya great for hot or cold salads, but it is also perfect as a boiled potato, cooked and served in its skin, just tossed in butter and parsley.

SUFFOLK ASPARAGUS WITH LOBSTER AND ANYA POTATOES *serves* 4

Here is a combination of three simple earthy flavours that deserve one another. Lobster is one of our great British luxuries, but unfortunately, we are often scared to cook and serve it at home. Overcooking is the main problem and rubbery old lobster meat is not appetising. The RSPCA recommends freezing live lobsters briefly before cooking, as they then go into a deep sleep.

2 live lobsters, each weighing about 500g

500g Anya potatoes in their skins

150g butter

salt and freshly ground black pepper

500g sprue asparagus, trimmed of woody stalks

1 tablespoon finely chopped parsley (reserve the stalks for the court bouillon)

for the court bouillon

1 onion, peeled and quartered

2 carrots, peeled and roughly chopped

1 bay leaf

a few sprigs of thyme

1 teaspoon fennel seeds

10 black peppercorns

First make the court bouillon: put all of the ingredients for it into a saucepan large enough to fit the lobsters. Cover with cold water and add the parsley stalks, bring to the boil and simmer for 10 minutes. Drop the lobsters into the court bouillon, simmer for 5 minutes and leave to cool in the liquid.

Meanwhile, cook the potatoes in boiling salted water for 12–15 minutes, until just cooked, and leave to cool.

When the lobsters are cool enough to handle, halve them with a heavy chopping knife and remove the meat from the shell, reserving any juices. Cut the meat into bite-sized chunks. Crack the claws and leg joints with the back of the knife and remove the meat.

Put the shells in a clean plastic bag and smash them up with a hammer or rolling pin and put the shells into a saucepan with any juices. Add the butter, season, cover and simmer the shells very gently for 5–6 minutes, then strain through a fine-meshed sieve.

Cook the asparagus in boiling salted water for a couple of minutes until tender.

To serve: toss the asparagus, potatoes, lobster and parsley in the butter and season, then arrange on plates and pour any excess butter on top.

Hillfarm rapeseed oil

When we decided to take the cross-country route from Southwold to Gunton Park in Norfolk, it certainly paid off. A quick pit stop at a farm shop between Orford and Aldeburgh found me a new and essential store cupboard ingredient for purely British dressings.

Rapeseed oil seems to be an obvious by-product of those acres and acres of yellow flowers you pass in the car in the spring months. Well, there it was, just sitting on a wooden trestle table alongside asparagus and strawberries, freshly harvested from the farm. Packaged in a nicely presented bottle with the words 'cold-pressed', 'extra-virgin' and 'high in omega 3', it was a by-product not to be passed by. I've always struggled to find purely British oil for my recipes, as imported olive oil seems to rule the shop shelves and it's just not native to these islands. Well, this one, made by Hillfarm, has a great golden – almost saffron-like – colour, with a unique nuttiness that worked perfectly with cider vinegar and Suffolk mustard for my crab salad.

Sam and Pippa Fairs' family have been cultivating their 700-1,000 acres of rapeseed for several generations and, when a friend reminded Sam of the exceptional properties of the oil for cooking – like the 6% saturates compared to most oils having 10–14% – he went to work on getting some cold pressed for the kitchen. He bought a German cold-press and began bottling the resulting oil for farm shops and delis. Within a year, it won a gold in the 'Great Tastes' Awards.

Saffron

Saffron is the most expensive spice in the world, but as it takes 5,200 autumn-blooming, purple-flowered crocuses to produce 30g of saffron, it's understandable.

These days, saffron is rarely associated with English cooking, yet it played a huge part in the history of English gastronomy from the fifteenth to the early eighteenth centuries. The saffron crocus is native to the eastern Mediterranean, the Balkans and Near East, but none has been found to be indigenous to India, Egypt, the Himalayas, Arabia, Britain or America.

It is an unusual spice, produced by the sex organs of a flower – the only other flower spice of any significance is the clove. There is much debate about the original home of saffron, but it came into England both from the East, via the Italian Mediterranean ports, and from Spain. The cultivation of saffron in England was supposedly introduced by a pilgrim on his return from the Holy Land to his native Chypping Walden in Essex, with a single saffron corm smuggled in his hollowed-out staff.

From there on, the commercial cultivation and export of this spice became a very profitable industry, bringing great wealth and fame to the town, which, by the early sixteenth century, had changed its name to Saffron Walden. The cultivation of saffron spread to surrounding villages, such as Cherry Hinton, Duxford and Littlebury, and it was also grown in neighbouring Suffolk.

Crocus corms were planted in July and harvested in September. Wet stigmas were spread on canvas and dried in kilns, before being made into cakes for sale, supposedly a much superior way of drying it than that favoured by the Spanish, which was said to give an inferior product. There was also much local demand, particularly from dye-works and textile producers, but the industry did suffer its ups and downs, with decline finally setting in during the late seventeenth and early eighteenth centuries, when the importation of cheaper saffron began, and the export market declined. Ultimately, it was the development of other materials for dyestuffs that saw its end, and by 1726, Littlebury was the only village in the area still producing. The last trace of saffron cultivation was in the area of Duxford, by a man named Knott in 1816.

There have been various efforts to reintroduce the saffron crocus into the region over the years, but not on a commercial basis, and instead in private gardens like that at Cherry Hinton by Heather Coppock. Her rare English saffron corms are available, though, at the historic Saffron Walden Museum, if you fancy having a go at it yourself.

The saffron crocus was also cultivated in Stratton in the north of the country, and also in Cornwall. When the Saffron Walden plantations died out in the late 1700s, the use of saffron was still popular throughout the country, mainly for baking. The Cornish still kept growing it in Launcells, near Bude, and the famous Cornish saffron cake survived. Traditionally saffron buns would be eaten with clotted cream on Good Friday – a bit like Simnel cake in other parts of the country.

DAMSONS WITH SAFFRON CUSTARD

serves 4

Custard is a great thing; add saffron to the milk and cream, though, and you have the most amazing accompaniment to stewed fruits like rhubarb, gooseberries or plums. However, you do need to be careful when you cook with saffron, as its taste can totally overpower your dish. A small pinch goes a long way and, infused like this, you don't need much at all.

500-600g damsons, halved and stones removed

200g granulated sugar

for the custard

pinch of saffron strands (see above)

300ml double cream

6 egg yolks

60g caster sugar

2 teaspoons cornflour

First make the custard: put the saffron and cream into a small saucepan and bring to the boil. Remove from the heat and leave to infuse for about 10 minutes.

In a bowl, mix together the egg yolks, sugar and cornflour. Then, using a whisk, mix well with the cream and saffron infusion. Return to the pan and cook gently over a low heat for a few minutes, stirring constantly with a wooden spoon, until the custard thickens – but don't let

it boil, though. Remove from the heat and give a final mix with a whisk and transfer to a clean bowl. Leave to cool, then cover with clingfilm and refrigerate.

Put the damsons in a pan with the sugar and cook over a low heat, stirring every so often, and simmer with a lid on for about 10–15 minutes, until the mixture is thick and syrupy. Leave to cool

To serve, spoon the damson mixture into bowls and spoon the custard on top. If you prefer, you can brûlé the custard by sprinkling it with caster sugar and burning it with a blowtorch. You can also spoon the fruit into a serving dish or dishes, then cover with the custard.

Mrs Temple's Cheeses Apart from making the finest cheeses in East Anglia, Catherine Temple also manages to have a part-time job as a medication pharmacist for the local NHS and social services, basically checking that the local old folk on medication are taking the right pills at the right time, and not getting them mixed up. I was surprised to hear that she had only been making cheese for 4 years and previously lived in Malawi for 9 years, working on tea colours and flavours for the Tea Research Foundation on a cooperative, with her husband Stephen, who was a crop-drying technologist.

Catherine was brought up in Melton Mowbray and told me how she used to make a local Colwick-style fresh cheese at home and spread it on toast with hedgerow jam, and this was how her first cheese, Wighton, came about. She found some haloumi moulds in Greece, which she has used ever since for the cheese, to give it that characteristic wicker-like exterior. Catherine reckons that the older community love this cheese as they remember that sort of home-style, simple cheese made using leftover milk.

Her second cheese, Walsingham is a kind of mature Cheshire-style cheese with a natural mould rind. She started making this cheese three years ago and used boiled sheets from the Salvation Army to wrap it. Today, she assures me, she uses proper muslin.

Her newest and most successful cheese is the delicious semi-soft Binham Blue, which was the first of her cheeses I discovered, in a farm shop near Cromer. It was Lorraine, who runs the cheese-making operation, who persuaded Catherine to make a blue cheese, as her parents live near the place where the famous Irish Cashel Blue is produced

and, funnily enough, the cheeses do have some similar characteristics. As we agreed over coffee, however, most cheese-makers are influenced by a famous cheese or two.

Modestly, Catherine tells me that she has won a couple of medals at the British Cheese Awards, but never a gold. Another interesting award they are really proud of, though, is the North Norfolk Environmental Award for Stephen's energy-saving wood chip and straw burner, which is used to operate some of the cheese-making machinery, and in the first year it saved them £6,000. She brought out the award, which was made by the local deaf school from of all sorts of plastic waste like hoops and CDs, and decorated with plastic tassels.

Catherine's cheeses deserve more recognition, so on my return to London I put all three on the Ivy menu as stand-alone cheeses for the week, and the best thing was that Catherine hadn't even heard of the restaurant.

Childwickbury Goats Cheese This is very much a 'Good Life' story in Hertfordshire for cheese-makers David and Elizabeth Harris. Many of the farmers I have met that keep goats seem to have similar stories of how the goats eventually got the better of them. Elizabeth used to be an environmental scientist and David ran a landscaping business. He needed some land for his machinery, and a plot came up on Stanley Kubrick's Childwickbury Estate near their home in St Albans. A small farm also became available on the estate and the temptation of giving everything up and living off the land was irresistible.

Initially they kept ducks, chickens, geese and pigs, and a few goats. The goats were let to roam around and things got a little out of hand. They were then kept in a barn with continuous outdoor access. The Harrises leave their billy goats with the females for most of the year, which means kidding and milking is staggered throughout the year, so their goats' cheeses can be made all year round.

Up to now, they have a mixed breed herd of over 100 goats, which began in the early nineties with pedigree Toggenburgs, Saanens and British Alpines, all chosen by Elizabeth on the basis of their high yield and quality milk. Since then, inevitably, the goats, with their free and easy lifestyle, have crossbred, and their resulting milk produces two of the finest cheeses in the county: Childwickbury, a fresh cheese available for sale 24 hours after production, and Verulamium, available fourteen days after production, with a more mature and slightly cheesier taste than Childwickbury and named after the old Roman town near St Albans.

TRINITY BURNT CREAM *serves* 4

Is this delicious dessert French or English in origin? It's difficult to say, as burnt cream seems to have been around for as long as crème brûlée. Even as early as the Norman Conquest, we were influenced by the French, and vice versa. It may even have been that both were derived from *crema Catalan.* They are all ways with custard, and whoever had the idea of putting a mirror of burnt sugar on top deserves our eternal gratitude. There are lots of versions of both crème brûlée and burnt cream, but, like most successful dishes, the simplest ones seem to work the best.

This creamy pudding is often called Trinity pudding, or Trinity cream, after the Cambridge college, although there is a story that the recipe came from an Aberdeenshire country house and was offered to the college back in the 1860s by an undergraduate. Earlier recipe books of the 1700s refer to a similar pudding as well, but I suppose at the end of the day it's just a good simple way to use up excess cream.

600ml thick Jersey or double cream

8 egg yolks

75g caster sugar

The day before you want to serve: bring the cream to the boil and reduce by one-third.

Meanwhile, mix the egg yolks with 1 tablespoon of the caster sugar in a heatproof bowl. Pour the reduced cream on to the egg yolks and mix well.

Return the mixture to the pan and cook over a low heat, stirring constantly and without allowing it to boil, until the mixture coats the back of a spoon. Remove from the heat.

Pour into 1 large or 4 individual heatproof gratin dish(es), like ramekins, and leave to cool overnight in the fridge.

An hour before serving, sprinkle an even layer of caster sugar over the cream and caramelize under a preheated hot grill or with a blowtorch.

NORFOLK TREACLE TART *makes one 26cm tart*

I have come across so many treacle tart recipes in my time, and all of them differing slightly from one another – some with cream, some with lemon and oats, or breadcrumbs to hold it all together. My preference is the deeper, lighter tart version, with that subtle hint of lemon.

It's arguable whether Norfolk is as famous for its treacle tart as the North East, and both versions also differ, depending on the maker. The Norfolk treacle tart is sometimes referred to as 'Norfolk treacle custard tart', but, actually it is just a lighter and less dense version of a normal treacle tart.

There is something good and old-fashioned about treacle, and the cans of treacle and golden syrup just haven't changed for years. Although, they are still a pain to keep clean; there just always seems to be congealed syrup hanging around the rim of the can.

Treacle is the general term for the uncrystallizable syrup that is a by-product of sugar refining. It refers to the dark molasses-like syrup and also the golden syrup from which the treacle tart is generally made, although I do like to use a bit of each. Golden syrup wasn't sold in Britain until the late 1800s, so the history of treacle tart only really dates back to that period.

for the sweet pastry
110g soft butter
135g caster sugar
225g strong flour
½ teaspoon baking powder
pinch of salt
125ml double cream

for the filling
225g golden syrup
50g dark treacle
220ml double cream
75g oatmeal or fresh white breadcrumbs
2 eggs, beaten
1 tablespoon lemon juice
extra-thick or clotted cream, to serve

Make the pastry a couple of hours ahead: cream the butter and sugar together, then sieve the baking powder and flour together and stir into the butter mix with the salt. Slowly pour in the cream until well mixed. Chill for about 30 minutes before rolling.

On a floured table, roll out the pastry to about 5mm thick. Use to line a 26cm flan or tart tin, about 3-4cm deep, and leave to rest in the fridge for 1 hour.

Preheat the oven to 160°C/gas 3. Meanwhile, make the filling by mixing the golden syrup, treacle, double cream, oatmeal and beaten eggs together, then stir in the lemon juice. Fill the flan ring with the mixture and bake for 40-50 minutes, then leave to cool.

Serve warm with some good extra-thick or clotted cream.

Mersey   Northumberland   Teesside   Tyne and Wear   Yorkshire

THE
NORTH

THE FOOD OF THE NORTH is generally considered working man's grub. Indeed, many Northern dishes are often based on economical ingredients and use all types of offal rarely seen in other parts of the country, such as tripe – often served as tripe and onions – brains, chitterlings, sweetbreads, pigs' trotters and cow heel. Black puddings are a great favourite: made from pig's blood and oatmeal, and there are lots of secret recipes and international competitions for the best ones. The coiled Cumberland sausage is another of the North's most recognized products.

The dales and moors of England's largest county, Yorkshire, are home to cows, sheep and pigs. Cows' milk is used to make the original Wensleydale cheese, and pork has always played an important part in the region's diet, York hams being celebrated at home and abroad. In Northumbria, Craster kippers come from the village of the same name and smokehouses use a traditional light cure. Pease pudding 'hot' is one of the most famous dishes of the region, sold by street vendors around Newcastle in medieval times. The North West also has many traditional products such as Morecambe Bay shrimps, and Lancashire and Cheshire cheeses.

Lancashire was one of the first counties to grow potatoes on a large scale as cheap food, so you can see where the marriage to battered fish comes from. Although history tells us that our famous British dish started in London, over the years it has become one of the symbols of Northern fast food. Baked goods are one of the region's great strengths: for example, oatcakes, parkins, gingerbread and Geordie stottie cake, and Lancashire

There's not much in the way of produce you can't get your hands on up North. It's without doubt one of the most interesting food regions in the UK and, likewise, has some of the most passionate and interesting producers. Like many Northern chefs, Nigel Howarth proudly names his producers on his menu at the Three Fishes in Lancashire – a fine example of a pub serving good simple local food.

If you're a regular visitor up North, you may have noticed food shops named Booths, who've been trading since 1840, when tea was their mainstay. Today they stock lots of local produce. Chairman, Edwin Booth has a passion for good produce and it's unusual to meet a supermarket owner who actually knows producers personally. He has a genuine excitement about local food, and the Northern food 'renaissance'.

was the birthplace of all manner of confectionery, including treacle toffee.

On my many visits to the North to see my daughters, Ellie and Lydia, who live with their mother near Manchester, I've come across some great producers through knowing local chefs like Paul Heathcote and Nigel Howarth. They have a real bond with one another and hold annual food festivals, inviting chefs from other parts of the country to display their culinary skills in the North to their local suppliers, restaurateurs and general foodie public.

The food culture in Lancashire is probably one of the best I've come across in the country. All the chefs, producers and growers seem to know and support each other, and in a real way have put Lancashire on the culinary map. The regional food bodies are strong, and associations like North West Fine Foods have annual producer competitions to keep everyone on their toes and let the rest of the country know that they are very serious about what they are doing.

LANCASHIRE HOT POT *serves* 4

There are various versions of Lancashire hot pot, one of the best-known dishes in the North, but the main ingredients are almost invariably flavoursome cuts of lamb (like the neck, which is traditionally cut on the bone like chops), potatoes and onions. Kidneys – and even black pudding – can be added to the potatoes and onions. Back in the days when they were cheap, a few oysters would be put under the potato, but that is largely a thing of the past, although well worth trying.

The pot in which it is cooked is important, and it took me some years to find an appropriate deep-glazed terracotta pot that was suitable and looked the part. Amazingly, I eventually found it in a junk shop in Romiley, along with a couple of old cookbooks, all for £3.50.

Pickled red cabbage is the traditional accompaniment to Lancashire hot pot. You may think it a strange pairing, but it works as well with a simple hot pot as it does with a plate of cold cuts.

salt and pepper

1 kg lamb or mutton neck chops, cut into rough 3-4cm chunks

flour for dusting

vegetable oil for frying

60g unsalted butter, plus a little more for brushing

450-500g onions, thinly sliced

a few sprigs of thyme

800ml lamb or beef stock (or a good-quality stock cube dissolved in that amount of water)

1 kg large potatoes, thinly sliced

for the Pickled Red Cabbage

1 litre red wine vinegar

1 teaspoon freshly ground black pepper

1 tablespoon pickling spice

1 tablespoon caster sugar

1 tablespoon salt

1 head of red cabbage, quartered and finely shredded

Several weeks ahead, make the pickled red cabbage: in a non-reactive pan, bring the vinegar to the boil with the pepper, pickling spice, sugar and salt, and leave to cool. Mix the shredded cabbage into the cooled pickling liquid in a non-reactive bowl and leave in the fridge overnight.

The next day, pack the cabbage into sterilized jars and top up with the vinegar. Seal the jars and store in a cool place for a minimum of 4 weeks, or up to 12 months.

When you want to cook the hot pot, preheat the oven to 220°C/gas 7. Season the pieces of lamb and dust with flour. Heat a couple of tablespoons of vegetable oil in a heavy-based frying pan and fry the lamb, a few pieces at a time, on a high heat until nicely coloured.

Clean the pan and heat another couple of tablespoons of vegetable oil, then fry the onions on a high heat until they begin to colour. Add the butter and continue to cook for a few minutes until the onions soften. Dust them with a tablespoon of flour, stir well and gradually add the lamb stock, stirring to avoid lumps, then sprinkle in the thyme. Bring to the boil, season with salt and pepper, and simmer for about 10 minutes.

Now you're ready to assemble the hot pot. Take an ovenproof casserole dish with a lid or similar, cover the bottom with a layer of potatoes, followed by a layer of meat with a little sauce, then another layer of potatoes. Continue until the meat and sauce has all been used. Finish the top with a layer of nicely overlapping potato slices. Brush the top with a little of the sauce and cook in the oven for about half an hour, then turn the oven down to 130°C/gas 1 and leave in the oven for 2 hours.

Remove the lid from the dish and turn the oven back up to 220°C/gas 7. Brush the top of the hot pot with a little melted butter and return to the oven to allow the potatoes to brown for a final half hour.

Serve piping hot, with the pickled red cabbage.

Peter Ashcroft's red cabbage and other vegetables

On a trip to Lancashire, during Nigel Howarth's food festival at Northcote Manor, I went to Tarleton to check out Peter Ashcroft, who had a bit of a reputation in the area for the famous red cabbage to be pickled to accompany Lancashire hot pot. I'd heard he had grown a couple of fields' worth for a certain well-known chef. Unfortunately, they were still sitting there in pallets awaiting pickling when we visited. He seemed unworried, though, as he had been putting his energy into lots of other seasonal goodies, like purple sprouting broccoli, trendy little dumpy Chantenay carrots and amazing golden beets. Peter's main crop, however, was summer cauliflower and he had several large greenhouses of seedlings ready to plant out after the frost. He's a modern-day experimental farmer and will grow more or less anything within reason for local chefs' menus, although he may grow a few less red cabbages next year. This is the way farming needs to go – being more responsive to customers' needs – and I think that the successful farmers of today are prepared to accommodate modern tastes and food trends, and develop relationships with the chefs and restaurants where the product ends up.

YORKSHIRE PUDDING *makes 6–8 or 1 large*

Every Sunday, hundreds of thousands of helpings of our favourite accompaniment are cooked in this nation's homes, restaurants and hotels. When I worked at the Dorchester Hotel, we used to make large Yorkshires in trays under the ribs of beef to catch the cooking juices, which is still the way I prefer cooking them today.

Originally known as 'dripping pudding', the crisp delight more commonly used to accompany mutton. In 1747, it was renamed Yorkshire pudding by Hannah Glasse in her famous book, *The Art of Cookery.* She says, 'It is an excellent good pudding; the gravy of the meat eats well with it'. In Yorkshire, it is often served with gravy as a first course, but it's more generally popular with roast beef in the main course – although it does occasionally feature afterwards with jam and cream.

250g plain flour

good pinch of salt

4 medium eggs, beaten

500-600ml milk

Preheat the oven to 220°C/gas 7. You need to start cooking your Yorkshires about 25 minutes before the beef is due to be ready and your beef would ideally need to be sitting directly on the oven racks at this stage to allow the juices and fat to drip into the pudding.

Put some of the roasting fat or some dripping in a large roasting tin or individual Yorkshire pudding moulds and preheat them for about 5 minutes until the fat is smoking-hot.

Meanwhile, mix the flour and salt together in a bowl, then whisk in the eggs and a little of the milk until the mix forms a good paste. Carefully mix in the rest of the milk, trying not to beat it too much, until a thick pouring consistency is achieved. Pour the batter into the tin(s) and cook in the oven under the beef for about 30 minutes, until well risen and crisp on the outside.

Pugh's Piglets

Barry and Gillian Pugh have a nice little bespoke – if you can call it that – business, selling suckling pigs in Garstang near Preston. You would expect a pig farm to be a bit of a smelly sort of place and that's exactly why Barry owns up to sourcing his rare-breed pigs from other pig farms in the surrounding local area, as he likes the family home, Bowgreave House Farm, to remain as clean as possible, and I don't blame him.

Their business has been going since 1965, originally under the name of Barry Pugh, which is the name some of his vans still bear. You will often see Barry's vans delivering to Chinese restaurants in London's Chinatown, with the driver normally hefting a baby piglet over his shoulder. They also deliver to many established restaurants in London and around the country.

Suckling pigs are an expensive commodity and fetch a

similar price at market as their fully mature parents. They are the perfect beast for celebratory feasts and I often cook one at Christmas, much to the disgust of my daughters Ellie and Lydia.

Over the years, Pugh's have developed their product into a superb porcetta, which is an Italian speciality of boned and rolled suckling pig, sold plain or stuffed with rosemary and garlic (there is also a Christmas dried fruit and spices version). With each piglet making two such rolls, this is a much more economical way to serve the pig, especially if you don't like the look of the whole thing, head and all.

ROAST SUCKLING PIG
WITH QUINCE SAUCE *serves 8-10*

A whole suckling pig will weigh up to about 5 kilos, serve 8–10 people and will cook in a relatively short time in a domestic oven. The only problem is that a standard domestic oven will probably not take the whole beast, so you may need to chop it in half. Domestic ovens are increasing in size, though, and keen cooks like to get an oven close to the size we use in restaurants, so if you have one, there's no problem squeezing the little beast in.

1 suckling pig, about 3–4kg

olive oil

sea salt

for the quince sauce

3 quinces, peeled, quartered and the cores removed

100g sugar

2 cloves

juice of ½ lemon

good knob of butter

Preheat the oven to 200ºC/gas 6. First, flatten the pig on its belly, then rub it all over with olive oil and season it with sea salt.

Cook the pig directly on the rack of the oven (with a roasting tray set below it to catch the juices and fat) for 1½–2 hours. (You can cook your potatoes in the roasting tray and baste them in the juices.)

While the pig is cooking, make the quince sauce: put the quinces into a saucepan, cover with water and add the sugar, cloves and lemon juice. Bring to the boil, cover and simmer for 1 hour. Drain the liquid off, add the butter to the pan and mash the quince coarsely with a potato masher, or in a food processor.

To serve, cut the suckling pig into joints with a heavy chopping knife and serve the quince sauce separately.

LIVERPOOL LOBSCOUSE *serves 4-6*

I just love the name of this dish. Perhaps the original version, made with salted meat, was eaten by seamen in the days of sail ships and they dreamt of eating lobster. The more down-to-earth reality is that it's a sort of typical poor man's meat and vegetable stew with pulses to bulk it out – and it's why Liverpudlians are known as Scousers.

The modern-day version of this dish can be made with any stewing meat, ideally cuts like shin of beef and neck of lamb to give the broth a rich flavour. It is incredibly easy, economical and tasty too.

50g beef dripping or 3 tablespoons vegetable oil

750g neck of lamb fillet or shin of beef, cut into rough 2cm cubes

salt and freshly ground black pepper

1 large onion, chopped

3 carrots, roughly chopped

500g medium potatoes, quartered

200g dried peas, soaked overnight

a few sprigs of thyme

2 litres beef or lamb stock

50g pearl barley

Melt the dripping or heat the oil in a heavy-based frying pan. Season the meat with salt and pepper and fry quickly on a high heat until nicely coloured all over.

Add the rest of the ingredients, bring to the boil, lightly season with salt and pepper and simmer gently for 2-2½ hours until the meat is tender. That's it.

Serve with buttery cabbage or mashed root vegetables.

York ham

The York ham is probably the most famous of all British hams and so much so that it is copied worldwide, especially by our European 'cousins'. A couple of years ago I was given a chunk of 'jamón de York' for Christmas by one of our Spanish suppliers, and delicious it was too, with a gentle mild smokiness to it. So there is some credit if the best producers of ham in the world have been influenced by our Northern ham-making traditions.

What's happened over the years, it seems, is that the York name has been used more generally to describe a curing style rather than a local product. Opinions vary, too, as to whether the ham should be smoked or not. The most common story seems to be that in the Middle Ages, the hams were cured and smoked over shavings from the wood left over from the 100-year build of York Minster.

So, what is so special about York hams? Back in 1747, the celebrated food writer Hannah Glasse reckoned that the quality of the salt used was much finer and superior to that used in London. One of the best – and few remaining – curers of note still producing York hams seems to be Scotts butchers in York, a third-generation family butchers, now run by Stephen Bailey. 'Mr Bailey',

as he's known locally, seems to dismiss the tradition of smoking as a bit of a myth and he cures his hams and always has done as unsmoked – or green – hams, as they are known in the trade. I may be wrong, but the York ham tradition does seem to be dying, except at Christmas time.

Another style of York ham is the Marsh York Ham, which is probably the most widely available outside the county. A green ham like Stephen Bailey's, it became popular at the end of the last century, when Alfred Marsh began production in Brierley in Staffordshire. They are now made using the same traditional method by Harris-Leeming Bar in Northallerton.

The hams are cured with salt, saltpetre, sugar and sal prunella, a highly regarded preserving salt used by the best ham-makers worldwide. The hams are rubbed and turned daily for a month. Two or three times during the process, the mixture is washed off and a fresh one used. The hams are then hung at a slightly higher temperature until no liquid drips out. They are then hung in calico bags to mature for 4 months. Each will take a slightly different time to cure and this is determined by regular inspection. The result is a very fine texture and flavour.

Andrew Sharp's Herdwick lamb and mutton

If there is an advocate for mutton, it's got to be Andrew Sharp. Back in London, Andrew Sharp is among the denizens of the buzzy Borough Market, where he displays every cut possible of his Herdwick lamb and mutton and Galloway beef. You may be wondering why I'm banging on about mutton? By now, as you read this, I hope it's becoming a popular dish again on tables up and down the country. And in restaurants. A small group of us – cooks, food writers and members of the farming industry – are trying our best to get mutton back in the kitchens through the Mutton Renaissance Committee, with the support of HRH Prince Charles.

In Cumbria, Andrew Sharp is eagerly watching his flock of Herdwicks in the Great Langdale Valley. They are a hardy breed suited to mountainous terrain, but Andrew keeps a close eye on them as they prefer to be up on the fells, wandering, rather than in the lambing fields. The great uncle of Farmer Sharp, was Tom Storey, Beatrix Potter's shepherd, so his roots are firmly embedded in sheep farming, where he has made a very successful career keeping cooks and food lovers who want

to know the provenance of their product very happy.

Not content with the fresh products, Farmer Sharp has developed air-dried mutton, which in effect is a mutton ham. On his Borough Market stand you will get a better idea of what 'Sharpie' is all about – the passion for his product and how the user should understand what they are going to do with their mutton when they get it home.

Over a beer, we often natter about where mutton is going, both in restaurants and in the home. The conclusion generally is that it's down to us to convince the public of its superior cooking and eating qualities compared to lamb. A sheep of 2 years plus has a bit of flavour about it and suits long, slow cooking, perfect for dishes like Lancashire hot pot or pies and, of course, Asian dishes like curry. The problem from a marketing point of view lies in the name. Mutton, like tripe, has this image problem of being 'a thing of the past', and also of being old and second-rate. This should be where clever cooking comes in, as long cooking cuts need to retain texture and flavour, and that's exactly where that slight gaminess of mutton comes into play.

COW HEEL AND BLACK PEAS *serves 6–8*

This recipe is from some friends of mine, Annette and Barry Broadhurst. They serve this and tripe at their annual festive bash, which happens between Christmas and New Year, along with the usual festive goodies, and it's quite delicious. The trickiest part of the dish is finding the black peas, also known as maple peas or carlings, which are more traditionally eaten at Easter, rather like pease pudding.

I ended up asking Annette where the hell to get the things, as it was driving me mad. I ended up in the market at Hyde, near Stockport, and asked a couple of traders, who sent me to the pet stand. Why? I wondered. Then, when I eventually found the stand, they had stopped stocking them and they told me to try the spice and Asian stall. There they were, bagged up in little packets, so I promptly bought up a couple of kilos, just in case I never found the things again. I then stumbled across a little gem of a place, run by Jack Curvis, the tripe dresser, who also had a stash of them, and we got chatting about tripe (see opposite).

salt and freshly ground black pepper

475g shin beef, cut into rough 3cm cubes

1 tablespoon vegetable oil

2 large onions, sliced

1 cow heel cut into 8–10 pieces on the bone

400g black peas, soaked overnight

3 litres beef stock (or a couple of beef stock cubes dissolved in that amount of water)

Lightly season the pieces of beef and fry on a high heat in the vegetable oil for 3-4 minutes until browned all over. Remove the meat from the pan and put to one side. Add the onions and cook over a low heat for 2-3 minutes until softened.

Put the beef, onions, cow heel, peas and stock into a large heavy saucepan, bring to the boil and simmer gently for 2½ hours until the beef is tender. The cow heel should have broken down by now and the liquid thickened. Adjust the seasoning, if necessary.

If you have any left after the meal, it can be set in a container and eaten like brawn.

The tripe dressers of the North

I've always been intrigued by the term 'dressers' used for the Northern tripe sellers. The preparation of what was once a very popular food among the workers is now sadly a dying art. My late father-in-law, Fred, liked to remind me of these shops and his tripe-eating experiences, much to the disgust of other members of the family. Tripe was one of his favourites, but like most wives, probably, Doreen wasn't prepared to cook it for him. Whenever I broached the subject, it really brought a smile to his face. He would explain to me about 'thick seam', 'thin seam' and 'blanket' tripe, and how it would be eaten just as it was with a sprinkling of vinegar and salt. I would always try to give him a tripe treat whenever possible, and the tripe in black bean sauce at the Yang Sing restaurant in Manchester always won him over.

On a hunt for the carlings (in the recipe opposite) on a cold Saturday afternoon, I was directed to one of the few tripe dressers left in the north, Jack Curvis, who sells his wares from the market hall in Hyde. He still trades in a traditional way and displays all the cuts – 'black', 'thick seam', 'honeycomb' and 'cow heels'. He sells non-brewed malt vinegar, dripping, brawn and all the other bits and pieces expected from a traditional tripe dresser.

As we waffled on about stomach linings, he proudly pulled out a book called *A Most Excellent Dish, Tales of the Lancashire Tripe Trade* by Marjory Houlihan. 'How weird!', I thought as I reached into my bag. I had picked up exactly the same rare book in a funny old book shop that morning for £3.50 and promptly pulled out my copy, much to his surprise; we bonded and continued chatting on, much to the dismay of my daughters.

It's the first time I've actually come across a proper tripe dresser, and the way the trade is going it may well be the last. The book lists about five hundred Lancashire tripe dressers and dealers, but, sadly, Jack is now among the small handful left trading in the area.

TRIPE AND ONIONS *serves* 4

Most tripe you buy has been chemically bleached to make it completely white, and boiled to further rid it of the unappealing brown colour (and, sometimes, off-putting taste), unless you come across a trader like Jack Curvis. I have, however, bought it from France, where they tend to keep it more in its natural state, so you can really give it a good, long cooking. Properly cooked with wine and a dash of cream, it is a revelation.

40g butter

4 medium-sized onions, thinly sliced

1 teaspoon chopped fresh thyme

30g flour

4 tablespoons white wine or dry cider

1 litre chicken stock (or good-quality stock cube dissolved in that amount of hot water)

1 kg fresh tripe, preferably untreated (see above), washed and cut into 6-8cm pieces

salt and freshly ground white pepper

2 tablespoons double cream

Melt the butter in a heavy-based pan, add the onions and thyme, cover and cook gently until the onions are soft. If they begin to colour, add a tablespoon of water to the pan and stir well.

Stir in the flour and cook over a low heat for another minute. Gradually add the wine or cider and the chicken stock, stirring constantly. Bring to the boil, add the tripe, season with salt and pepper and simmer gently for 1 hour until tender. A little more stock or water should be added if the sauce is getting too thick. Different types of tripe will have different cooking times, so keep an eye on it and cook it for a bit longer or shorter as necessary.

Finish by stirring in the double cream and adjust the seasoning with salt and pepper if necessary. Serve with mashed potato.

Sillfield Farm

Peter Gott is one of those guys who doesn't need much PR. If you have witnessed his array of pork and wild boar products in London's Borough Market or Liverpool and Manchester farmers' markets, served by staff in bowler hats, you will know exactly what I'm on about. He has taken the tradition of Cumbrian ham-making to another level. While wandering around the market for inspiration, I regularly buy a few rashers of his wild boar bacon and sausages, and occasionally a homemade pie to snack on, but Peter's business is more about the raw ingredient, the beast itself.

Peter's passion is rare-breed pigs and a visit to Sillfield Farm, which runs either side of the M6 in Endmoor near Kendal, Cumbria, is like an A to Z or living history of the pig. He breeds Tamworths, Middlewhites, Saddlebacks and many more, as well as his trademark wild boar and Iron Age, which are a wild boar and Tamworth cross.

Most wild boar in this country are nearer to pigs than real wild boar, but Peter has an array of cross-breeds. He also has many of the real thing that won't come anywhere near him and vice versa, and just stay in the woods with their young, breeding and occasionally popping into the barn area for bits of food when there's no one around.

Peter's enthusiasm for food is astonishing and, what's more, he's got a bigger collection of cookbooks than me – both antiquarian and new – and last year he was even in the process of writing a book himself.

Peter's involvement in the Slow Food Movement and regular visits to the Turin Slow Food Festival have won him several awards for his wild boar prosciutto, and his products are up there with the serranos of Spain and prosciuttos of Italy.

Unlike your run-of-the-mill pig farmer, Peter has really gone to town on developing by-products from his pigs, as well as the normal everyday cuts like classic Cumbrian hams and wild boar sausages and bacon. On a visit to his coldroom, you will see pancetta and speck, and experimental salamis and chorizos, although he admits he's got to do a bit of work on the chorizos yet. Peter's wife, Christine also makes the most wonderful range of tasty pies using the rare-breed pork and wild boar.

Peter talks ardently about his aims to reintroduce extinct breeds like Cumberland, crossing Middle Whites and British Lops, or even Lincolnshire Curly Coat – which is now only a memory, existing only in old photos. Hopefully, he'll succeed in reinstating breeds, and they will become as popular on menus as Gloucester Old Spot.

SILLFIELD WILD BOAR STEW WITH HAWKSHEAD BEER *serves* 4

This dish is basically a cook-up of Peter Gott's fresh, cured and prepared wild boar produce, with a little local ale thrown in. In France, a dish like this would be cooked, normally in red wine, for a hunting party. It's difficult to know what to do with boar and, unlike pork, there are few cuts that are tender enough to cook as you would pork. I came up with this idea over the phone with Peter, but he's yet to try it out. It may have to come with us in a tiffin box on a fishing trip, when he gets his boat in the water.

salt and freshly ground black pepper

1½ tablespoons flour, plus more for coating

1kg wild boar meat, cut into rough 3cm chunks

2 tablespoons vegetable oil

200-250g wild boar pancetta, ordinary pancetta, or a piece of smoked streaky bacon, cut into 3cm chunks

1 onion, roughly chopped

2 garlic cloves, crushed

1 teaspoon fresh thyme leaves

1 teaspoon tomato paste

500ml Hawkshead red ale

2 litres beef stock

2 wild boar sausages, each about 100g, or 4 small ones

Preheat the oven to 180°C/gas 4. Season and lightly flour the wild boar, shaking off any excess flour. Heat half of the oil in a heavy frying pan and brown the pieces of boar, a few at a time. Fry the pancetta in the same fat and put into an ovenproof dish with the boar.

In another pan, gently cook the onion, garlic and thyme in the rest of the vegetable oil for 3-4 minutes until they begin to colour. Add the 1½ tablespoons flour and the tomato paste, and stir well over a medium heat for 2-3 minutes.

Gradually add the beer, stirring well to avoid lumps forming, then add the beef stock. Bring to the boil, season and add to the casserole with the boar meat and pancetta. Cover and cook in the preheated oven for 1½ hours.

Meanwhile, twist each sausage in half and cut across. Grill them under a hot grill for about 2-3 minutes on each side, then add to the stew for the last half hour in the oven. Check the pieces of boar to see if they are tender; if not, return to the oven for another 30 minutes or so.

Serve with mashed potatoes or other root veg.

Black Pudding

The black puddings of the North West are renowned and come in all sorts of shapes and sizes, from the 'berries' (small individual rings) to larger hoops and puddings set in trays and sliced. The celebrated Bury black pudding, or 'burrie', is documented as far back as 1820.

The relationship of such blood puddings to the French *boudin* is a close one, but they are fairly different in taste and texture, and the Spanish *morcilla* are different again, and even sold semi-dried as a kind of cross between a chorizo and a salami. (I haven't forgotten the Scottish and Irish versions; they're in the appropriate chapters!) I favour the softer, spicier puddings myself and am always curious to try black puddings all over the world, just to check out the different spice levels. Even here, spice mixtures vary from region to region and each maker gives the recipe his, or her, own little twist. The usual flavourings are anything from celery seed and pennyroyal to mint, thyme and marjoram. As a nod to some of the European cousins, some add pimento to give it a little zing, or even coriander seed.

Chef Paul Heathcote makes his own using apples and raisins – a little French influence I think. He makes them in large tubes and slices them before cooking. I must say that I prefer the individual round shape of the Bury black pudding myself; it keeps the moisture in during cooking, so they stay soft and present well.

When I visited Stuart Higginson of Higginson's in Grange-over-Sands, his great butcher's shop was blocked with a double queue of customers either side. He makes great homemade pies under the guidance of his wife Pauline, who also makes black pudding to an old recipe of Stuart's mother's. She makes it in a tray and bakes it like a loaf, which can then be sliced and grilled or fried.

Over in Bury, Andrew Holt at R.S. Ireland makes award-winning black puddings that appear on the menus of many local chefs, like Nigel Howarth at the award-winning The Three Fishes at Mitton. Andrew makes the traditional 'burrie' and strives to improve on his recipe and create new variations like his duck black pudding.

Reg Johnson's Goosnargh poultry

I've known Reg a few years now, through chef Paul Heathcote. Reg farms poultry in Goosnargh, pronounced 'Goozna', and his ducks, chickens and geese are the real deal. He inherited the business from his stepfather, Thomas Swarbrick, when it was then a mixed farm of dairy cattle, battery chickens and sheep. Paul badgered Reg to breed decent ducks and chickens, like French poultry, as he couldn't find an English product that matched up to his needs, and wanted to buy local.

When Reg first started experimenting for Paul, he tried and tested various breeds of both ducks and chickens, settling for an Aylesbury and Peking cross.

You'll commonly come across his Goosnargh poultry on Northern menus and he's slowly creeping into the London market, but is understandably reluctant to expand too much too fast. When customers first try Reg's chickens, they're just blown away by the flavour and surprised by the shape of the seemingly slim breasts. This conformation is actually as a real chicken should be and the full flavour is almost guinea fowl-like, which is achieved by proper feed, with no growth promoters and only being killed at 60-70 days (50-60 for ducks).

On my visits to Reg, his mother, Winnie cooks breakfast, which includes a plate of Goosnargh cakes. They're thick and shortbread-like, with caraway seeds through them. On our way to Ruth Kirkham's (page 150), I thought what a good match they'd be with her cheese, though I'm sure somebody has thought about it before.

POT ROAST GOOSNARGH CHICKEN WITH ROOT VEGETABLES *serves* 4

The best way to cook a chicken of this quality is simply, and on the bone. If you have a spit-roast facility on your cooker, that will produce a perfectly flavoured roast chicken and you can let the juices run into the vegetables while they are cooking. You can vary the vegetables according to the season, and in the summer, you may want simply to roast the bird and serve it with a garden salad or a selection of beans.

1 chicken, weighing 1.2 –1.5 kg

1 onion, quartered

2 carrots, cut into rough chunks

1 small swede, cut into similar-sized chunks

2 small parsnips, cut into rough chunks

a few sprigs of thyme

½ tablespoon flour

good splash of white wine

500ml chicken stock

for the stuffing

good knob of butter

1 medium onion, finely chopped

60g chicken livers, cleaned

2 tablespoons chopped parsley

2 teaspoons thyme leaves

60g fresh white breadcrumbs

salt and freshly ground black pepper

Preheat the oven to 230°C/gas 8. To make the stuffing, melt the butter in the pan and gently cook the onion for 2 minutes, giving an occasional stir, then add the chicken livers and cook for a couple of minutes on each side. Remove from the heat.

Remove the livers from the pan and chop into small pieces, then mix with the onions, parsley, thyme and breadcrumbs, and season. Spoon the stuffing into the large cavity of the chicken; rub the outside with butter and season.

To cook the chicken, put the vegetables in a roasting tray with the thyme and place the bird on top. Cook for 15 minutes, then turn the oven down to 200°C/gas 6 and cook for another 45–50 minutes, basting every so often.

Remove the chicken and the vegetables from the roasting tray and put the tray on a low heat on the oven top. Stir in the flour, then gradually add the wine and chicken stock, stirring well to avoid lumps forming. Bring to the boil and simmer for about 10 minutes, until the gravy has thickened, then strain through a fine-meshed sieve.

Cut the chicken into joints, or carve the breast and cut the legs in half, and serve with the vegetables and roast potatoes if you wish, preferably cooked in goose or duck fat.

GOOSNARGH CAKES

Reg's mum, Winnie always seems to have these in her kitchen, or maybe its just when I'm in Lancashire. On my last visit, we were off to see the famous cheese-maker, Mrs Kirkham, after Winnie's compulsory breakfast and cakes. Mrs Kirkham's farm is just up the road and, on the way, I thought to myself that the Goosnargh cakes and the crumbly Lancashire would make a perfect combo. I'm not sure they are intended for each other, but they are certainly neighbours, and suitable for that sweet biscuit and cheese partnership

275g plain flour, sieved

225g unsalted butter, cut into small chunks

20g caster sugar

2 teaspoons caraway seeds

icing sugar for dusting (optional)

Preheat the oven to 150°C/gas 2. Put the flour and butter into a bowl and rub together with your fingers until the mixture has a breadcrumb-like consistency. Add the caster sugar and caraway seeds and mix well, then form the mixture into a smooth dough.

Roll out on a lightly floured surface to about 1cm thick. Cut into 7-8 cm rounds, or smaller if you wish. Dust with a little sugar (not if you are serving it with cheese though) and bake for about 20 minutes until just coloured.

Dust again with sugar while they are still hot and leave to cool on a wire rack.

George Taylor, 'King of the Egg Shows'

I wasn't aware of George Taylor until Peter Gott (page 133) mentioned him and showed me an article on him in *Cumbria Life*. Peter reckoned he lived up the hill and pointed vaguely across his farm to George's place 600 feet up on the outskirts of the village of Crook, near Kendal, appropriately called High Farm.

So, what's so interesting about George Taylor? Well, he's in the *Guinness Book of Records* for the number of first prizes won in a year. He established his place as a world record holder in 1999 with 536 firsts – I didn't realize there were that many farm shows. He then got it up to 596, and in his 50-year farming career, he's had an incredible 7,300 wins.

George reckons he has one leg shorter than the other, through all the walking up and down the hills over the years on his 174 acres of craggy land. Four successive generations of George Taylors have farmed and lived on High Farm, and George and his son, George the Fourth, rear sheep and cattle, as well as the 250 or so free-range hens, ducks and the one goose.

Until I met George, I didn't realize that showing eggs was such a serious business. It used to make good commercial sense, as George sold all the eggs locally, and I suppose a premium egg deserved premium prices. Unfortunately, it would seem that the new EU egg stamping regulations have made it difficult for him to continue selling them. The breeds involved in producing the eggs are Leghorns, Araucanas, Welsumers, Marans and Hamburg Bantams, chosen as they're the ones that produce eggs to meet stringent show standards.

FRIED EGG WITH BLACK PUDDING AND DUCKS' LIVERS *serves* 4

When you have two great products like George's eggs and top-rate black pudding from Andrew at R. S. Ireland or Stuart Higginson (see page 141), you really need to do very little to them. You can use ducks' or hens' eggs for this dish, or goose eggs if feeling really adventurous.

vegetable oil for frying

12 slices of black pudding from a small burrie, or about 60-80g per person

salt and freshly ground black pepper

200g duck livers, trimmed

100g butter

1 tablespoon chopped parsley

4 ducks' eggs

Heat a tablespoon or so of vegetable oil in a frying pan and lightly fry the black pudding slices for about a minute on each side, then keep them warm in a low oven.

Season the duck livers and sauté them in the same pan over a high heat with a little more vegetable oil for about 1½ minutes on each side, until nicely coloured but still pink in the middle. Add the black pudding, butter and parsley, and remove from the heat.

Fry the eggs in a little vegetable oil, transfer to warmed serving plates and spoon the black pudding and livers around, with the buttery juices.

The shrimpers of the Sefton coast

Morecambe Bay and the Sefton coast have been famous for brown shrimps for many years, and the local dish of potted shrimps has been produced since the late 18th century. Some of the coastline may look a bit of an eyesore – with rusty tractors and derelict-looking rowing boats on the beach – but these are the vehicles that earn the local shrimpers their living on the flats at low tide.

The brown shrimp, *Crangon crangon*, although not as tempting in the raw as its slightly inferior pink cousin, is the most common for potting, as they soak up more butter. In France, you may well have had them on a *plateau de fruits de mer*, where they're eaten whole, head and all.

I initially spoke to Andrew Lanagan at his fishmonger's shop in Lytham, where he supplies local chefs with cooked shrimp to pot in butter. John Fisher (appropriate name!) works for Andrew and used to be a shrimper himself until he caught pneumonia and decided to study marine biology instead. If you're going to pick someone's brains on this subject, then a marine biologist is the man, especially when the shrimps are apparently getting scarcer in the Bay. 'When the water is like gin, you won't find the shrimps; the water needs to be a bit murky,' says John. Something I remember well from my childhood prawning days. John also does a bit of fishing and bass seem to be the species most commonly found in the area, as they feed on shrimps, rather as the salmon does.

When we spoke to John, the shrimp season had not quite started. Not that there is an open and closed season but, as with my elver experience (page 57), the water needs to be the correct temperature. John's theory was that they were not migratory like elvers, but they would bury themselves and hibernate until the water warms up.

I returned up North a month or so later, when it was a bit warmer. The flats themselves are evidence of what the coastline has to offer. On certain parts, especially near Piel Island, you'll see nothing but mussel beds and empty shells, and further down you find only cockle shells.

What I did discover were native oyster shells on the flats, which must have come from the oyster beds at Walney just up the coast. Since the early 1980s, oyster seeds have been reared on Walney Island, which is an extension of the South East of England oyster fishery in Seasalter near Whitstable. The company Seasalter (Walney) Ltd was founded in 1883 and started breeding oysters to restock its beds in Kent.

Down in Flookburgh, I visited Les Salisbury, who is well known in the shrimp business and owns the Morecambe Bay Potted Shrimp Company and Furness Fish. Les is an old shrimper himself, who now cooks, processes and pots local shrimps. He uses a high-tech Dutch machine that heads, shells, cleans and grades, with no human involvement. I've always wanted to see one of those gadgets in action, because it fascinated me how they can get shrimps that small completely clean.

I suppose the real fun is to be had actually out catching them. The old method would have been horse and cart, just pulling a trailer with a shrimp dredger either side. Today the only difference is the horse being replaced with a tractor and, in some cases in deeper water, a boat.

POTTED SHRIMPS *serves* 4

This is a classic potted shrimp recipe as was once used to preserve the catch and enable us to savour the sweet flavour of the delicate and labour-intensive peeled shrimps, but now has now become a pricey starter in many restaurants.

180g unsalted butter

juice of ½ lemon

good pinch of ground mace or freshly grated nutmeg

pinch of cayenne pepper

small bay leaf

1 teaspoon anchovy essence or paste

200g peeled brown shrimps

salt and freshly ground white pepper

to serve

2 lemons, halved

good-quality brown bread

Melt the butter in a pan, add the lemon juice, mace, cayenne pepper, bay leaf and anchovy essence, and simmer on a low heat for 2 minutes to infuse the spices. Remove the pan from the heat and leave it to cool until just warm.

Add the shrimps and stir well, then season with salt and white pepper. Put the mixture into the fridge and stir every so often. When the butter starts to set, fill 4 ramekins with the mixture or spoon it on to plates.

If not serving them that day, return the ramekins to the fridge and cover with clingfilm. It's important not to serve the shrimps straight from the fridge, as the butter will be too hard to spread nicely on to the toast.

Serve on or with hot buttered toast and lemon halves.

Craster Kippers

Kippers are yet another old method of curing fish that has sort of stuck with us in a funny sort of way - as their smell does for hours. Perhaps that's why they're no longer in vogue, although I'm sure they'll be reappearing in some form on British food pioneers' menus.

Kippering is a method of preserving rather like the way salmon is smoked – split down the back, cured and smoked. In 1843, a John Woodger had the idea of doing this to herring in Seahouses in Northumberland, as previously herrings were cured as red herrings in hard blocks that more or less lasted forever and took days to reconstitute; or as bloaters which were like Arbroath smokies (see pages 110 and 188) and didn't have much shelf life. The kipper was a combination of the two, with a bloater's eating qualities and the shelf life of red herring.

In Craster in Northumberland, the long tradition of curing herring still exists and Craster has kept the kipper reputation going through the vagaries of food fashion. L. Robson and Sons Ltd, based in Craster, is a fourth-generation family business specializing in kippering with the traditional method of oak-smoking. The fish are still cured in the original 130-year-old family smokehouse.

The quality of the herring is paramount, as they must be plump and have the correct oil content before machines (which replaced the old 'herring girls' that used to split the herrings by hand) split them. They are then brined and hung on tenterhooks, and finally they go off to the smokehouse, where they have a good 16-hour hot smoke.

FILLET OF SEA BASS WITH SAMPHI, SHRIMPS AND COCKLES *serves* 4

On my shrimping expedition, it seemed quite natural that the ingredients available there – bass, shrimps, cockles and samphire should be married up in a dish all of their own. Now this is what British cooking is all about, not just reviving the classics, but also marrying up affinitive ingredients that all bear a relationship to the locality.

If all the ingredients are not available, then you could quite easily use either cockles or shrimps or leave out the 'samphi' as the locals call it. The brown shrimps can be eaten whole, as the shell is soft; or, if you prefer, buy them peeled. They are the same species as the *crevettes gris* that you will find on French *plateaux de fruits de mer*.

250–300g cockles

salt and freshly ground white pepper

4 sea bass fillet portions, each weighing 150-160g, skin on, scaled and boned

good knob of butter

3 tablespoons dry white wine

100g samphire, woody stalks trimmed

60g cooked shrimps, peeled or whole

Cockles tend to contain a lot of grit in their ribbed shells, so immerse them in a bowl of cold water for 30 minutes and agitate them every so often with your hands to dislodge the grit. Then rinse under cold running water for 10 minutes and drain.

Preheat the oven to 200°C/gas 6. Season the sea bass fillets, then put them in an ovenproof dish and rub each fillet with butter. Cover with greaseproof paper and cook in the oven for 15 minutes.

Meanwhile, put the white wine in a saucepan with the cockles and samphire, season, cover and cook on a medium heat for 2-3 minutes, or until the cockles are all opened.

Add the shrimps and any cooking liquid from the sea bass and stir well.

To serve, put the sea bass fillets on warmed serving plates and spoon the cockles, shrimps and samphire over, with the cooking liquid.

Ravens Oak We feature Ravens Oak Dairy cheeses fairly regularly on our cheese boards in the restaurants, as they make a perfect mellow match to most hard and blue cheeses, without taking over the board. Mike and Sandra Allwood have run the dairy since 1999, and are the eighth generation of the farming family. Nowadays, they keep only an organic flock of cattle on their 230-acre estate near Nantwich, and have a portfolio of a dozen or so cheeses made from cows', sheep's and goats' milk, and they also make cheese from the milk of water buffalo. (Imagine running into one of them in Cheshire – well, we did and it scared the hell out of us.)

Each of their cheeses is made and sold in three types: a fresh cheese, a Brie-style and a log variety. The dairy joined forces with Lancashire-based Butlers Farmhouse Cheeses in 2004, but expansion hasn't affected production standards in the slightest. Over the years, the Ravens Oak range of cheeses have won many awards, establishing them firmly in the British cheese premier league table.

My favourites are the Burland Green, which is a cows'-milk, Brie-style cheese and probably their 'flagship' cheese, although every time I read the cheese press, one of the others has scooped up a prize. Whitehaven, which is a similar Brie-style goats' cheese, comes a close second, along with Radmore, a sheep's milk cheese again in the same style. In fact, they are all great cheeses and can be eaten in a very fresh state or slightly more mature.

H. S. Bourne John Bourne and his wife Juliette-Anne are familiar faces at London's Borough Market. John Bourne produces fine, traditional organic Cheshire cheese on The Bank Farm in Malpas, Cheshire. Six or so cheeses are produced on the farm, as well as organic butter and soft curd cheese, all from unpasteurized milk from their 80 black and white cows. The milk literally travels about 50 yards from the parlour to the cheese press. I like the simplicity of John's cheeses and the confidence that he can put his family's names on the labels as John Bourne's Organic Cheshire, Tom Bourne's Oak Smoked Cheshire and Mrs Bourne's Mature Cheshire. Who will be next, I wonder?

Mrs Kirkham's Lancashire Cheese On the two occasions I've visited Ruth Kirkham's Lower Beesley Farm just outside Goosnargh, she's literally had her hands in the curds each time. Mrs Kirkham's Lancashire is the most famous of all Lancashires and even in London, you see it on menus wherever the chefs care about the provenance of their produce. The great thing is that the farm is a modest, humble place that seems to tick over with all the family mucking in. Graham, her son, runs the dairy now and I've even seen his son moulding cheese one morning – under very close supervision from his Gran of course.

All of her cheeses are made with milk from her own cows, with a 3-day curd from 6 milkings. This is what gives it its unique creamy crumbliness. They are matured anywhere from 2 to 6 months. They see the whole process through, except sadly where it ends up. They are just too busy getting the product right. Lancashire is the softest of the English pressed cheeses, but the texture differs according to the maker and to the age of the cheese, as the Kirkhams amply demonstrated to me while I was there. The best have a wonderful combination of crumbliness and butteriness. Lancashire is widely considered the 'king of toasting cheeses', but in the case of Mrs Kirkham's, this might seem sacrilege.

Wensleydale Creamery Cheese-making in this part of the Yorkshire Dales had started way back in 1150 in a monastery built at Fors a few miles from Hawes. The unwelcoming locals and the bad weather caused the monks to move to Jervaulx Abbey in lower Wensleydale. The French Cistercian monks from the Roquefort region had brought with them their special recipe for cheese made from ewes' milk, which continued to be made at Jervaulx until the dissolution of the monasteries in the 16th century. The art of cheese-making then lived on in the region with the local farmers' wives, although it was usually made from cows' milk and changed considerably in character.

In the late 1800s, however, flour and corn merchant Edward Chapman of Hawes was so shocked by the quality of some of the cheeses he was getting from locals as trade for his products that he was inspired to make cheese himself. Much to the surprise of his loyal customers, instead of trading his corn and flour for cheese, he began asking for milk instead and then began making cheese in 1897, first in his flour mill then moving to a converted wool mill in Hawes. His creamery became an important part of the community as the farmers who once made the inferior cheeses now had a guaranteed outlet for their milk and this time could get back some decent cheese.

Chapman's creamery did well until depression hit in

RIGHT Ruth Kirkham and her son Graham at work in the dairy at Lower Beesley Farm, near Goosnargh

the 1930s and the business fell into debt. The Wensleydale farmers who were owed money by the dairy were offered contracts by the Milk Marketing Board to take the milk from Dales to one of their national dairies miles away. The farmers had an affiliation with the dairy and, although they were creditors, wanted the dairy to continue running as it was. One of their fellow farmers, Kit Calvert gathered a meeting in the local town hall and raised enough support to keep the dairy going and it remained the only dairy producing cheese in the heart of Wensleydale.

Kit managed the dairy successfully for well over 30 years. He also bought dairies further east including the then popular Fountains Dairy. As retirement time came close, the Milk Marketing Board made another approach and ended up buying both dairies and planned heretically to move production of Wensleydale cheese to Lancashire. However, Fountains maintained its independence with a management takeover in 1987 and Hawes followed suit five years later.

Sadly, demand outside the area had dwindled almost entirely and, by the early 1990s, it looked as if this brave last stand was doomed, until help came from the most unlikely quarter. Mention of Wensleydale in the highly popular Wallace and Gromit animated films suddenly brought this crumbly cheese, with a delicious balance of honeyed sweetness and acidity, back into the public's ken. Apparently, animator Nick Park lit on the cheese as he thought the name would afford him interesting animation possibilities. Nick has now done the same with Charles Martell's Stinking Bishop cheese (see page 75) in the most recent W&G film, and it will be interesting to see what effect that exposure might have on such an artisanal product.

CHESTER PIE *serves* 6-8

I discovered this recipe in an old cookbook, *Warnes Model Cookery* by Mary Jewry, the new edition of 1868 . . . well not that new. This could well have been the precursor of that American favourite, the lemon meringue pie, as Liverpool was the great port of American emigration. Rather as with crème brûlée and burnt cream, you never quite know where it started, but with the proximity of Chester to Liverpool it might well be.

for the pastry

60g unsalted butter, softened

30g caster sugar

grated zest of ½ lemon, reserving the juice

1 small egg, beaten

125g plain flour, plus more for dusting

butter for greasing

for the filling

100g butter

grated zest of 2 and the juice of 3 lemons
(you have the juice from the lemon used
in the pastry already)

225g granulated sugar

8 egg yolks, reserving the whites

2 tablespoons ground almonds

120ml double cream

for the topping

whites of 2 eggs

60g caster sugar

First make the pastry: in a food processor, mixer or by hand, cream the butter and sugar together with the lemon zest and egg until smooth and creamy, scraping the sides of the bowl down every so often if you are using a mixer, until they are mixed well, then slowly fold in the flour and mould the dough into a ball.

Lightly grease an 18-20cm x 3cm deep straight-sided flan ring on a buttered tray or, better still, a flan tin with a removable bottom. Roll the pastry out on a floured table to about 3mm thick, then use it to line the flan ring/tin. The best way to do this is to roll the pastry around the rolling pin, then roll it over the flan ring/tin and ease the pastry into it with your hands. Press the pastry firmly into the corners of the flan ring and patch up any holes by pinching the pastry together or use some of the excess pastry. This pastry is quite forgiving and a bit of patching up wont be noticeable when cooked. Roll the rolling pin across the top of the flan ring to trim off the excess pastry and neaten up the edges by going round and pinching the edges of the pastry with your thumb and forefinger. Leave to rest in the fridge for 20-30 minutes.

Preheat the oven to 190°C/gas 5. Line the pastry case with a large disc of greaseproof paper or foil and fill with baking beans. Bake the pastry for 25 minutes, or until lightly coloured. Remove from the oven and leave to cool a little. Reduce the oven to 150°C/gas 2.

While the pastry case is baking blind, make the filling: melt the butter in a saucepan over a low heat. Remove from the heat and beat in the lemon zest and juice, sugar, egg yolks, almonds and double cream. Return to the stove and stir on a low heat until it thickens, but don't let it boil. Remove from the heat, give a final stir and cover with clingfilm to stop it forming a skin.

Remove the greaseproof paper and baking beans from the pastry case and pour in the lemon filling. Bake for 10-15 minutes until just set, then remove from the oven and increase the temperature to 220°C/gas 7.

Make the topping: clean a stainless steel mixing bowl and a whisk (preferably electric) with boiling water and dry with a clean cloth to remove any traces of grease. Whisk the egg whites until stiff, then add the sugar and continue whisking until they are stiff and shiny. Spoon the mixture over the filling with a spoon and return to the oven for about 3-5 minutes until lightly browned.

Taylors of Harrogate

We do rather take our daily brew and our inherent passion for tea drinking for granted. Tea is one of those commodities that is an integral part of our life and culture, but no one really gives a second thought as to how it got into the teapot. By the mid-1800s our tea drinking was becoming quite a sophisticated pastime, with its associations with travels to the Orient and India, and the spur of the establishment of new tea plantations. In 1886, teas from remote corners of the British Empire were showcased at the 1886 Colonial Exhibition that followed the Great Exhibition of 1851, and China exported 170 million pounds of tea to England in that year, a record never to be repeated to this day. This is all the more remarkable as tea was still an expensive commodity and a bit of a luxury. When Queen Victoria started serving tea in the afternoons at Buckingham Palace, it started a bit of a craze. Then especially with the opening of the Suez Canal and the triumph of steam over sail ships, this did now mean that tea was accessible to all, and an affordable treat. Tea rooms started opening across the country, and serving cakes, and the genteel idea of afternoon tea was born.

In that year of 1886, after serving an apprenticeship in London in the heart of the tea trade, Charles Taylor took advantage of the tea boom and established his family tea merchants in the heart of Yorkshire. After beginning a small business blending different batches of tea to suit different water types across Yorkshire, he then decided to open tea and coffee kiosks in the towns across Yorkshire – and as far afield as St Anne's-on-Sea in Lancashire – selling tea for two shillings a pound. His flagship, though, was the Café Imperial in Harrogate itself, and it soon become the place for ladies to meet for afternoon tea in this, one of the most fashionable spa towns in the country. By 1920, Harrogate boasted well over a dozen of the country's leading tea houses, all serving Taylors teas.

After Charles Taylor's death, the business joined forces with another famous Yorkshire family tea house called Bettys. Taylors of Harrogate is still a family business and one of the very few remaining independent tea merchants in Britain. They work closely with tea growers around the world, paying premium prices to support tea plantations.

YORKSHIRE TEA CAKES *makes 8*

I remember eating toasted tea cakes as a kid at the local golf club after a round. It seemed to be a traditional thing to do and they were always available, and I wasn't in Yorkshire by the way. Yorkshire tea cakes were first known as just good old Yorkshire cakes back in the early 1800s but by the end of that century the term 'tea cake' was commonly being used and mentioned by Cassell the historian in 1896: 'A hospitable Yorkshire housewife would consider her table was barely spread if it were not liberally supplied with these delicious cakes, constant relays of which should be served steaming hot.' This connection with Yorkshire is now not so commonly held and, as I experienced, they were commonplace in the Dorset golf club, although I'm fairly sure Eddie the Steward had a broad Yorkshire accent.

    450g strong plain flour
    1 teaspoon salt
    50g lard, cut into small pieces
    15g yeast
    300ml tepid milk
    50g sugar
    2 eggs, beaten
    115g currants
    25g candied peel
    butter and preserves, to serve

Sift the flour and salt into a large mixing bowl and rub in the lard.

Mix the yeast with a couple of tablespoons of the milk and a teaspoon of the sugar and leave in a warm place for about 20 minutes until it ferments.

Add the yeast mixture, the milk and the half the beaten egg to the mixing bowl and knead to a smooth dough for 3-4 minutes, then knead in the currants and mixed peel. Put the dough into a bowl, cover and place in a warm place for about 30-40 minutes, until doubled in size.

Knead the mixture again and divide into 8 pieces. Roll into rounds with your hands and place them on a lightly greased baking tray about 6-7cm apart to allow for expansion. Prick them lightly with a fork and leave them again to double in size.

Preheat the oven to 200°C/gas 6 and bake the tea cakes for 20 minutes, then brush with the beaten egg and return to the oven for 5-6 minutes to glaze.

Allow to cool on a wire rack, then halve and toast them. Serve piping hot, with butter and preserves.

PARKIN

I've never been too much of a cake person, but there is something warming about the parkin, hence the old association in the North with eating it on Guy Fawke's Night. It probably doesn't get served on that particular night much these days and on the nights I've attended bonfire parties with my daughters, Ellie and Lydia, there wasn't a slice of parkin in sight.

Parkin can take on names of the counties it's made in and you may well come across Yorkshire, Lancashire and Derbyshire parkins, and occasionally you may see it called the old name of 'thor' or 'tharf' cake. Moggy, another version of parkin made with wheat flour and with a really sticky texture, is my favourite way of eating parkin and you basically need to undercook it, as opposed to going the other way, when it can turn out really dry.

October, November and up to Christmas would have been the traditional time to use spices in cooking and a way of being a little extravagant, although nowadays we eat them all year round because spices are relatively cheap. Dorothy Hartley suggests it was popular practice to make an extra panful of parkin mix to serve hot with apple sauce, almost like a sticky toffee pudding.

    115g butter, plus more for greasing
    225g plain flour
    1 teaspoon bicarbonate of soda
    2 teaspoons ground ginger
    1 teaspoon ground cinnamon
    1 teaspoon mixed spice
    ½ teaspoon salt
    110g coarse (pinhead) oatmeal
    175g dark muscovado sugar
    3 tablespoons golden syrup
    115g black treacle
    150ml milk
    1 large egg, beaten

Preheat the oven to 180°C/gas 4 and grease a (preferably non-stick) loaf tin with butter. Sift the flour, bicarbonate of soda, spices and salt into a bowl. Stir in the oatmeal and sugar and make a well in the centre.

Melt the butter, syrup and treacle over a low heat, whisking to emulsify. Remove from the heat and let cool.

When cooler, mix into the flour mixture with a wooden spoon, then beat the milk and egg together and stir into the mixture until well mixed.

Pour the mixture into the tin and bake for 45-50 minutes, leaving the mixture slightly soft to the touch.

Leave to cool for 30 minutes or so before turning out.

The Rhubarb Triangle

Rhubarb is generally classified as a fruit these days, as it more often than not lends itself to being used like a fruit, but it is, in fact, a vegetable. It's a hybrid of several species, first grown on the banks of the Volga in Siberia and transported down the old Silk Road to China for medicinal purposes, and there are records of this trade dating back to 2,700 BC. Marco Polo was said to have brought it to Europe and it was recorded in Britain by the sixteenth century. Up until the nineteenth century, it was only really the root that was used, dried as a laxative, and for stomach, colon and liver complaints. Its culinary life really only developed in the nineteenth century.

So, what do we have against rhubarb? Memories of school meals of stewed rhubarb and lumpy custard maybe, or when mum didn't quite put enough sugar into the pot. It probably goes back further even than my generation all the way to war rationing and cold winters perhaps. Like spinach, you were always being told how good it was for you, and those memories seem to have stayed with many of us. There is, however, undoubtedly a rhubarb revival coming, with lots of new and interesting recipes hitting the streets, along with well-made old classics.

Go back even further than those school memories and Janet Oldroyd Hulme, 'the queen of Yorkshire rhubarb' will recite tales of the Chinese hijacking British troops' rhubarb supplies during the Opium Wars in the hope that their resulting constipation would force them to give up and go home, and Henry VIII taking rhubarb (then costly as gold) to his deathbed in an attempts to fend off syphilis.

Janet owns the country's largest rhubarb forcing shed in Carlton near Wakefield. It is part of what is commonly called the 'Rhubarb [or 'Pink'] Triangle' in a 30-mile area between Bradford, Leeds and Wakefield. Farmers here grow the country's finest rhubarb and, until the 1960s, this same area grew 93% of the world's forced rhubarb.

The climate in that part of the North is particularly suitable for growing as it forms a frost pocket, which Janet tells me is a good thing, and when the heat in the forcing sheds is turned on you can hear the buds popping to reveal the shoots. Sadly, there are only a handful of rhubarb growers like Janet left in and around the rhubarb triangle. At one time there were 190 of them and the process of rhubarb growing used to involve dressing an area of land with 'shoddy', the waste from the textile industry, to provide nitrogen-enriched fertiliser.

The new rhubarb plants stay outside for the first two summers before they are replanted in the windowless forcing sheds and from then on the new shoots naturally grow rapidly, looking for light. They are not cut outside in those first two years, just left to grow and die off so a great mass of energy is built up in the roots ready for their long stint indoors.

In the forcing sheds, they'll grow to harvesting point in 5–6 weeks and the first will be harvested around mid-January, with other varieties continuing up to March.

The day I spoke to Janet was 'firing day', which was the old term for firing up the old coal fires (when the area was a mining centre) to bring on the rhubarb. These days they use a more modern heating system, but Janet remembers her father harvesting the first rhubarb in early December, which goes to show how our climate is changing.

Janet grows several varieties of forced rhubarb: the earliest is Timperley, which is a salmony-pink colour, then follow the main-crop varieties, Stockbridge Arrow - one of Janet's favourites, this is a deep blood-red in colour and has arrowhead-shaped leaves. The other two are Queen Victoria, again a deep red colour, and a tricky one to grow but yielding double the quantity of Timperley; and her premium grade is Crimson Crown, which are the best sticks you can buy, according to Janet.

Talking to her, it suddenly occurred to me that we often don't name our rhubarb varieties on menus, but you often see the term 'Champagne rhubarb' used by some people to refer to forced rhubarb.

The outdoor varieties are harvested in April and these are generally much greener than the forced rhubarb, because of photosynthesis. The most popular of these is the Cawood Delight, which has a relatively small yield. Many people prefer the smaller stems, but in terms of flavour you are better off with the thicker stems as they tend to stay intact during cooking.

Janet told me that only five years ago business was incredibly tough, with interest in rhubarb at an all-time low, but since then things have turned full circle and she is now producing 200 tons of forced and 600 of the outdoor type.

Until the 1960s the railway ran a 'Rhubarb Special' that took crates of the stuff to London for Covent Garden market and if you looked from the air around Leeds, all you could see was just fields and fields of rhubarb.

Rhubarb is causing so much interest these days that rhubarb growers in the area have declared January the 14th 'National Gourmet Winter Rhubarb Day'.

RHUBARB PIE *serves 4*

1kg rhubarb, trimmed and chopped into rough 2cm pieces

1 large cooking apple, peeled, cored and roughly chopped

300g granulated sugar, plus a little extra for the top

a little extra butter for greasing

thick custard or clotted or thick Jersey cream, to serve

for the sweet pie pastry

110g soft butter

135g caster sugar

½ teaspoon baking powder

225g strong flour

pinch of salt

125ml double cream

Put the rhubarb and apple in a heavy-based pan with the sugar, cover and cook on a medium heat for 3-4 minutes, stirring every so often. Remove the lid and continue to cook for another 15-20 minutes over a fairly high heat, until the rhubarb is soft, most of the liquid has evaporated and the mixture has a jammy consistency. Remove from the heat and leave to cool.

Preheat the oven to 200°C/gas 6. To make the pastry, cream the butter and sugar. Sieve the baking powder and flour together and stir into the butter mix with the salt, then slowly pour in the cream until well mixed. Chill for about 30 minutes before rolling.

Grease a 17–18cm x 2–3cm flan ring with a little butter and roll two-thirds of the pastry to about 2–3mm thick. Line the flan ring with the pastry and trim the edges.

Then line the flan ring with a circle of greaseproof paper or foil and fill with baking beans. Bake the tart for 15-20 minutes, or until the pastry is lightly coloured.

Meanwhile, roll the remaining pastry out to a circle just a little larger than the tart. You can make a straightforward pie top, or cut the pastry in strips about 1cm wide to lay on top in a lattice pattern. If you have a lattice cutter, use this.

Remove the baking beans and paper from the tart and spoon the rhubarb mixture in. Lay the rest of the pastry over the top, trim the edges and press on to the edges of the pastry base with your thumb and forefinger. Brush the top with the egg white and scatter some granulated sugar on top. Bake for about 30-35 minutes until the top is a golden crisp. Leave to cool to room temperature and serve with thick custard, or clotted or thick Jersey cream.

WALES

As with Scotland, the food of the principality owes its origins to both Celtic tradition and a geography unsuited to all but the hardiest crops. Long after the Romans had introduced a variety of vegetables to Britain, the only two grown in Wales were the emblematic leek and the cabbage. Cooked with bacon – the pig was the mainstay of the local diet – these form the 'national dish', cawl.

This shortage of cultivated greens may also explain the fact that the Welsh make much use of laver bread, edible seaweed. The lengthy coastline also gave rise to a productive fishing industry, famed particularly for its sewin or sea trout, cockles and the great shoals of herring and mackerel caught off the west coast.

The hilly regions also favoured sheep farming and the salt-marsh lamb of the Welsh coastal regions is quite justly prized. Today, ewes' milk is used to produce award-winning yoghurt and cheeses, and Welsh goat's-milk cheeses are also now widely available. Rachel's Dairy in Aberystwyth is today among the most respected manufacturers of organic yoghurt in the British Isles.

Of course, the best-known Welsh dairy product still remains moist, crumbly Caerphilly cheese. One of the most enduring traditions in Wales is the weekly bake, and items like bara brith ('speckled bread') and Welsh cakes like teisen lap (fruit cake), teisen sinamon (cinnamon cake) and teisen mêl (honey cake) endure as family teatime favourites.

Wales is the land of home cooking and the Welsh really cook from the heart, using simple ingredients. Some of the producers are well-preserved hidden treasures, whose produce often rarely leaves the principality. I stumbled across some great little producers on my travels, who really care about what they produce and who they sell it to. Each producer led me to the next in a friendly, organic kind of way.

Tourism in Wales is on the up, and their country house hotels seem to retain some of the qualities a country house hotel should be about. Places like Tyddyn Llan in Denbighshire, run by Bryan Webb, who used to run Hilaire in London, fit the bill. Tyddyn Llan is a 12-bedroom Georgian house in the beautiful Vale of Edeyrnion, on the very edge of Snowdonia National Park, surrounded by sheep-studded hills.

Meals in Wales tend to reflect the main householder's occupation and in north Wales there was at one time a meal known as the 'quarry supper' (*swper chwarel*) at five in the afternoon, when the men returned to the light from the depths of the slate caves and the coal mines. With such quarrying and mining fast disappearing, this type of meal is becoming a thing of the past.

My findings have unravelled a host of great food producers in both north and south Wales and I usually get invited to the Abergavenny Food Festival every year, where foodies, journalists and chefs gather to pay homage to Welsh food, and check out if there is anything they are missing 'over the big iron bridge'. While there last year, I got rudely awakened at 5am to go salmon fishing after a long night on the grappa at the Foxhunter Inn with Mitch Tonks and Jason Lowe. Mr Lowe resumed his sleep on the riverbank; hence, we have no photos of frisky, early-morning sewin being landed.

A friend's wedding in Anglesey (which locals proudly call 'the food island') led me to several great food producers in just one day, each one of them proudly leading me to another within the 20-mile stretch. Before the wedding celebration, I headed off to probably the best sea salt producer in the country, Halen Môn, and then on to a couple of relatively unknown cheese producers who need putting on the map and an oyster grower that time had forgotten in London and that hasn't supplied a London restaurant for 10 years, since my predecessor at the *Independent*, Simon Hopkinson, was chef at Bibendum. Wherever I end up, I do seem to come across a producer of some kind who still remembers Simon.

Cockles and laver

We British are not generally a nation of seaweed lovers and, for most of us, the nearest we get to seaweed crossing our lips is probably samphire. The one ingredient that is quite unique to the Welsh kitchen is laver – or laver bread as it is known once cooked and prepared – the delicate purplish seaweed harvested from rocks in south Wales. It is rather confusing calling it laver bread, as it has nothing to do with bread at all. For you Japanese food lovers, the nori sheets in which sushi rolls are wrapped are made from the same laver seaweed, which may or may not change our minds a little.

On a laver mission with my guides Horace Cook and Dai Daniels, the latter being a fish buyer with a coracle licence (see page 166), by accident we stumbled across a small-time producer of this nutritional seaweed pulp. After checking out a couple of large-scale and not-so-interesting cockle and laver bread producers, Horace just recognized the house in Penclawdd from which he had bought laver bread a couple of years ago.

The place was a breath of Welsh fresh air and we drove literally into its back garden, where we met Jeff and Liz Williams. They had just finished boiling a batch of laver, and it was sitting there freshly minced to a pulp and stacked up in large metal trays. This was a proper family business, concentrating on local cockles, mussels and laver processing. Jeff let me stick my finger into one of the stacked-up trays of steaming laver. It was quite delicious and you could just taste the nutrients.

The raw seaweed gets washed several times in Jacuzzi-like machines before being boiled in lightly salted water for 7 hours. It then gets minced and that's it. While Jeff showed us around, Liz got out a tub of freshly cooked plump shelled mussels to nibble on. It was the first time I've tasted a shelled mussel of that quality. Some of their laver bread goes to be canned and the rest is sold fresh at local markets, butchers and fishmongers, or from their little retail unit at the back of the house.

Laver bread has lots of possibilities, whether being served with meat like mutton, or grilled or steamed fish, or as a side dish. I've even spread it on toast to use up the last of a tub. It can be mixed with oats and fried in cakes for breakfast, served with rashers of bacon. Simmered with cream and a squeeze of lemon juice it makes a perfect sauce to accompany sewin (sea trout) or scallops.

Liz and Jeff recommended serving their laver bread with Albert Rees's Welsh cured bacon and cockles. Albert, who is at Carmarthen Market on Wednesdays and Saturdays, is known as 'Rees the Ham' as he is among

several stallholders with the same name. He's the only pig butcher in Wales to dry-cure his hams to the stage where they're similar in style to Parma, Bayonne and Ibérico.

Laver bread and cockles seem to go hand in hand in Wales, and those who gather and process laver, like Liz and Jeff – and Alyson and Brian Jones of Selwyn Penclalawdd Seafoods just up the road – still continue the old tradition of cockle collecting themselves. In the old days, it was usually the wives of miners too ill to go back down the pits who did the gathering. In many areas over the years, they got superseded by donkeys, men and sophisticated machinery. The Bury Inlet, however, still paints a traditional picture and, fortunately, its sands are still rich with cockles – as you'll see by the empty shells piled high outside Selwyn's Seafoods. These get taken off to be used to make paths on golf courses and in gardens.

The Bury Inlet, where the local cockles are gathered, is one of the few remaining areas of hand-collecting. Gathering by hand in the traditional way is pretty hard work, very time-consuming and thus obviously more costly than with modern mechanical methods. Welsh cockles are highly rated around the country and the Penclawdd Bury Inlet is deservedly proud to be judged a sustainable-rated fishery and an environmentally responsible area by the Marine Stewardship Council (MSC). It has resisted the temptation over the years to let the Dutch, or anyone else, into their fishery with mechanical harvesters, and their self-imposed quotas are carefully monitored, as are the licences given out and daily quotas carefully adjusted according to stock levels.

Jeff tells me that the local cockles are at their best and plumpest during the autumn, but are harvested up to Christmas time, when they're still sweet but not as plump.

BACON CHOP WITH LAVER BREAD AND COCKLES *serves* 4

Here I've used a bacon chop, which can be cut from a piece of whole back or streaky bacon, or better still a piece that's been cured and smoked on the bone. A good old-fashioned pork butcher will sell a piece of whole bacon joint, or you could settle for thick rashers of bacon. If using a whole piece of bacon joint, simmer it for an hour and let it cool, then slice it into 2cm slices before cooking. Depending on where you live, you will find laver bread fresh or canned. Try to buy the fresh if possible, as there is a world of difference.

350g fresh cockles

4 thick bacon chops, each weighing about 120-150g (on the bone they will be heavier)

200-250g laver bread

good knob of butter

salt

If you are using cockles, leave them in a bowl of cold water, agitating them every so often with your hand to loosen any sand, then rinse under clean running water for 5 minutes.

Preheat a lightly oiled grill or griddle pan and cook the bacon chops for 4–5 minutes on each side.

Meanwhile, put the laver bread into a pan with a knob of butter and gently reheat. Put the cockles into a large saucepan with a little water and a teaspoon of salt, cover and cook on a high heat, shaking the pan every so often, until the cockles open. Then drain in a colander.

Spoon the laver bread on to 4 serving plates, place a bacon chop on each and scatter over the cockles.

The Lobster Hatchery of Wales

Apart from their famous sea salt, David and Alison Lea-Wilson have also been quietly busy running a lobster hatchery at their sea zoo next to the Halen Môn. They started a small-scale pilot hatchery in 1989, where fisherman would sell them berried females (i.e., those carrying eggs). When the larvae hatch, they are put into tanks called 'up welling bins', where fast-moving water is pumped around to keep the larvae moving. This emulates sea currents and stops them eating each other. Once they have built up some strength and have gone through four stages of growth, known as moults, they are transferred to individually compartmentalized trays, rather like mini wine boxes, where they are left to grow for 4–6 months, so they are strong enough to be released into the sea.

In 2002, the hatchery was awarded 'objective one money' from Europe, which goes to the poorest industrial areas of Europe. This allowed the fishery to expand and increase the amount of lobsters brought in.

All female lobsters released back to sea are clipped with a V-shaped notch in their tales, which means that, if and when they are caught, they are released regardless of their size, otherwise heavy fines are enforced on the fishermen. This also applies to berried females released after they have released their eggs.

So, as well as having a top-notch and successful salt business, the Lea-Wilsons are also doing their bit for conservation and the future of our lobsters, funded by the sea zoo entrance fees and tourism.

The Lobster Pot

What a find this was – a last-minute recommendation for a lobster feast from our B&B, Penyrorsedd Farm. I'm sometimes a bit sceptical about restaurants that are signposted for miles on the roadside, as they often disappoint when you eventually get there. This was certainly no disappointment; in a great location, down a winding road overlooking Church Bay, it was a traditional old whitewashed cottage, which started its current life as a guesthouse selling lobster teas to the public 50 years ago. Chefs Steffan and Wendy Coupe have now taken over, and have kept the same homely, family atmosphere for which

the place has become renowned While we sat in the bar, I spotted fish identification charts on the wall from Bridport Gundry, a net maker back in my home town. They must have dated back to the 1960s by the look of them – before towns had phone codes. An inviting bowl of complimentary local winkles sat on the bar as a teaser and, I must say, they were some of the best winkles I've ever tasted.

The menu consists of about thirty per cent lobster dishes, from salads to simply grilled, as well as some classics from Escoffier's repertoire. My friend, Niru ordered grilled lobster, and 3 halves showed up at the table. We also

sampled a bowl of the sweet plump Menai mussels that we discovered were at their best in July, when talking to Shaun Krijnen (see page 169). There should be more places on the map like this, serving local produce to both locals and tourists.

Coracle fishing

Over the years, I've come across lots of interesting methods of catching salmon and trout, other than using rod and line. Of all of them, the coracle is one of the most fascinating of the old ways of fishing, although it's actually a fishing craft and not a direct means of catching them. The coracle is the most ancient watercraft in these islands, along with a very similar vessel in Ireland known as the curragh, and its design remains virtually unchanged.

The coracle is a tiny keel-less, bowl-shaped fishing boat – if you can call it a boat – that barely holds one person. They are made with willow frames, covered in calico and coated in boiling pitch to make them watertight. These old-style coracles are still made today by Bernard Thomas in Llechryd, 'The Welsh Coracle King'. Although, as with most boat-making, the modern fibreglass version is fast replacing the original type.

They are light enough to be carried on the fisherman's back to the riverbank, with the ash paddle tucked behind the seat to provide leverage and act as a handle. Older versions would have been made with hide and be much heavier, and not so manoeuvrable. The actual design of the coracle will vary slightly from river to river, as some waters are faster than others. There is a wooden seat in the centre of the coracle and users fish in pairs, with a net that can be up to 20ft long slung between them.

When they have trapped salmon or sewin (sea trout), the fishermen draw a rope to close the mouth of the net. The coracle fishermen will then offload their catch on the bank and continue fishing. Coracle fishing is an extremely efficient way to fish, although these days licences are pretty restricted, and good rivers like the Towy have only 10 pairs of licences granted.

Dai Daniels is one of the licence-holders and when the season kicks off, on March 1, he will be out most nights. Most of the Towy fishermen use fibreglass coracles these days, as they're pretty maintenance-free. As well as being manoeuvrable in all waters, coracles can fish in water only inches deep. They can also be used for fly fishing and angling, where wading is impossible.

FILLET OF SEWIN (SEA TROUT) WITH CUCUMBER SAUCE *serves 4*

A freshly caught sea trout, simply cooked, is a memorable treat. Although my quest to catch one on the fly is still ongoing, I'd like to think by the time the book comes out that the quest will be fulfilled.

1 tablespoon vegetable or corn oil

4 portions of skinless sea trout fillet, each about 150g

for the sauce

2 small shallots, finely chopped

4 tablespoons fish stock

4 tablespoons double cream

1 small cucumber, halved lengthways and the seeds scooped out, and the flesh cut into small (5mm) dice

salt and freshly ground black pepper

a good knob of butter

1 tablespoon finely chopped chives

Heat the oil in a heavy-based or non-stick frying pan. Season the fillets and cook for 3–4 minutes on each side, skin side down first. The cooking time will depend on the thickness of the fish; fillets from a smaller fish will take about half the time.

Meanwhile, make the sauce: gently simmer the shallots in the fish stock until it has almost all evaporated. Then add the cream and cucumber, season and simmer for a couple of minutes until the sauce has thickened. Stir in the butter and chives. Season to taste.

Spoon on to warmed plates and place the pieces of fish on top.

Halen Môn – The Anglesey Sea Salt Company

I first met David and Alison Lea-Wilson at the International Food Exhibition in London's Docklands about 3 or 4 years ago. What a breath of fresh air – a new salt company to complement our world-famous Essex counterpart. The salt crystals had an interesting shape and the salt itself seemed rather different from the sea salt we'd been used to, so I couldn't wait to pay a visit.

My trip to Brynsiencyn, where they're based, turned out to be quite a productive foodie trip before my mate's wedding in Roscolyn. In 1981, David and Alison fell in love with Anglesey after leaving university, but had no cash. Their first business venture was breading oysters and selling wet fish to local hotels and restaurants from their small shop. The fascination their customers had with their fish display was incredible, and they seemed more interested in the fish themselves than cooking them.

From this curiosity of the general public, David and Alison had the idea to start a sea zoo in 1983 as a tourist attraction, and it was attracting some 150,000 people a year, but a sea zoo was never going fulfil their ambitions.

They came up with the idea of making sea salt from the water they already had a licence to pump ashore. No sooner had they had the idea, than they got a pot of sea water on the Aga overnight and started experimenting. The next morning, they harvested the very first batch of white flaky Halen Môn sea salt. Next, they bought some old tin baths and camping stoves, and tried the idea on a larger scale. In 1997, they started selling commercially.

I was curious to see how the process differs from salt-making I've witnessed in places like the Camargue in France and Trapani in Italy. Down in the salt-making buildings, three or four locals tend to the gently heated water pumped from the Menai Straits. Sea water only actually contains 3% salt, so it's a pretty laborious process to turn that into sellable salt. As the water releases steam, which is then reused to heat the sea water, it is concentrated into a very salty brine When the concentration of salt in the water is high enough, it's transferred to shallow crystallization tanks with overhead radiant gas heaters to imitate sunlight and thus help crystallization.

Tiny delicate crystals form on the surface, then sink to the bottom as they grow. The local workers harvest the salt crystal by hand, then put them into mesh trays and move them around, washing them in the same brine, then finally drying them. This manual process is the secret to the unique formation and shape of the crystals, and watching the guys in action really makes you appreciate a commodity we take so much for granted, like salt. The drying of the salt is done in fan ovens at around 60°C overnight and then its ready for packaging.

David and Alison's Halen Môn salt is gaining worldwide respect, and restaurants like Iroco in Madrid have their salt featured in six dishes on the menu. Spain and Italy are among their biggest customers, although these countries produce a lot of salt themselves, and the Japanese, of course, go mad for sea salt crystals.

Celery salt

The familiar commercially made brown powder is made with celery seeds, and the idea of sprinkling pretty homemade green celery salt on gulls' eggs, or into a Bloody Mary is much more appealing.

Take a head of leafy celery (producers tend to cut off all the leaves, so you'll need to search for a head with plenty of leaves from a farmers' market). Remove and chop the leaves, and use the rest for a soup, stock or salad. Set your oven to its lowest temperature. (With some modern ovens. you can get away with just using the fan; an Aga warming oven is also ideal.) Scatter the celery on 1 or 2 baking trays lined with greaseproof paper and leave in the oven overnight until the pieces are dry and crisp, but don't let them brown. Depending on how watery the celery is, you may need longer. Once dry enough, put into a food processor with a handful of sea salt flakes and briefly blend to a powder, then sieve if necessary.

Menai Oysters

I managed to catch Shaun Krijnen doing a bit of DIY on his day off, so he was probably glad of some company and a bit of a tea break, I'm sure. Shaun, like lots of oystermen I've come across, studied marine biology and has a masters in shellfish biology from Bangor. Although Shaun was passionate about shellfish, he struggled to find a job after leaving university, and ended up signing on. He soon got bored with that and doing nothing all day, and went to work for a small local oyster farmer, Rod Jones. He ended up buying him out in 1994 and started up his own company, Menai Oysters.

The oysters are Pacifics, and Shaun tends to grade them in just the one size, mediums, as production is relatively low. After downing a couple of specimens from the purifying tank for breakfast, I said to Shaun that I was surprised I'd never seen them on London restaurant menus. Shaun said he used to sell them to Simon Hopkinson at Bibendum many years ago, so we will have to see what we can do about that. I'm quite sure we can find a space on the J. Sheekey menu and most certainly at Scott's.

Oysters and mussels historically grew wild in the Menai Straits, but, as with lots of natural oyster fisheries around the British Isles, pollution destroyed them and many of the farmers were forced to give it up. The water is much cleaner these days and suitable for rearing shellfish once more. A few years ago, Shaun saw a gap in the market for Menai mussels and just bought a few bags from a wholesaler to test the market and his regular local customers. The response was great, so Shaun decided to lease an existing mussel bed and expand his business. Unusually, his mussels are at their plumpest and sweetest in July, as I experienced the night before at the Lobster Pot (see page 165). We tend not to buy mussels during the summer as the meat is pretty small, so again I'm sure we can find a space on a menu for these little gems.

Since my visit to Anglesey last summer, Shaun has had an entry in the *Guinness Book of Records*. He stumbled across a 1.4kg specimen, which is the largest recorded in Britain and was probably about 30 years old. However, the world record is held by a 3.7kg native flat oyster from Virginia – theirs would be bigger!

1 smoked ham hock, soaked overnight and rinsed well

1 neck of lamb or mutton, cut into chunks

2 onions, roughly chopped

10 black peppercorns

2 garlic cloves, sliced

a few sprigs of thyme

1 bay leaf

3 carrots, cut into rough chunks

2 medium leeks, halved, roughly chopped and well rinsed

1 small swede, peeled and cut into rough chunks

2 tablespoons roughly chopped parsley

salt and freshly ground black pepper

Put the ham hock, lamb, onions, peppercorns, garlic and thyme and bay leaf into a large pan, cover well with cold water and bring to the boil. Skim and simmer for 1½ hours.

Add the carrots, leeks and swede, and continue cooking for another hour, or until the meat is tender.

Add the parsley, adjust the seasoning and simmer for a further 10 minutes.

Remove the ham from the bone in chunks and serve with pieces of lamb and vegetables, and the liquid.

CAWL *serves* 4

Bacon remains today an essential and favourite food of the Welsh. Together with leeks and cabbage, which were until relatively recently very much the only two vegetables cultivated in Wales, it forms the basis of what was virtually the national dish, cawl. There is no precise translation for the word 'cawl'; in Welsh, it signifies a soup or broth, but is actually much more of a meal in itself, a classic one-pot dish, originally cooked in an iron pot over an open fire. Fat home-cured bacon and scraps of sweet lamb would form the basis of the stock, then vegetables would be added at the end of cooking.

Recipes for cawl vary from region to region, village to village, even house to house, and ingredients will be added according to what's in season. In some cases, the broth would be served first and the meat and vegetables served as the main course, rather like a French *pot-au-feu*. I often find myself making this kind of soupy broth at home if I have cooked a ham hock, as I just hate wasting anything that I can turn into another dish.

BRAISED FAGGOTS WITH PEAS *serves* 4

These bring back fond teenage memories of faggots and gravy from the chippy after youth club or swimming. Faggots are found in many parts of Britain and sometimes referred to as savoury ducks in the North. They are most likely to be of Welsh ancestry, although Northerners may well disagree. They are one of the best ways to use up all of the offal and are generally made around pig-killing time. It's a real working man's dish and easily transportable, a bit like the pasty, hence their popularity among the mining communities.

The wrapping of caul fat, or pigs flead as its sometimes referred to, the lacy-thin marbled membrane that lines the pig's stomach, is quite essential to keep the filling moist, though it's not a general stock item for most of our butchers nowadays, so you will need to pre-order some.

We ate faggots in a working-man's-lunch sort of way with Dai Daniels and Horace Cook (page 163) before a spot of laverbread hunting and a night's sea trout fishing.

2 medium onions, finely chopped

1 tablespoon vegetable oil

1 garlic clove, crushed

⅓ teaspoon ground mace

1 teaspoon chopped fresh sage

1 teaspoon chopped fresh thyme

400g pork liver, coarsely minced or chopped in a food processor

250g pork mince, with a good proportion of fat

100–150g fresh white breadcrumbs

100–120g caul fat, well washed

olive oil, for frying

for the peas and gravy

100g dried green peas, soaked in plenty of cold water overnight

salt and freshly ground black pepper

2 large onions, finely chopped

1 tablespoon vegetable oil

30g butter

30g flour

½ teaspoon tomato paste

1 litre beef stock (a good-quality stock cube dissolved in that amount of water will do)

a few drops of Worcestershire sauce

First prepare the peas and gravy: drain the peas, rinse them well and cook in lightly salted water for about 45 minutes, or until tender. It's difficult to put an exact cooking time on dried pulses, as you never know how long they've been dried, so you may have to be patient on cooking times.

While the peas are cooking, gently cook the onions in the vegetable oil in a covered pan for about 5 minutes or so until soft. Turn up the heat and allow the onions to colour. Add the butter and then stir in the flour, and cook over a low heat for a minute or so. Add the tomato paste, stir well and gradually add the beef stock, stirring well to avoid any lumps. Bring to the boil, season with Worcestershire sauce, salt and pepper and simmer for 1 hour on a low heat. Remove from the heat and add the drained peas

Also, while the peas are cooking, start to prepare the faggots: gently cook the onions over a low heat in the vegetable oil, together with the garlic, mace, sage and thyme, for about 4 or 5 minutes. Remove from the heat and leave to cool.

Mix the pork liver and minced pork together with the breadcrumbs and cooked onion mixture, and season with salt and pepper. Divide the mixture into 4 balls and refrigerate for 30–40 minutes.

If you are not using caul fat, wrap each faggot in clingfilm a couple of times and steam them over a pan of simmering water in a steamer or a colander for 20 minutes, then leave to cool.

If you have caul fat, rinse it well under cold running water for about 10 minutes and pat dry on some kitchen paper or a clean tea towel. Lay it out on a table and cut it into 12 rough squares big enough to wrap around each ball of meat a couple of times, then carefully wrap them up in it.

Preheat the oven to 220°C/gas 7. Lightly oil a deep roasting tray and put the faggots in it, with the join of the caul fat on the undersides. Roast for about 20–30 minutes, until they are lightly coloured. Then drain off any excess oil from the tin and pour in the gravy. Turn the oven setting down to 160°C/gas 3, cover the faggots with foil or a lid and braise them for about 1 hour. If you are not using caul fat, unwrap the faggots and roast and braise as above.

Serve the faggots with the peas spooned over and around them.

The Thomas's Welsh Blacks

Before I went up to see Brian and Ffiona, I was proudly shown an article in a local paper by Richard, the husband of Margaret Davies (see page 174) about the dense population of female company directors in Anglesey. There was a photo of the Thomases, both dressed up in the field, with their famous ancient breed Welsh Black cattle, so I thought I was on the way to see a couple of posh well-to-do farmers.

I was pleasantly surprised, when I sat in their living room with a mug of instant coffee, that, like the other producers in the area, they were totally down-to-earth as well as passionately into their farming.

They run three farms between them. Ffiona farms Welsh Blacks at Wilpol Farm just down the road and Brian farms with his 82-year-old father at Chwaen Goch Farm, and also has an organic, Soil Association-registered farm, Plas Coedana, where he rears the ancient breed Welsh Black cattle and Black Welsh Mountain ewes and Suffolk tups.

Brian is an ex-chairman of the Welsh Black Cattle Association and, after the family sticking strictly to these breeds all their lives, they decided to diversify their farming routine and sell their meat to the general public themselves in the year 2000 under the name Beef Direct. They set up a cutting unit in a converted barn and travel to farmers' markets in the North East, including the Wirral, Liverpool and Altringham, selling their meat and by-products, like sausages and burgers.

Brian actually drives up to the markets himself and had just finished loading the van with various cuts of beef and lamb, and kilos of sausages, when I met him. He says he just hasn't got enough meat to keep up with the demand. You can also buy the meat, in various cuts, by mail order, and it will be on your doorstep within 36 hours of ordering.

Back in their living room, Ffiona proudly paraded her Black Welsh Mountain Lamb rugs, which are going on sale at the markets as another very sensible by-product, along with a prototype rocking lamb made of wood and sheepskin, with leather curly horns . . . the lot. I included a rug with the first order of Welsh Black rump for the restaurant, which went down a treat with the local carnivores – the beef that is, not the rug . . . that's on the floor in the bedroom.

BEST END AND BRAISED NECK OF BLACK WELSH MOUNTAIN LAMB *serves 4*

Pairing a popular well-used cut with a less popular cut that is actually really tasty provides an interesting contrast. The neck is a great cut for a braise, and is full of flavour, while the best end is an easy cut to cook – roasted or grilled as cutlets – and you can keep it a touch on the pink side. I love experimenting with different cuts of meat, not that a neck is an unusual cut, but cutting it through the bone into rounds gives it an interesting shape when braised, rather like an osso buco or oxtail. You can serve anything seasonal with this, and my favourite with lamb would be a Welsh Onion Cake (see opposite).

salt and freshly ground black pepper

4 neck of lamb steaks, each about 200g, cut through the neck about 2cm thick

1 tablespoon flour

2 tablespoons vegetable oil

a good knob of butter

1 small onion, finely chopped

1 garlic clove, crushed

1 teaspoon chopped fresh rosemary

½ teaspoon tomato paste

1 litre beef or lamb stock (a good-quality stock cube dissolved in that amount of water will do)

1 small leek, trimmed, well rinsed and finely chopped

1 celery stalk, peeled if necessary, and finely diced

1 small carrot, finely diced

One 8-bone rack of lamb

Season the neck chops and lightly flour them with about ½ tablespoon of the flour. Fry them in the oil for about 2–3 minutes on each side over a high heat until nicely coloured.

Melt the butter in a medium heavy-based saucepan add the onion, garlic and rosemary, and cook over a low heat for 2–3 minutes, stirring occasionally. Stir in the rest of the flour and the tomato paste, then stir in the lamb stock a little at a time.

Add the pieces of lamb, bring to the boil, cover and simmer gently for an hour. Add the leek, celery and carrot, and continue to simmer for another hour, or until the meat is tender. It's difficult to put a cooking time on a cut like this it may well take another 30–40 minutes.

While this is cooking, preheat the oven to 220ºC/gas 7. Season the best end of lamb and roast it with the fat down for 15 minutes, then turn it over and cook for another 10 minutes. Remove and leave to rest in a warm place.

While the lamb is cooking, remove the neck chops from the cooking liquid, skim off any fat and reduce the cooking liquid until it has thickened.

Carve the best end between the bones, plate the neck and spoon over the sauce, then arrange 2 cutlets on each.

WELSH ONION CAKE (*Teisen Nionod*)

serves 4–6

This is a bit like the famous French *pommes boulangère*, in which the potatoes are cooked in meat stock. If you are roasting a joint, I would strongly recommend you finish cooking it on top of the onion cake, so the juices are absorbed into the potatoes and onions.

800g large potatoes, thinly sliced

500g onions, sliced

100g butter, melted, plus extra for brushing

salt and freshly ground black pepper

Preheat the oven to 200ºC/gas 6. Wash the potatoes briefly in water and dry on a tea towel or kitchen paper. Put them in a bowl, season with salt and pepper and mix with the 100g melted butter.

Butter a shallow ovenproof serving dish and layer the potatoes and onions alternately, beginning with the potatoes and finishing with a neat layer of overlapped potatoes on top.

Cover with foil or a lid and bake for 1 hour, then remove the foil, brush with a little more butter and cook for another 15–20 minutes to allow them to brown.

Cheeses of Wales

Gorau Glas Cheese This is yet another of Anglesey's great success stories. I had yet to taste or set eyes on the famous Gorau Glas cheese and eagerly made my way to the farm from the sea salt company. It's a good job everyone knows each other around here, because I managed to get completely lost on the brief 5-minute car journey.

Margaret Davies, who has always worked the Quirt Dairy Farm with her husband Richard, modestly gave me the rundown on her, thus far, short and highly successful career as a cheese-maker. Her son Huw, who grew up on the family dairy farm and took a banking degree, decided to do his dissertation on a fictitious Welsh cheese-making business. This gave Mum the idea to go on a cheese-making course at the local Coleg Menai Food Technology Centre. The course involved making everything from feta to Brie, and her course homework was creating a blue-veined cheese.

Margaret experimented at home with her basic Brie-style cheese by inserting stainless-steel needles at random points in the cheese to create the blue veins. This was about the time in 2002 that dairy farmers' milk dropped to a ridiculously low price, so this new cheese-making hobby turned into an interesting and real prospect to add value to the farm's milk business.

Margaret eagerly started making a few cheeses for some local markets with her daughter Catrin, and launched her Gorau Glas cheese at the county show. In the same year of 2002, she won a gold at the British Cheese Awards and got a first at the Nantwich Show – not bad for year one.

When she discovered I also cooked, I became the guinea pig for some experimental cheeses she had stashed away to mature. A couple were snapped away from under my nose before I could get them on my oat biscuits. The most successful, though, was a blue that she had moulded in a colander to form a flatter cheese than the cylindrical Gorau Glas, to give it a unique shape and exterior texture, and a piquant 6-month maturity, as opposed to the younger gold medal winner.

Gorau Glas, or 'blue moon' as it translates, has not made it to London yet, as the production is relatively small. Although, as I was leaving, Richard her husband called her in to deal with a Cheshire wholesaler's order enquiry. It will certainly be going on our cheeseboard, even as part of a trio with the young unveined version, the blue and the flat mature blue, possibly with a slice of bara brith (see page 177).

Caws Cenarth Thelma Adams bought Glyneithinog Farm with her husband Gwynfor in 1961, after they got married, and they ran it as a dairy farm. In 1984, Thelma decided to do some market research on cheese-making and went on a short cheese-making course in Nottingham, then spent some time in Devon with Rita Ash, an author who wrote *Cheesecraft, a Manual for Cheesemaking*. Rita was running a course on cheese-making and Rita's husband also makes bespoke cheese-making equipment, so this really gave Thelma an insight into the business she was about to get involved in.

After that little stint with Rita, she visited several cheese-makers in Devon and Somerset, to get a feel of exactly the kind of cheese she should be making. Thelma started production in April 1987, with her version of traditional Welsh farmhouse Caerffili, made with unpasteurized milk from their Friesian Holsteins, which they called Caws Cenarth. The cheese has quietly gained a great reputation in the cheese world and won a silver medal at the British Cheese Awards in 2002 and at the 2005 Awards was Welsh Cheese of the Year.

Thelma's son, Carwyn joined the family making cheese business in 2000, after studying at agricultural college. Carwyn really got into the cheese-making and showed an interest in taking over the family business at some stage, which he did in 2003. They decided to rent out their farm where the cows were and sold the cows to the farmer. They now buy back the organic milk from there for their cheese – a sensible move, allowing them to concentrate on the cheese-making.

Carwyn is now making his own style of cheeses on the farm. His first cheese was Perl Wen ('white pearl'), which is a Brie-style cheese with a white bloom rind and won a silver for the best new cheese in the 2001 World Cheese Awards. Perl Las ('blue pearl'), a hard blue-veined cheese, was next, a year later.

Perl Las got Carwyn the joint best cheese at the *Mail on Sunday* Soil Association Organic Food Awards and since then he has won two golds at the Welsh Taste Awards 2005 and a gold in the blue class in the 2005 British Cheese Awards as Best Blue Export Cheese. Carwyn has just started making Golden Cenarth, which is a smear-ripened, semi-soft cheese that will no doubt be on the awards lists this year.

One of Thelma's proudest moments in her cheese-making career was after she had a visit to the dairy from Prince Charles. When he was leaving, he invited Thelma up to Highgrove to have a look around the farm, so she

LEFT: Gorau Glas cheese; RIGHT: Margaret Davies and her daughter Catrin with some of their cheese in the kitchen at Quirt Farm.

took him up on the offer and spent the day with David Wilson who runs the farm. During the course of that day, David suggested that Thelma makes a cheese with milk from their Highgrove organic Ayrshire dairy herd as a surprise for Prince Charles's 50th birthday. Thelma spent a couple of days under cover at Highgrove, bringing her own cheese-making equipment up in the back of the van and went to work making some Caerffili for the party.

HRH was so impressed that he rang Thelma and asked if she would mind making some more cheeses for him. She agreed and a tanker with 480 gallons of milk turned up, which is way over what they would normally make in a day's production. They finally got it all finished just before midnight, borrowing moulds and making do with what they had.

Thelma runs the dairy as a bit of an open farm, where tourists can come and tour the dairy, then buy cheese from the shop afterwards. This saves Thelma going to the farmers' markets herself; they have to come to her.

Llanboidy Cheesemakers Our directions to Llanboidy to meet Sue Jones seemed pretty straightforward until we got to the chocolate farm(!), which we were told was next door to Sue's Dairy. Now what would a chocolate farm be doing in the middle of Welsh countryside you may ask? Well, me too. We pulled into the chocolate farm to ask directions. I just couldn't resist it, the whole thing was bizarre – chocolate fountains, chocolate café, chocolate cinema, the whole thing – and not a cocoa tree in sight.

I asked the young girl serving in the chocolate café if she knew where Llanboidy cheese was, thinking she would be wondering what the hell we were doing asking

for a cheese producer. She immediately replied, 'My mum's not there at the moment. I'm her daughter. It is Sue Jones you're after, I presume'. I chuckled. She was obviously not interested in cheese-making, or maybe she was and was earning a few bob in the holidays. Anyway, she pointed us in the right direction and rang her mum to tell her we were on the way.

Sue uses the rare-breed Red Poll cattle that I came across up in Norfolk a couple of months ago. I was more interested in their meat at the time, and didn't even consider there might be cheeses from their milk. Sue started out as a teacher, but kept a few goats and made a bit of soft cheese and yoghurt as a hobby, selling them in the market at Tenbury Wells in Worcestershire. Sue kept a few Red Polls and Friesians, and decided to dig up a bit of history on the rare old breed, to discover that in the 1800s Red Polls were widely used for cheese-making. Sue explains that their milk on its own is just so creamy, and with a flavour all of its own, it is just bound to produce a unique cheese.

Sue eventually phased out the Friesians and developed the Red Poll side to make a unique cheese. She brought in her sister, Alison to assist with her cheese-making. She refers to Alison as 'a bit of a scientific cook', but not on the Heston Blumenthal level, I presumed – just precise with her measuring and timing, which is, of course, essential in cheese-making. That was over 20 years ago and Alison is still there, as an essential ingredient of Sue's cheese-making process.

Sue now has over 100 Red Polls, which produce considerably less milk than conventional dairy cattle, but they are certainly producing a quality product to start the cheese-making process. Sue has the only Red Poll dairy herd in Europe and, being unconventional dairy cattle, they come with their problems. Often her farmer has to pull a bull out of the herd because of bad behaviour, and fertility can be a problem too. However, she has decided to stay with them, as she has a unique product. They have even installed brushes for the cows, so that they can rub themselves against them in the winter as a sort of self-relaxation treatment.

Her main cheese from the beginning was the Llanboidy, a cheese that is sold in varying stages of maturity. It's a full-fat, hard-pressed cheese and similar in texture to a Lancashire perhaps, although comparing cheese textures with cheese-makers is always dangerous and, at the end of the day, it's a unique farmhouse cheese with nothing added and nothing removed. It won her a British Cheese Awards gold medal in 2001. She has also experimented with lacing the cheese with laver bread to great effect, and that cheese won a silver in 2000.

To expand her cheese-making, she decided to bring in some local organic Pembrokeshire milk and produce a new cheese called Cilowen Organic, which has a slightly caramel-like flavour, with hints of wild flowers from the red clover where the cows graze. This has won her more awards than any of the other cheeses, including Best Organic Cheese at the British Cheese Awards in 2001 and subsequent golds there in 2001, 2002 and 2003.

Sue still pursues the farmers' markets, as these outlets form a key part of her business, keeping in touch with her personal customers and getting real feedback.

WELSH RABBIT *serves* 4

No, I haven't made a spelling mistake. For years, like most people, I thought 'rarebit' was correct and 'rabbit' was a misprint or used by someone who had been getting it wrong since the inevitable childhood misunderstanding. If anything, it's the other way round. After reading what reputable food writers, such as Jane Grigson, have to say on the subject, I've become determined to see the return of 'rabbit'. Even Dorothy Hartley's *Food in England* (1954) and Hannah Glasse from 1747 confirm it – the original name for cheese on toast. That's what it started off, as in the early 1700s, when there was a difference between English, Scottish and Welsh rabbits. Maybe the 'rarebit' adaptation was a Welsh joke that caught on, or it was thought to sound more refined. Anyway, Welsh rabbit is a refined cheese on toast with savoury additions. Ideally, you should use a Welsh cheese like Caerphilly; if not, Cheddar will suffice, or you could use a mixture to suit your taste.

5 tablespoons stout

5 tablespoons double cream

250g Caerphilly or Cheddar cheese, or a mixture, grated

2 egg yolks, beaten

2 teaspoons Worcestershire sauce, or more if you wish

1 teaspoon English mustard

salt and pepper

4 slices of bread (a small bloomer-style loaf is ideal)

In a small heavy pan, simmer the stout until it has reduced by half. Add the cream and then reduce this by half again until it is really thick. Leave to cool.

Mix this together with all the other ingredients, except the bread, and season to taste.

Toast the bread on both sides, and keep the grill on at medium heat.

Spread the cheese mixture on top of the slices of bread, about 1cm thick, and to the edges to avoid burning. Grill until nicely browned.

BARA BRITH

I must say that I had never tried bara brith until I grabbed one from Hooton's roadside farm shop in Brynsiencyn. In Wales, it is a variation of a weekly loaf and can be eaten on its own, buttered or – as I did – with a lump of Margaret Davies' Gorau Glas cheese (see page 174). I'm not sure how the locals would have reacted to eating it with cheese, or maybe they would have welcomed it. The original version uses yeast as a raising agent, though some recipes now use baking powder.

150ml milk

50g brown sugar

10g dried yeast

450g wholemeal flour

1 teaspoon salt

1 teaspoon mixed spice

75g butter, cut into small pieces, plus more for the loaf tin

75g seedless raisins

75g currants

25g chopped candied peel

Heat the milk until tepid, dissolve the sugar in it and mix with the yeast in a small bowl. Place this somewhere warm for about 15 minutes until it begins to froth.

Meanwhile, mix the flour, salt and mixed spice together, then rub in the butter. Make a well in the centre, add the yeast mixture and mix to a smooth dough. Cover with a clean damp cloth and leave in a warm place until doubled in volume (about 1–1½ hours).

Knead the dough, then work in the fruit and peel. Butter a warmed loaf tin and carefully push in the dough. Leave in a warm place for another 1–1½ hours, until it has doubled in volume again.

Preheat the oven to 220°C/gas 7. Bake for 20–30 minutes, covering the top of the loaf with foil for the last 10 minutes of cooking. Leave to cool and serve buttered.

SCOTLAND

W HAT CHARACTERIZES MOST SCOTTISH food is the canny frugality of a northern European peasant tradition. As in Wales, the inhospitable terrain and climate made oats the staple grain, giving rise to the oatcakes, bannocks and porridges at the heart of Scots eating. Warming and filling broths based on barley or lentils and flavoured with mutton; offal dishes like mealie pudding and the world-renowned haggis; tasty preserved fish like smoked salmon, kippers, finnan haddies or Arbroath smokies– all speak of a need to make the very best of what is available and to set food by for harsher times.

Of course, in season, the Highlands are also rich with many types of game bird, like red grouse, capercaillie, partridge, pheasant, grouse and snipe; there is magnificent venison from the deer; and the fast-flowing burns teem with salmon and trout. Highland livestock, like the world-famous Aberdeen Angus cattle and Scots Blackface lamb, also provide some of the tastiest meat in the world. There are also surprising pockets of market gardening, like the cultivation of those fruits that thrive in a cooler climate with long summer evenings, such as raspberries, tayberries, loganberries, etc.

Scotland also has a strong tradition of baked goods, from Forfar bridies (the Scottish 'pasty') to delicate shortbread and glorious Dundee cake. Finally, Scotland has given the world whisky, the 'water of life'; which is used judiciously in some of its favourite dishes, as in whisky sauces for venison and in Atholl Brose, the sublime honey and oatmeal dessert.

Of all the regions of the British Isles, Scotland must boast

Driving through most parts of Scotland is always a mouthwatering experience for food lovers. No sooner have you passed a famous fishing water than you are driving through fungi-friendly tree-lined roads and I find it difficult to keep my eyes on the road. Scotland is a food heaven, although much of its glorious produce gets immediately exported out of Britain.

BELOW LEFT The aftermath of a highlands grouse shoot

When you are actually deep in the heart of Scotland, you can really see why so many people come from all over the globe for fishing, hunting, golf, walking, or just for a relaxing vacation.

It is a unique corner of the world, and some parts of it have managed to stay almost entirely unspoilt, despite that very wealth of visitors – and, with any luck, they will remain that way.

some of the finest produce. Do we make enough use of it, though? On my journeys through the amazing countryside, my answer had to be no. What does happen to the stuff? I'm convinced that the majority of restaurants and pubs just are not making use of what's around them. I struggled to find a local restaurant that was proud to serve local cheeses. I know for a fact that produce such as squat lobsters, langoustines and razor clams go straight to France and Spain, as you rarely see them on menus and you hear stories that a couple of decades ago they couldn't give the stuff away.

One of my memorable Scottish feasts was years ago in Port Appin on a shellfish 'recky' to check out scallops and langoustines, or prawns as they are called in Scotland and Ireland. We lunched at The Pierhouse, a modest local restaurant on the quay and, as we sat, a local fisherman walked in with a creel full of prawns straight out of the water. That brief moment was memorable enough, but when the large ones, known as 'Number Ones' in the business, were split in half almost immediately and just simply grilled with butter, and the smaller ones brought to the table just boiled, it became a complete gastronomic pleasure.

So why is something so simple such a pleasure you may ask. Well, that's exactly the answer. It was so simple and so fresh, and no one had tried to mess with it, and we saw the product arrive, live and kicking. If this type of eating was more common, maybe the price would be lower and there would be no excuse to export any more of our finest fare.

Rannoch Smokery

There is so much venison in Scotland that it seems a shame not to do something more inventive with it rather than stick to the obvious traditional ways. I have, though, often wondered what exactly people's perception of eating it in a traditional way is? Like a cow, it can be divided up into all the prime cuts and joints, and the hindquarters can also be broken down into the various muscles. Some of these are really tender, so don't need braising, like the central seam joint in the middle of the leg, which is the equivalent to the topside, and can be roasted or cut into escalopes and pan-fried. The rest of the leg, being slightly tougher, is then best braised. Other cuts, like the saddle and the small under-fillets, are very tender and need little cooking, so are perfect for roasting pink or, again, pan-frying or grilling. Of course, smoking is one of the oldest and most flavoursome ways of preserving meat, and seems the obvious way to treat an abundance of wild venison.

The Barclay family – Leo, Sarah and son Richard – up at Rannoch in Perthshire, thought exactly that in the early 1980s, when they were faced with a large deer cull and a heavy snowstorm blocked the roads. Leo built a wooden box in the backyard and began smoking some of the premium cuts of venison 'for a bit of fun'.

The family subsequently took over the 500 acres of land overlooking Loch Rannoch from Leo's parents, who historically farmed sheep. On my visit, Richard, who now runs the family's smokery, was busy sorting out packaging dilemmas in the HQ of their now very successful meat-smoking business. Those cuts of venison from the surrounding heather-clad hills now feature as high-end

products on deli counters in major foodie stores across the UK, along with other products that they have developed, like smoked goose, duck, lamb and chicken.

Richard's style of smoking is fairly traditional, with no 'bells and whistles' except for the now common, modern-day electronic smoking ovens. The process basically follows a brine soak, and the meats are then smoked over whisky cask chips from a Speyside distillery – which Richard gets in trade for his smoked meats in a bit of good old-fashioned bartering.

Although 60-80 or so deer are culled on the estate each year, Richard also needs to source wild deer from other local game dealers to keep up with demand. After a guided tour up the hills, we sat down to a feast of cold- and hot-smoked meat. Like that for cured and smoked hams, the consumer market for smoked meat is fickle and some foodies prefer the hot-smoked products to the cold. My preference was definitely the cold-smoked venison fillets, but that's me.

As we were eating lunch, a curious thing happened: a Royal Bank of Scotland van turned up and I thought it was delivering wages or collecting cash. Richard informed me that it was actually a mobile bank, and I promptly went out to the car park with my switch card and got fifty quid in cash with no pin number required, just a signature. That really brought home to me that there is something to be said for self-sufficient life in the country. I promptly left for the airport back to London with a promise to Richard that I would be back in the autumn to help him improve his fungi knowledge.

FILLET OF VENISON WITH HAGGIS AND BASHED NEEPS *serves* 4

When I was up on Ben Weatherall's grouse moors (see page 194), I couldn't help pulling a few turnips from their kitchen garden. Now, I'm actually talking about white turnips here, not the yellow ones (swedes). I do find it totally confusing the way the Scots call turnips swedes and vice versa. Anyway, swedes when they are mashed up, or 'bashed' as the Scots put it, are just delicious with meats like game or, traditionally, with haggis. On that subject, I quite like to add a few spoonfuls of haggis to neeps to give them a real taste of the Highlands.

Silvy, Ben's wife has everything there to feed the family all the year round without having to shop. The ground has plenty of manure dug into it, which always helps to produce a good crop, and it seemed such a shame to throw the turnip leaves into the bin, or the compost in Silvy's case. I decided to bastardize the classic recipe and blanched the leaves, then mashed them in with the turnips and butter. After all, in Italy, turnip tops, or *cime di rapa*, are a sought-after and popular vegetable, and there the white roots probably go into the bin, or compost.

4 trimmed venison saddle fillets, or under-fillets, each about 150g

½ glass of good red wine

6 juniper berries, crushed

a few sprigs of thyme, chopped

salt and freshly ground black pepper

150ml beef stock (or ¼ good-quality stock cube dissolved in that amount of hot water)

a little cornflour (optional)

30g butter

vegetable oil for frying

150g-200g good-quality haggis, skinned and meat crumbled or spooned into pieces

500g swedes or turnips, peeled and roughly chopped, plus the leaves, if available, destalked and roughly chopped

60g butter

The day before, put the venison fillets to marinate in a non-reactive dish with the wine, juniper and thyme. Cover with clingfilm and place in the fridge overnight.

Next day, remove the venison from the marinade, pat the fillets dry on kitchen paper and season with salt and freshly ground black pepper.

To make the Bashed Neeps, cover the turnips with water and season with salt and pepper. Bring to the boil and simmer gently for 10-15 minutes until they are soft enough to mash. Drain in a colander, then coarsely mash with a potato masher. Adjust the seasoning, if necessary, and stir in the butter.

While the neeps are cooking, cook the leaves in a separate pan of boiling salted water until just tender. Drain and toss in with the neeps. Keep warm.

Also while the neeps are cooking, put the marinade into a saucepan and boil it rapidly until it has reduced to a tablespoon. Add the stock and any juices from the venison and boil for about 5 minutes or so until the sauce has thickened. If the sauce is not thick enough, dissolve a little cornflour in some water and stir it in, a little at a time, until it thickens. Strain it through a fine-meshed sieve and whisk in the butter.

Heat a little oil in a heavy frying pan and cook the fillets for 2–3 minutes on each side for medium-rare or a few minutes longer for medium. Let them rest on a plate to catch the juices, covered with foil to keep them warm.

Reheat the bashed neeps if necessary and fold the haggis into them. Spoon into the centre of each plate. Slice each venison fillet into 4 or 5 pieces and arrange on the neep mixture, then pour the sauce around.

'Great chieftain o' the puddin race'

While in Scotland, I discovered two really good haggis producers, although there are probably lots of small local butchers producing equally good versions. Simon Howie started in the trade as an apprentice in Rattray's butchers in Perth. It was an old-fashioned shop that made use of the whole carcass, and a part of that process was, of course, haggis. Simon ended up buying the shop at the height of the BSE crisis in 1995 and continued the haggis-making tradition with a few personal tweaks on the way. He has won many awards since, including the Best Butcher in Scotland and the Best Shop in Scotland.

Simon is a relatively new haggis maker, compared to better-known makers like MacSweens, and, for me, his are among the top for taste and texture – not too dry and a good level of spice. Although, when I watched them being made from scratch, the proportion of spice looked pretty high, but this did mellow when cooked.

Talking of the other ingredients, for those of you who know and love haggis, I needn't mention what actually goes into it – or should I? Simon's recipe, which I ate in miniaturized canapé form, uses the following ingredients, although I was sworn to secrecy as to the exact quantities (or I may have ended up in the mincer as well). Laid out before my eyes were: kibbled onions, which were sort of sliced and dried; medium and pinhead oatmeal for the texture; flaked barley; and the best bits, lungs, liver, heart and fat; then the secret spice mix of pimento, cloves etc. This all gets minced and mixed, then filled into the appropriate casings and boiled for 45 minutes.

Simon produces about 4,000 pounds (1,818 kilos) of haggis per week, some in the natural casing of sheep's stomach and the rest, for the less discerning eaters, in a plastic sleeve. In the week of Burns Night, the production goes up, not surprisingly, to 250,000 pounds.

I asked the boys in the factory which of them actually ate haggis and only a few hands showed, although I did learn it's a big thing in Scottish chippies, sliced, battered and deep-fried, with tatties and neeps. Sounds good to me, although I'm not sure if I could manage the deep-fried Mars Bar to follow.

Stuart Houston, a Dumfries butcher, makes an equally delicious haggis. He is a third-generation family butcher, working out of the family premises. I detected a slight variation in spices, but that's a personal thing and a safely kept secret, I'm sure. If you're not a local, then you can buy these directly from Ben Weatherall's website (www.blackface.co.uk).

Fishing on the Dee

I've long been looking forward to an opportunity to fish on the River Dee, one of the best salmon rivers in Scotland - well, in the UK, in fact. As well as enjoying great fishing opportunities, we were fortunate enough to stay in the lodge belonging to Jim Grey, overlooking the stretch of the river he owns. It was the beginning of the salmon season and kelts – fish that have spawned and are off back to sea –- were leaving the river, and fresh fish were on their way up the 60-mile stretch of the Dee. We observed this activity over breakfast from the lodge, getting our adrenalin going for the day.

Snow, blizzards and rain are not ideal conditions for fly fishing, especially in April. I've never experienced such diverse weather: one minute we had a job standing up against driving snowstorms and five minutes later the sun was out and the wind had totally dropped. The extreme weather made little difference, though, to activity below water and we managed to pull a good few fish out of the river.

Rules on salmon fishing vary from river to river around the country, and some will allow you to keep one fresh fish (not the newly spawned kelts though) and others further down south insist that all fish must be returned to the river until a set date after the spawning season is over.

Having never experienced a real salmon fishing trip, I was intrigued by the river's gillie, Jim Paton. I've heard lots of gillie stories over the years from my fishing and hunting chums, and now was my chance to hear them straight from the man himself. I was advised to buy my flies from the gillie, as this was a way of indicating respect for local knowledge, and he might also then be more inclined to put you in a good spot for the day. There were no flies for me to buy in Jim's cabin, although a bottle of the local brew and a few dinners seemed to do the trick. Jim was also partial to a bowl of cullen skink, prepared by our host Alex Fisher, to his own recipe, I may add, although I did offer up my version as opposite.

A gillie's job is not just about coaching, fishing and putting clients in the right spots. Jim's stories dealt with all the aspects of his duties, like warding off poachers, chasing kids trying to steal the giant protected mussels from the riverbed and, best of all, dealing with the casual trespassers on his boss's estate. In a broad local accent and with some fruity-sounding local words thrown in, his

CULLEN SKINK *serves 4–6*

This was the most comforting dish I experienced on our River Dee trip, along with the Aberdeenshire butteries on page 188, that is. Alex Fisher, our host on the trip and a big player in the food business, quickly responded to my request for cullen skink, and even missed a morning's fishing to buy the ingredients. Alex left the skin on his potatoes, but that's entirely up to you. Smoked haddock just produces the best flavours, whether in a soup, poached with an egg or in kedgeree. Avoid the yellow-dyed smoked haddock, though, and buy the lighter-coloured genuinely smoked fillets or Finnan haddock. Cullen is a harbour town in Banffshire on the southern shore of the Moray Firth and 'skink' is just the Gaelic name for a broth or soup.

good knob of butter

1 leek, chopped into rough 2cm dice and well rinsed

1 litre fish stock (or a good-quality fish stock cube dissolved in that amount of water)

1 small waxy potato, about 200g, peeled and cut into rough 2cm cubes

1 bay leaf

300g undyed smoked haddock fillet

salt and freshly ground white pepper

3 tablespoons double cream

1 tablespoon chopped parsley

Melt the butter in a pan, add the leek, cover and cook gently for a few minutes, until soft. Add the stock, potato, bay and haddock. Season lightly. Bring to the boil and simmer for 15 minutes. Carefully remove the haddock from the pan with a slotted spoon. When cool enough to handle, remove the flesh from the skin of the haddock, checking for bones, then flake it into the soup. Blend a ladleful of the soup in a liquidizer and return to the pan. Stir in the double cream and parsley. Simmer for another 2-3 minutes, then adjust the seasoning, if necessary, before serving.

normal tactic for passers-by who fancied picnicking or barbecuing on private property and wouldn't budge, was to ask for their address and promise to pop by for a picnic with his family on their front lawn.

Jim tells us that currently each year about 60,000 salmon and sea trout pass through the lower Crathes/ Western Durris stretch of the Dee, heading up river. With stories across the country of salmon not returning to our UK rivers as they used to, this is more encouraging news. There are obvious reasons for this, like all the fishermen who use nets being bought off the river, so the fish have a decent chance to enter, spawn and escape the river again. Other more natural threats that are more difficult to deal with, however, are the seals that make their way 12 miles upriver in search of prey. A dozen or so are spotted each year and often mistaken for logs, until they take off after salmon. Surprisingly, the brown trout are an even greater threat, as they eat the salmon eggs.

The salmon was once the king of fish in Britain and elsewhere, but widespread intensive farming has somewhat downgraded its status on the fishmonger's slab. However, I would say that a fishing trip on a good salmon river soon restored its status for me.

BUTTERIES *makes 16*

I'd never heard of Aberdeen butteries – or rowies, as they're also called – before the fishing trip. The rest of the party warned me of the high fat content of these morning rolls, and the fat turned out to be lard as well as butter. My first impression was a sort of cross between naan bread and a croissant, but one thing I discovered is that they must be eaten warm or they 'donae gi doon weel'.

While munching on my butteries, I was conjuring up all sorts of ideas for these little flatbreads. Wild mushrooms perhaps, sautéed in more butter with wild garlic leaves, pocketed and stuffed with cheese for a mid-morning snack or dunking in your soup.

2 teaspoons active dried yeast

1 tablespoon soft brown sugar

450ml warm water

500g plain flour

good pinch of salt

250g butter, softened

125g lard, softened

Mix the yeast, sugar and a tablespoon of warm water. Put in a warm place for 15–20 minutes, until it bubbles.

Mix the flour, salt and yeast mix to a smooth dough. Cover and leave in a warm place to rise for 30–40 minutes.

Cream the butter and lard together and divide into 3. Once the dough has doubled in size, knead it on a lightly floured surface for a couple of minutes. Roll out to a rectangle about 1cm thick. Spread ⅓ of the butter mix over ⅔ of the dough, fold the remaining ⅓ over the butter mix and fold the other bit over that, giving 3 layers. Rest in the fridge for 30–40 minutes. Repeat the entire process twice, using up the rest of the butter mix.

Preheat the oven to 200°C/gas 6. Cut the dough into 16 pieces and shape each into a rough circle. Place on a lightly greased baking tray and bake for 15 minutes until risen and golden.

The Arbroath smokie

Despite high unemployment and modern town planning, the fishing town of Arbroath, on Scotland's east coast, still retains its charm, with its blue and pink fishermen's houses along the harbour. Lobster pots sit on the harbourside and nets get repaired by local fishermen killing time between tides and bad weather.

The Spink family have a long fishing history in Arbroath. Bob Spink, a fifth-generation Spink, now runs the family business, as well as redesigning his smoking kilns with his brother to give his Arbroath smokies (hot-smoked haddock, whole apart from their heads) an authentic smokiness and as close as can be to the original taste, when they were smoked over wooden barrels all those many years ago. After years of campaigning, the family's artisan product, has been awarded the EU's PGI status (Protected Geographical Indication), meaning that only haddock smoked in the traditional method within 8 kilometres of Arbroath can be sold as the real thing, so their smokies can now sit alongside products like prosciutto de Parma and Champagne.

Back five generations ago, there was obviously no refrigeration and the only methods of preserving fish for transportation were salting, pickling and smoking. Bob proudly brought out a photo album with shots from 1885 of local families preparing and smoking fish in the village. In those days, the men would fish and the wives smoked the catch. He found these amazing pictures in the attic of a house he bought and has set up a website to share these amazing shots, www.thefrasercollection.com.

Bob's brother, Ian also has a desire to retain a bit of smokie history and demonstrates the original method of smoking at local shows, digging a hole in the ground and smoking haddock in a wooden barrel.

Nowadays, the smokies are left for 3 hours in dry salt, then the tails are tied up in the traditional way with thick string, known as the strum, and they are then smoked for 50 minutes in the kiln. The combination of the smoke and steam from the fish gives the smokies that moist eating quality.

LEEK AND POTATO STOVIES WITH ARBROATH SMOKIES

serves 4 as a light meal or for breakfast

Stovies are traditionally made with leftovers on the stove, rather like English bubble and squeak. After visiting Bob Spink, I was scratching around for an appropriate recipe that wouldn't offend the smokie purists, especially Bob. What would you do with leftover smokies though? A smokie stovie maybe! You can make individual stovies if you have one of those tiny non-stick egg (or blini) pans, or make one large one and cut it afterwards.

2 medium leeks, halved, well rinsed and coarsely chopped

salt and freshly ground black pepper

good knob of butter

2 large baking potatoes, boiled in their skins until cooked but still firm, then peeled

1 Arbroath smokie, weighing around 250g, skinned and boned, or the same weight of undyed smoked haddock fillet

2 teaspoons freshly grated horseradish

2 tablespoons chopped parsley

vegetable oil for frying

4 eggs

Cook the leeks in boiling salted water for 5–6 minutes, until tender. Drain well, then transfer to a bowl.

Coarsely chop the potatoes and add to the leeks with the flaked smokie flesh. Add the horseradish and parsley, season and then mix well.

Heat a tablespoon of oil in one or two frying pans, preferably non-stick. Divide the mixture into 4 and shape each into a cake with a spatula. Let the cakes cook for 4–5 minutes, until it begins to colour nicely underneath, then flip it over like a pancake. Alternatively, you can turn them out by inverting them on to a plate, then heating a little more oil in the pan and sliding the hash back into the pan(s). Cook for another 4-5 minutes.

While the stovies are cooking, fry the eggs in some oil and butter, and serve on top of the stovies.

Rope-grown mussels

In and around Loch Fyne is a hive of fishing industry, and a trip out on the barge-like, open-decked mussel boat is something of an experience. We rarely get to see mussels fresh out of the water, as they're normally bought live in net or plastic bags from our local fishmongers, usually ready-scrubbed, debearded and all set to drop straight into the pot.

On a chilly October morning, we ventured out on the Loch in a small boat with an outboard motor. We soon moored up alongside one of the many rows of mussel rope buoys and climbed aboard the mussel boat to check out how the mussels were developing on the ropes beneath the surface.

It's quite fascinating to see how the newly spawned mussel seeds just latch on to anything suspended in the water. Each buoy has a 30ft rope with pegs every few feet to stop the mussels sliding off. Each rope has about 100 kilos of mussels attached to it, at varying stages of maturity. When harvested, they get graded and sorted on board, and the ropes – along with the small spats (the tiny young mussels) get returned to the water.

MUSSEL BROSE *serves 4*

The term 'brose' can mean a number of very different dishes, from hearty soups to a sweet atholl brose, all of which are thickened or contain, oatmeal. I suppose a dish as simple as a mussel brose is rather similar to the classic *moules marinière*. You can add many other flavourings instead of the parsley, such as dill or chopped spring onions and a splash of wine, to suit your taste. When wild garlic leaves are in season in springtime, a handful of them just torn into the soup will really give it a special flavour.

    1 onion, finely chopped
    good knob of butter
    250ml fish stock
    150ml milk
    salt and freshly ground black pepper
    1kg mussels, well scrubbed and any beards removed, discarding any mussels that stay open when tapped
    3 tablespoons fine oatmeal, lightly toasted
    2 tablespoons chopped parsley

In a large pot, gently cook the onion in the butter for 2–3 minutes until soft. Add the fish stock and milk and lightly season. Then add the mussels, cover with a lid and cook over a high heat, stirring or shaking the mussels, until they begin to open.

Drain the mussels in a colander over a bowl to catch the liquid. Pour the liquid back into the pan and stir in the oatmeal. Cook over a medium heat for a couple of minutes until the liquid thickens slightly and then add the parsley.

Put the mussels into warmed serving bowls and pour over the hot liquid.

Braden rost

This is a delicious way to eat smoked salmon and is, sadly, not that well known. On a visit to Loch Fyne a few years ago, we were treated to Loch Fyne oysters and this special kiln-roasted salmon in the house of John Noble (the late founder of the Loch Fyne company) overlooking the loch. Oysters and braden rost washed down with some crisp Chablis, followed by a trip to the smokehouse, was a memorable way to enjoy a one-day trip to the Highlands.

In fact, I'm wrong to call braden rost an alternative to traditional smoked salmon, as its taste is miles away from that of a cold smoke, and it has a flavour and texture all its own. It almost seems as if it could have been invented by accident, and when that was suggested, it brought a cheeky grin to the face of Kenny, the smoker. I suppose, after a few drams, the kiln temperature could easily have been increased and the next morning the product was cooked.

The Loch Fyne cure for the braden rost is sea salt and unrefined brown sugar, then it is smoked at ambient temperature, as for smoked salmon, for 12 hours before extra fire boxes are lit and the fillets then cooked through.

SCOTCH (MUTTON AND PEARL BARLEY) BROTH *serves 4-6*

Mutton is without doubt the best meat to use for a Scotch broth like this. You will probably need to ask your butcher to order it in advance, although butchers are coming round to the fact that mutton is back into vogue (see page 136). A broth like this is perfect to take in a Thermos on a day's fishing or shooting

250-300g mutton or lamb neck fillet, or boned shoulder of mutton or lamb, cut into rough 1cm dice

1/2 teaspoon chopped thyme leaves

30g pearl barley, soaked in cold water for 1 hour, then drained

50g dried split peas, soaked in cold water overnight, drained and rinsed

2 litres lamb or chicken stock (or a couple of good-quality lamb stock cubes dissolved in that amount of hot water)

salt and freshly ground black pepper

1 small leek, well rinsed, trimmed and cut into rough 1cm dice

2 carrots, peeled if necessary and cut into rough 1cm dice

1 celery stalk, peeled if necessary and cut into rough 1cm dice

1 small swede, peeled and cut into rough 1cm dice

a few leaves of green cabbage, stalks removed and cut into rough 1cm dice

1 tablespoon chopped parsley

Put the lamb and thyme into a large pan and cover with the stock. Season with a little salt and freshly ground black pepper, bring to the boil and simmer for 1 hour.

Add the barley and split peas, and simmer for 30 minutes more.

Add the vegetables, except for the cabbage, and simmer for another 30 minutes.

Add the cabbage and parsley, and simmer for a further 10 minutes. Season again with salt and pepper, if necessary, and serve.

Glen Fyne beef

It took us some years in the restaurants to find a piece of steak that had the flavour and cutting qualities that really suited the expert and well-travelled carnivores who regularly eat in our establishments. Our mission to Loch Fyne, apart from checking out the rope-grown mussels, smoked fish and oysters, was exactly that – to source the ultimate steak, although we did get persuaded to sample all the produce for lunch, overlooking the Loch.

We butchered and cooked various cuts of the Highland cattle breeds that grazed the hills surrounding the loch. The cut I was really interested in was the French-style côte de boeuf as a single portion. The one we tried was spot on, with a good proportion of fat that gave the meat the perfect eating qualities.

A few minutes' drive from the loch's edge, on the hills by Eagle Falls, you'll see these beautiful shaggy cattle grazing in their natural habitat, where they stay all 12 months of the year, feeding on grass and wild herbs. They are naturally slow-maturing, traditional Scottish cattle, which gives them their great eating qualities.

A piece of this pedigree meat doesn't need much cooking treatment, except a red-hot chargrill, or a short stay on a ribbed griddle plate, with some chips cooked in beef dripping. . . delicious! If not into chips, then a bowl of Scottish chanterelles, sautéed in butter with parsley and garlic, or wild garlic, would satisfy just as well.

GRILLED RIB OF BEEF WITH CHANTERELLES *serves 4*

For me the best eating cut for grilling or roasting has got to be the rib. The mention of fat is disconcerting for some, but on a cut like a rib, it's an essential part of the deal, as the tasty fat melts during cooking, naturally basting the meat and keeping it moist.

A barbecue or ribbed griddle pan is the perfect way to get maximum flavour from a rib of beef, as the exterior gets charred and the interior stays moist and rare. Earthy chanterelles with the beef are a marriage made in heaven (well not quite as much so as chips, of course).

You will need to ask your butcher to cut your beef rib steaks on the bone, a slice through the bone should yield 2 good steaks, enough for 4 people

2 best-quality rib steaks with the bone, each about 350-450g

sea salt and freshly ground black pepper

vegetable oil for brushing

100g butter

400g chanterelle mushrooms

2 medium garlic cloves, crushed

2 tablespoons chopped parsley

Preheat a barbecue or ridged griddle pan. Season the steaks and lightly brush with oil, then grill for 5 minutes on each side for rare and allow another 3-4 each side for medium.

Meanwhile, heat a heavy-based frying pan with the butter until melted. Add the mushrooms, season and cook over a medium heat for 2-3 minutes, stirring every so often. Add the garlic and continue cooking for another 2-3 minutes. Add the parsley, stir well and keep warm.

To serve, slice the beef into 5mm-1 cm thick slices and arrange on 4 warmed serving plates. Serve the mushrooms on the meat or separately.

Moors fit for red grouse

Before starting this book, my last trip to Dumfries to visit Ben Weatherall was a sea trout fishing weekend on the river Nith. The aim of this more recent trip was to shoot grouse on the grouse moors he bought with his brother about six years ago. He has about 600 acres, which are also home to a herd of Blackface lambs, which graze in their natural habitat on heather and other wild stuff. Ben recently added 20 Galloway cattle, which would also have been native to the area, and he sells this meat through his mail order company Weatherall Foods. Ben has a real passion for food and is partner in another company, Yorkshire Game, which supplies London clubs, restaurants and hotels with game in season.

You may wonder why grouse fetches such a high price for such a small bird, but when you pick the brains of Ben and his gamekeeper, Sandy, on the subject, it's all so clear. Unlike pheasants and partridge, which these days are semi-wild and are encouraged to breed for sport, the grouse is still a completely wild bird, relying on heather and wild berries for food.

The heather plays a key part in a successful season for the grouse; it acts as both food and cover. In the run-up to the glorious 12th of August, when the season kicks off, the gamekeeper has his work cut out ensuring the heather is in prime condition. When there are hundreds of acres, this is some task, as some of the heather needs burning out in strips to encourage young shoots to grow as food for the grouse. The heather also needs to be checked for beetles, which will otherwise destroy it.

As well as heather maintenance, the gamekeeper needs to keep under control many predators on the moors, such as foxes, stoats, weasels and rooks. Allowing these too free a rein will affect the success of the season. Sandy shows us little wooden bridges with what look like giant mousetraps he's built across burns to trap the stoats and weasels, as they don't like getting their feet wet. Sandy also plots piles of grit for each covey (family) of grouse for them to eat to help digest the heather.

With all this in mind, the red grouse – commonly just called grouse – has, without doubt, earned its place at the table. Its unique taste, derived from a diet of heather and wild berries, steers off many a gourmet though, and the nineteenth-century French author, Alphonse Daudet did refer to it, while generally engaged in putting down British food, as tasting like 'an old courtesan's flesh marinated in a bidet'. That's just bad luck for those not appreciating one of our great delicacies.

Ben encouraged us to get dressed up in tweed plus-fours to shoot, and off we went, up on to the moors. I'd never shot a bird in my life and my only experience with a gun was when I was sent to shoot wild boar at Chasse de la Loire. As Ben had warned, the grouse were pretty scarce and he had counted only about 450 in the year. After about 40 minutes, we come across a covey of birds, and Ben shot a couple in the space of 5 minutes, as we made our way back to his hunting lodge. While Ben was retrieving his last bird, one took off out of the heather 20 metres in front of me and I nervously, without thinking too much about it, took a shot and, much to my surprise, the bird dropped. We celebrated my first bird with the first cartridge with a couple of tins of McEwans and Ben's wife, Silvy's homemade Scotch eggs, and local cheeses from Loch Arthur.

ROAST GROUSE WITH BREAD SAUCE AND ROWAN JELLY *serves* 4

Every connoisseur of game has their own preferences when it comes to cooking and hanging game birds. For me, grouse has such a unique flavour that very little needs doing to it. Too much hanging can destroy the fine flavour of the bird and, for me, quick cooking in a hot oven is the key to keeping it moist – not rashers of bacon, as this encourages the breasts to boil beneath the bacon and imparts the flavour of the bacon to the birds. I know it's difficult to change one's eating habits, especially if you've been brought up on game, but that's my theory on pure grouse pleasure. Also, the accompanying bread sauce is a must, and must be well made with care and attention.

Rowans can easily be mistaken for one of those other poisonous berries that you constantly remind kids to stay clear of on bushes. The rowan, or mountain ash as it's sometimes known, is common throughout the British Isles and is actually a small deciduous tree, so fairly unmistakable. While I was on a shooting trip in Scotland in autumn, I thought I'd better harvest a basketful for a jelly. In old Celtic culture they would often ferment rowan berries to make a strong spirit, but I had game in mind after a successful first shoot, and rowan jelly seemed like the obvious accompaniment. You can serve the rowan jelly with lots of cold meats like ham, tongue, or pâtés, or as an alternative to cranberry sauce with turkey.

4 oven-ready young grouse

salt and freshly ground black pepper

good knob of butter, softened

splash of red wine

cupful of game or chicken stock or water

a little cornflour (optional)

for the Rowan Jelly
(makes about 1–1.5 litres)

750g sweet eating apples, peeled, cored and sliced

1kg ripe rowan berries

preserving or jam sugar

for the Bread Sauce

1 small onion, peeled and halved

50g butter

3 cloves

1 bay leaf

500ml milk

pinch of freshly grated nutmeg

100g fresh white breadcrumbs

Well ahead, make the rowan jelly: cover the apples with water, bring to the boil and cook at a steady boil for 20 minutes. Add the rowans and simmer for 30-40 minutes.

Strain through a clean tea towel or jelly bag. Add 450g sugar to each 500ml. Return to a clean pan and bring to the boil, stirring so the sugar dissolves. Boil for 10-15 minutes, then spoon a little on a plate and put in the fridge to test if it sets; if not, return to the heat and test again after 4-5 minutes. Pour into sterilized jars, seal and leave to cool. Store in a cool place or in the fridge for up to 6 months.

Start making the bread sauce: finely chop half the onion and cook it gently in half the butter until soft. Stud the other half with the cloves, pushing them through the bay leaf to anchor it. Put the milk, nutmeg and onion in the saucepan with the cooked onion and bring to the boil. Season and simmer for 10–15 minutes. Remove from the heat and leave the sauce to infuse for 30 minutes or so.

Meanwhile, preheat the oven to 220°C/gas 7. Season the grouse inside and out and rub the breasts with butter. Roast for 15-20 minutes, for medium rare, basting every so often.

While the grouse cook, finish the sauce: take out and discard the onion, add the breadcrumbs and return to a low heat. Simmer gently for 10 minutes, stirring occasionally. Pour one-third of the sauce into a blender and process, then return to the pan and add the remaining butter. Stir until the sauce has amalgamated; check the seasoning and adjust if necessary.

Remove the grouse from the roasting pan and set aside in a warm place. Place the pan over a moderate heat, add the wine and stock or water and deglaze by stirring up the stuck-on sediment with a wooden spoon. Cook rapidly for a minute or so. For a thicker gravy, add some cornflour mixed with a little water and simmer briefly.

Serve the grouse on or off the bone, with the gravy, bread sauce and rowan jelly.

GAME SALAD WITH BLAEBERRIES

serves 4 *as a first course*

On our way back from my first successful grouse shoot, we stopped off for a blaeberry foraging opportunity. We looked hard in among the dense heather, and our eyes eventually focused in on the tiny wild blue berries that very few people bother picking. The blaeberry is the original, wild version of the blueberry, before they were cultivated and, although it may take you an hour to pick half a kilo, it's well worth it.

You can make this salad with any game, like grouse, pigeon, venison fillets, hare or rabbit saddles, and if you are a regular at shooting, then it's a good way to use birds that are damaged.

When we got back to Ben and Silvy's house, I went straight into the garden and grabbed a few edible weeds like chickweed – yes chickweed, it's perfectly edible and very tasty – along with some small leaves of celery, pea shoots, flat parsley and chives, and knocked up a salad.

salt and freshly ground black pepper

500g selection of game bird breasts and fillets

good knob of butter

50-60g small salad and herb leaves

30-60g blaeberries or blueberries

for the dressing

2 tablespoons sherry or red wine vinegar

6 tablespoons rapeseed or olive oil

Season the game and pan-fry very briefly in the butter, so they stay pink, then transfer them to a warmed plate and leave to rest, saving the juices.

Make the dressing by mixing the oil and vinegar together with any cooking juices, and season to taste.

Toss the dressing with the leaves and arrange on plates. Slice the game thinly and scatter over the leaves with the berries.

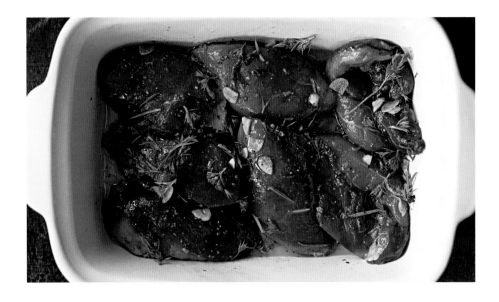

SCOTCH BLACK BUN

makes 10–15 good slices

I sort of knew about black bun, but had never set eyes on it. I eventually managed to find some sitting in among some other fruity cakes in a Scottish deli, and my first thought was 'giant Garibaldis'. Maybe the Garibaldi was the snack-sized version for carrying around in your pocket, because you certainly wouldn't want to be carrying this lump around in your pocket. I rather took a shine to the black bun and even Mr Lowe, our photographer, submitted and munched on it with his cheese after shooting. These days, black bun is traditionally eaten at Hogmanay, but originally it would have been eaten on Twelfth Night. Like Christmas cake, black bun should be made several weeks ahead of being eaten.

for the pastry casing

125g butter, cut into small pieces

250g plain flour

½ teaspoon baking powder

1 small egg, beaten, to glaze

for the filling

330g seedless raisins

500g currants

85g flaked almonds, chopped, or nibbed almonds

120g plain flour

80g brown sugar

1 teaspoon ground allspice

½ teaspoon each ground ginger, ground cinnamon, freshly ground black pepper

½ teaspoon baking powder

½ teaspoon cream of tartar

2 tablespoons brandy or whisky

about 3 tablespoons milk

Preheat the oven to 130°C/ gas 1. First make the casing: rub the butter into the flour, add the baking powder and mix with just enough cold water to make a stiff but rollable dough (usually 80-100 ml).

Divide the pastry into two and roll out the first piece on a lightly floured surface to a thickness of about ⅓cm and large enough to line a rectangular 16 x 26cm sponge tin, 5-6cm deep, allowing for a little overlap. Roll the second piece large enough to fit the top.

Mix all of the ingredients for the filling together, adding just enough milk to moisten the mixture. Spread into the pastry case and place the rest of the pastry on top. Pinch round the edge to seal, prick the top with a fork and brush with the egg.

Bake for 3½ hours. Leave in the tin to cool, then cut into useable squares. Store in an airtight tin

The Shawhead craft and produce show

It would have been a missed opportunity not to check out the local baking section in the village hall in Shawhead, near Dumfries. In fact, I was unofficially invited to give a hand with the judging of the baking section. This was a great first-time opportunity to check out some serious traditional local baking with some proper local girls who were old enough to be my gran. There was a homely array of doilys and paper plates with 30 or so different types of cakes and biscuits lined up and waiting to be critiqued on bare trestle tables. This was more nerve-racking than judging Junior Masterchef.

Keen gardeners who had been carefully manuring their vegetables, including Ben Weatherall's wife Silvy, had also brought in giant specimen vegetables like onions, marrows and cauliflowers, and I spotted a couple of the dreaded punky lollo rosso lettuces in among perfectly formed multicoloured tomatoes and beetroots, but I reckon size always wins on the vegetable table.

First up on the baking section was plain griddle scones, or girdle scones as the locals call them. They ranged from a couple of delicious light and thick versions to a couple of thinner ones that had slightly different characteristics, although they all tasted pretty good and the contestants and judge seemed to be old hands at this, so my opinions were best kept to myself.

Next in line were some pretty good-looking dropped scones, or Scotch pancakes, although we tend to call them drop scones for short, I think. I was told that these would all have been cooked traditionally, directly on top of the Aga or Rayburn, or on griddle plates. The quality of the eggs is very important, too much baking soda, could be a disaster and too thin would not have made the grade.

After another 10 or so categories, including treacle scones, cherry scones, oatcakes and scotch eggs, I was summoned by Ben to get going for our grouse shoot on the moors, so I had to leave the girls to it.

Annie Grierson's girdle scones

I was warned that Annie Grierson has the touch when it comes to the girdle pan. Her reputation and presence were sorely missed at the Shawhead show and, strangely enough, tattie scones, her speciality, were not even a judging category. Prospective competitors' fears of entering against her was the reason, I believe. A visit was arranged to Annie's house to witness real Scotch home scone-making. Annie tells me that she always used an Aga in her old farmhouse and cooked the scones directly on the hot plate. She now has a smaller house with an electric cooker, and has got used to her cast-iron girdle with the rounded, basket-like handle for easy turning of the hot plate.

When I arrived at the house, Annie had the girdle preheated and all the ingredients ready for her drop and tattie scones. Everything was weighed by her experienced eye, or by the cup as my gran would have done, and, as you can imagine, the results were remarkable from the experienced old hand. From a bowl of mash, mixed with some butter and milk, then a handful of flour, her tattie scones were rolled, cut with a saucepan lid, quartered and cooked to perfection. I couldn't help myself from devouring them as quickly as she scooped them off the girdle with her faithful old palette knife, which she has carefully looked after since she got it as a wedding gift.

These flat earthy scones would be perfect served just warm with smoked salmon and crème fraîche mixed with a little horseradish, or just eat them as the Scots do with butter and jam. They are also really great as part of a breakfast fry-up.

When I quizzed Annie on the shape of the scones, she replied, 'They like them neat and tidy at the show' and they were certainly very neat, and very tasty, and if she were showing, they would've got the first by my judgement.

SCOTCH PANCAKES, OR 'DROPPED' SCONES *makes* 16-18

I thought Annie's tattie scones good, but her Scotch pancakes were perfect, as if off a production line. That sounds like an insult to her baking skills, but each and every one was perfectly formed off her spoon. Her secret seemed to be the addition of golden syrup to her mix, or maybe that's the norm and it was her years of experience.

225g self-raising flour

1 teaspoon baking powder

30g granulated sugar

1 tablespoon golden syrup

2 eggs, beaten

250-275ml milk

butter for greasing and to serve

fruit compote, cream or fresh berries, to serve (optional)

Sieve the flour and baking powder into a bowl, then add the sugar. Stir in the syrup, eggs and enough milk to form a thick smooth batter that just drops off the spoon.

Heat a griddle pan, girdle or non-stick frying pan and rub it with a little butter. Drop in spoonfuls of the mixture and cook for 3 minutes until bubbles rise, then turn and cook on the other sides for another 2-3 minutes. Put them on some kitchen paper, while you cook the rest.

Serve warm or cold, with just butter, a fruit compote and cream, just butter or some fresh berries.

TATTIE SCONES *makes about 6-8*

> 500g floury potatoes, peeled, cooked,
> mashed and kept warm
>
> salt and freshly ground black pepper
>
> 80-120ml milk
>
> 100g flour, plus some for rolling
>
> a little vegetable oil for the griddle or girdle

Season the mashed potato and mix in just enough milk that the mash just drops off a spoon, then mix in the flour.

Roll the mixture into 6-8 rounds about 3mm thick.

Preheat a lightly oiled griddle (Annie rubs hers with a butter paper), heavy-based frying pan or cooler Aga hot plate. Cut the scones into 4 quarters and cook them for a couple of minutes on each side, or until they are just starting to colour.

Serve warm, or cold with butter, jam, or smoked salmon as I've suggested.

Dean's of Huntly

Shortbread is a perfect symbol of a Scottish tea time. I always end up eating some with a coffee on the train on a northbound journey. After visiting Dean's of Huntly, though, those have never tasted quite the same. Helen Dean started Dean's of Huntly in 1975, from the kitchen of their family home. It was never intended as a profit-making business venture, but her husband, Bill senior persuaded her to sell the shortbread to raise money for the Huntly pipe band, in which he was the drummer.

The shortbread soon got a reputation for its melt-in-the-mouth texture, due mainly to the Locherbie butter, wheat flour and cornflour, as used in Bill's mum's original recipe, although he remembered margarine being used when he was younger, as indeed did my grandmother.

Demand became high for private orders in the village, so Helen decided to open up a small bakery and shop close to the town centre. Helen and Bill's son, Bill junior, started working for them in 1987, and he now runs the business in their purpose-built factory.

Bill's mum's recipe is still used almost unchanged today, and their product looks as if it's just come out of a home oven, which is always a good sign in a fast-growing modern business. Dean's also now produce a range of innovative variations on the basic shortbread recipe, including shortbread crumbs for homemade cheesecakes and the like, and Bill junior is even proposing a new project of a restaurant and gallery, so the shoppers can see the production.

MacKays Dundee Marmalade

MacKays in Carnoustie are Dundee's only remaining marmalade and jam manufacturers, and are the largest producers in Europe still using traditional copper-bottomed boiling pans for production.

In 1995, Paul Grant bought the business and developed it into an international success, enhancing some of the jam and marmalades with alcohol, such as whisky. This helped Paul enter the Japanese market in a big way, and that is now their largest export market.

The factory looks almost as if it's been camouflaged so no one can see what goes on inside. From outside, it looks like a row of weavers' cottages, but inside it's the 'real MacKay'. Several copper-lined boiling pans bubble with golden syrupy marmalade. The basic MacKays brand targets everyday consumption and they also have their Mrs Bridges brand targetting specialist food shops and the gift market, with its cute oval bottles. The Mrs Bridges brand won six Great Taste Awards in 2004.

The history of marmalade as we know it now begins with grocer James Keiller, who first built a marmalade factory in Dundee in 1797. The term 'marmalade', from *marmelo*, the Portuguese for quince, was then widely used for any fruit preserve. Keiller is said to have bought a bargain job lot of oranges from a Spanish boat in Dundee Harbour without realizing they were the inedibly bitter Seville variety that the Arabs grew in southern Spain just for their medicinal qualities. His wife, Janet, made the lot into a preserve by shredding and boiling the fruit, but into less of a concentrated pulp, so the flavour was fresher and the consistency lighter and less solid. She also left the shredded peel in the conserve, reckoning its astringency would make it good for the digestion. Over the next century, Dundee marmalade became the breakfast favourite all over the British Empire.

ORANGE MARMALADE *makes 1.5-2kg*

Seville oranges are best for marmalade making and are available in the shops from around Christmas time until late February and March. This simple and fruity recipe, cooking them whole and then chopping them up, seems the easiest and best of all the recipes I've tried. You can adapt it to other fruits, such as grapefruit and lemons, or even a mixture. The pressure cooker, a forgotten kitchen utensil, is perfect for jam-making, as it cuts down the cooking time, although the pans tend not to be that big, so you have to make smaller batches.

1.5kg Seville oranges
3kg jam or preserving sugar or granulated sugar

Put the oranges into a large saucepan and cover with water. Bring to the boil, cover and simmer for about 1½ hours, or until the skins are soft and tender, and easily pierced with a small knife. Remove the oranges from the liquid, cut them in half and put them on a plate to cool.

Once they are cool, scoop out the seeds with any pulp and push through a colander with the back of a large spoon. This pulpy mixture is very gelatinous and will help to set the marmalade. Put the pulp mixture in the cooking liquid and discard the seeds. Cut the halves in half again and cut them into thin strips or chunks, according to whether you like fine or chunky marmalade.

Add the peel back into the cooking water with the sugar and stir until the sugar has dissolved. Bring to the boil and then boil rapidly for about 10-15 minutes, skimming off any white impurities every so often, until setting point is reached. The best way to test this is to drop a teaspoonful on to a small plate that has been in the fridge. If it sets after, say, a minute to a marmalade consistency, it's done; if not, continue boiling it and keep re-testing it. If you want a really thick marmalade, continue to boil until the sugar is almost caramelized.

Leave the marmalade to cool for about 30 minutes, stirring every so often, so that the pieces of orange suspend in the liquid. Then pour into sterilized jam or Kilner-type jars and seal well. Store in a cool place for up to 6-8 months.

The cheeses of Scotland

Whenever I'm in Scotland, I find myself on a bit of a cheese mission, because I know there are some great cheeses out there, but they're just not openly on offer. Scotland has such great produce, but few cheeses of real note. (I know I will probably be challenged on that one.) I've always made a point of asking staff in Scottish restaurants for some local cheeses and, generally, if I'm lucky, I get a piece of smoked Cheddar plus another indescribable lump with green bits running through it.

So why is a country with a noted dairy herd not producing? Or are they and, if so, why are they not shouting more about it? Fortunately, in London, thanks to Randolph Hodgson's pioneering efforts at Neal's Yard Dairy, a few quality Scottish cheeses are now embedding themselves firmly on the British cheese map.

The old Highland method of cheese-making was to sour the milk by leaving it in the sun, the cream would be skimmed off for butter and the remaining milk was scalded on the stove, causing the whey to drain. The resulting curds would be wrapped in muslin and hung to drain further. As soon as the cheese had stopped dripping, it was mixed with salt (and sometimes cream) and spooned on to oatcakes. This simple cheese preparation is known as crowdie, and been around since the days of the Picts, and is still made in many homes today.

The Cheddar-like Dunlop, Scotland's most famous cheese, first made in 1688 by farmer's wife Barbara Dunlop (née Gilmour) in the village of that name in Ayrshire, was so well received that it led to a general shift away from using skimmed milk and sheep's milk in Scottish cheese-making.

The Loch Arthur Creamery This outstanding producer deserves its place on the cheese-making map. The 500-acre estate overlooking Loch Arthur was set up in 1984 by an Austrian paediatrician, Dr Karl Konig, who founded the Camphill Village Trust. It was set up to provide work and homes for people with learning difficulties as part of the Camphill Movement and was one of six such communities scattered around Britain. The workers live in family houses within the community of co-workers and their children, and share domestic life and work according to their location and circumstances.

The Loch Arthur Community is run by South African, Barry Graham, who arrived a couple of years after it was set up. The dairy then just made butter and simple soft cheeses to accommodate one of the workers, Jorg, who

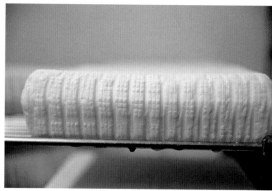

CLOCKWISE FROM THE BOTTOM LEFT
a Kebbuck cheese and two Criffels
at various stages of maturity,
from the Loch Arthur Creamery.

was given the job of churning butter, as he was disabled from his waist down and his strength was in his arms. He is now 50 and still working in the dairy, churning away at the butter.

Anxious to take the community production to the next level, Barry started producing an organic Cheddar-style cheese with milk from their own herd of Ayrshires. Not content with their organic Cheddar, they then pushed the boundaries and produced a small Coulommiers-style semi-soft cheese called Crannog, which has intriguing earthy aromas, almost mushroomy. Next, they went on to produce my favourite cheese, a semi-soft, washed-rind cheese called Criffel, which is shaped rather like a Taleggio, and has an interesting orange washed rind and a tangy sweet texture.

When I asked Barry if he had any interesting stories about the dairy, he went out the back to the fridge and pulled out an interestingly shaped cheese called Kebbuck, which looked a bit like an Italian Burrata. It was created accidentally when they had run out of moulds and one of the workers suggested they hang the curds in muslin. The shape is totally natural and each cheese will turn out a slightly different and unique shape. It has a smooth, creamy texture and won a gold medal in the 1999 British Cheese Awards.

The dairy has a changing group of workers, which is not the norm in a cheese-making environment, as consistency is key. This makes life interesting for Barry, and I was able to sympathize with him from my own experiences of restaurant kitchens, where you have to place each cook according to their best ability.

About 70 people now live and work in the community, along with 15 volunteers. The dairy will have 6 staff at any one time and 15 in total working shifts. Barry finds their best skills, and gears the work around them – that's how the dairy runs.

Other areas of the community produce biscuits and bread, and weave baskets. They also sell their own fruit and veg in the farm shop cum deli, so you can do a week's shopping there and feel you've helped a very good cause.

The history of the area was rich in cheese-making, then it almost disappeared. The Finnlay family, who were the last local cheese-makers, eventually gave up in the early 1970s, but continued selling their milk. Barry met up with them, when he first started up and had the idea of making hard cheese, and they kindly gave their old cheese presses to his dairy.

During the foot-and-mouth crisis, the Finnlays lost their entire herd, even though the animals were not infected. Barry went to the Finnlays to buy up their milk, which had just got organic certification, so Loch Arthur cheeses made with the Finnlay's milk went back into their cheese presses and, by a miracle, the last batch of cheese made in the presses using milk from the Finnlays' lost herd then won a gold for the farmhouse Cheddar.

H. J. Errington Of all the cheese-making stories on this tour - and I heard a few similar ones – none rivals how Humphrey Errington's Lanark Blue thankfully got through the nightmare legislation battles that most small-time unpasteurized cheese-makers dread.

Although Humphrey was the first cheese-maker this century to milk sheep for cheese commercially in Scotland, in 1994 he ended up battling with the Clydesdale Council, as his unpasteurized cheese was causing a bit of a stir with cheese-making legislation being tightened up.

'Big cheeses' all over the country supported his battle to keeps his blue sheep's-milk cheese from extinction when he was asked to recall all of his cheese because of a suspected listeria scare. He was almost forced to pack up further production as a sample test of his cheese showed the presence of *Listeria monocytogenes*. Humphrey fought the ruling on the grounds that the test did not discriminate between the dangerous and the non-virulent forms of the micro-organisms.

Cheese-making was Humphrey's life and he waited in anticipation, expecting the worse. Legal hearings continued for a year and costs built up, and supporters around the country helped fight and raised money to support his escalating legal bills. Finally, he was able to make cheese again.

Like many cheese-making stories across the country, if you're good enough and run a tight ship, then you will satisfy the Environmental Health Officer's demands. Humphrey certainly did that, and his famous blue cheeses, available from June to January, increased in popularity among the public and food writers.

If you've sampled one of his two great blues on a cheese board is Dunshyre – a cows'-milk blue of equal quality to Lanark Blue – you will appreciate the story of Humphrey's passion for his products.

The Oatmeal of Alford

My gran was right, of course, and a bowl of porridge really does seem to keep the cold out. Although I grew up on the South Coast, almost as far from Scotland as you can get in Britain, I learned to appreciate the connection between oats and golf. As a skinny kid, I'd be out straight after breakfast, playing golf in freezing, gale-force winds straight off the sea, with no weatherproof gear on.

The common oat was not introduced to Britain until the Iron Age, although it is thought to have existed in Europe since the Bronze Age. The oat was – and still probably is – the most important cereal in Scotland, due mainly to it being a hardy and resilient crop, able to survive in poorer soil and a harsher climate than cereals like wheat.

We were lucky enough to get to see the only working oat mill of its kind in Scotland, and it is one run by water at that. Mills are normally there for ornamental value these days, but not this one. It does a lot of the work at its own pace, and needs very little maintenance and few large repair bills.

We met up with Gwen Williamson, who runs the 180-year-old Montgarrie Mill in Alford, Aberdeenshire, for the Medlock family. The place was a silent piece of almost-forgotten industry, with just the faint sound of motion somewhere in the mill behind closed doors. It is strange what old-fashioned machinery really sounds like.

The oats mainly come from the Medlocks' farm, just down the road, or are sourced locally if demand is high.

Once they arrive at the mill, they are spread, two tons at a time, on to perforated metal floors, where they are dried for 3½ hours by coal fires, then allowed to dry naturally for a further week. Gwen turns the oats herself a couple of times weekly by hand, with an old long wooden-handled shovel. Gwen refers to the oats as 'corn' for some reason; I'm really not sure why and I didn't ask, after coming across all sorts of odd terminology, like the girdle and dropped scones, on my travels North of the Border.

The first stage of processing the dried oats is the shelling stone, operated by the water wheel. This slowly cracks open the husk and the oats are then transferred into tiny . . . well, elevators, I suppose, which are cleverly concealed in the beams and supports of the mill; clever stuff and very hygienic. They have small cups attached to a belt, which then takes the oats to a brushing machine. It was rather like watching a big model railway for the first time. The final stage is the millstone, after which they are sieved and graded into fine, medium, rough and pinhead oatmeal.

I was curious to take a closer look at the water wheel, as I'd only really ever come across an old one at the local brewery back in Dorset as a kid. This was a 25-foot monster that scooped up the water from the burn to operate the millstones inside. There is, however, nowadays a touch of electricity to operate some of the milling process, but this does not diminish the pleasure of witnessing a piece of milling history.

CRANACHAN WITH RASPBERRIES *serves 4*

This dessert is dead simple to make and it's full of flavour. You can use any soft fruit really, but raspberries are associated with Scotland and their size and sweetness are perfect. I did try using Drambuie instead of whisky, since I had some lying around in my larder as it's not my drink, and it worked pretty well. I've used this recipe occasionally as a breakfast dish and replaced some of the cream with yoghurt for a less rich result.

60g medium oatmeal
150g raspberries
600ml double cream
4 tablespoons runny honey
4 tablespoons malt whisky

Scatter the oatmeal on a baking tray and toast in a low oven or under a medium grill until golden. You'll have to watch it closely or it may burn.

Blend 50g of the raspberries in a liquidizer until smooth. Whip the double cream until stiff, then stir in the honey and whisky, and mix well but do not over-whip. Fold in 50g of the oatmeal, then carefully fold in the raspberry purée to form a rippled effect.

Spoon the mixture into glass coupes or a serving dish, then scatter the rest of the raspberries and oatmeal on top.

WHISKY AND WALNUT TART *serves 4-6 (makes a 26cm tart)*

For a drink as established as whisky, it would seem rude not to dedicate a dessert to it, although the cranachan does contain a wee dram. I have to hold up my hands on this one and confess that this is a converted pecan and bourbon recipe. But that's the fun of cooking and messing around with food.

for the sweet pastry
2 medium egg yolks
225g unsalted butter, softened
1 tablespoon caster sugar
275g plain flour

for the filling
3 medium eggs
200g soft brown sugar
220g golden syrup
125ml whisky
100g melted unsalted butter
1 teaspoon vanilla essence
pinch of salt
300g walnuts, roughly chopped

to serve
vanilla ice cream or thick double cream

Well ahead, make the sweet pastry: beat the egg yolks and butter together in a bowl, then beat in the sugar. Stir in the flour and knead together until well mixed. Wrap the pastry in clingfilm and chill in the fridge for an hour before use.

To make the filling, mix all the ingredients, except the walnuts, in a food processor or mixer until smooth. Then fold in the walnuts and mix well.

Roll the chilled sweet pastry on a floured table to a thickness of about 5mm. Grease a 26cm diameter tart tin, line it with the pastry, then trim the edges and refrigerate for an hour.

Preheat the oven to 190°C/gas 5. Fill the chilled tart shell with the walnut mixture and bake for 20-25 minutes until golden.

Serve with vanilla ice cream or thick double cream.

IRELAND

I RELAND'S RICH SOIL AND GENTLE CLIMATE made it ideal for growing the new-fangled potato when the vegetable arrived in Europe, and potatoes quickly became the basis for much of the island's cooking. They are used in soups, cakes, dumplings, bread, scones, pies and pancakes. The climate and resulting rich green pastures also make Ireland a major producer of lamb and beef, and a rich dairy production has helped it relatively recently develop some extremely fine cheeses, such as Gubbeen, Cooleeney, Milleens and Cashel Blue.

The embracing Atlantic Ocean has made it a great seafood producer, famed for its oysters, eels, sea trout and wild salmon, as well as Dublin Bay prawns. The famous Dublin Bay prawn, or langoustine, as it's more correctly known, is one of the culinary wonders of the world and needs nothing except mayonnaise and crusty bread, as do the oysters of Ireland. The Irish waters are amazingly clean, and a lot of English oysters start their life in Ireland, and are then grown in English waters.

Ireland has many traditional baked goods, including farls, soda bread, potato bread and barm brack fruit bread. Perhaps Ireland's greatest gift to the world of food and drink, however, is its stout, made famous by the Guinness brewery, and a common ingredient in many Irish dishes.

On many visits to both Northern Ireland and Eire, the vast range of produce – from both land and sea – and the total respect and simple passion the locals have for it has always

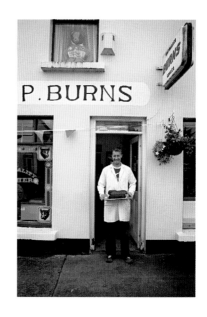

Ireland is becoming a major hub of food production and they are making some really wonderful stuff there. Cheese-makers, old and new, tend to dominate the scene, and their superb farmers' markets are going from strength to strength, both in the smaller towns and in the cities. At these, you can see both centuries-old traditional products and new artisanal creations.

Gone are the days when the only crop grown in all of Ireland was the potato – you can now find an amazingly wide range of fruit, vegetables and herbs grown and sold all over the island, worthy of many Mediterranean markets. Vividly coloured squashes, courgette flowers and multicoloured salad leaves vie with traditional carrageen moss and a whole new range of interesting roots.

impressed me. Not that I was expecting anything different, but it's just refreshing to find local oysters and shellfish on sale by the roadside and in tiny town markets, together with homemade bread and jams, etc.

Ireland is surrounded by water and has plenty of loughs and rivers running through its countryside, so even today there is a noticeable difference in eating habits of those that live on the coast and those inland. The contrast in the landscape almost dictates what there is to eat and what's on offer in local pubs and restaurants, rather as in Scotland.

However, it's the Celtic heritage that really dominates the still relatively simple eating and cooking, and I even found myself cooking traditional Celtic fare while staying in a friend's house in Caherdaniel, when there was no fish to be had. In midsummer, I managed only to find fresh marrowfat peas, which are a rarity over back in England, as a token of summer seasonality, and I ended up gathering young sea spinach leaves from the beach for a delicious green salad. I did love the challenge, though, and colcannon, made from leftovers of the previous night's dinner, that was often served up for breakfast. I was forced into cooking in the Irish manner, and a few simple and basic ingredients certainly do go a long way.

Irish potato dishes

There are conflicting stories as to how potatoes got to Ireland in the mid-sixteenth century: some say that Sir Walter Raleigh introduced them, and others claim they were discovered in wrecks of Spanish Armada galleons. A popular folk song, 'The Pratie [potato] Song' even contains the lines:

'The brave Walter Raleigh, Queen Bess's own knight, Brought here from Virginia the root of delight.'

However they got there, they have been a staple food of the country ever since and would be an important part of small and big-time farms, supporting families and the local community, as they were pretty easy to grow. The potato cultivation system was then known as the 'lazy bed' system, as it involved high raised beds that were easily accessible for harvest by hand without too much digging with a spade-like tool known as a 'loy' or 'fack'. The soil would generally be enriched with manure from cows and pigs kept on the small farms; or in coastal regions, seaweed would be used, which gives the potatoes a really distinctive flavour, rather as with Jersey Royals.

In the mid-nineteenth century, there was a nationwide failure of the potato crop caused by a fungus popularly called potato blight. By that time, potatoes had become the main source of food, so the failure caused widespread famine and disease. Over a million people died and many more than that ended up emigrating to the UK and the USA.

Until the twentieth century, potatoes would have been boiled in their skins in three-legged pots on the open fire, as there were no real cooking utensils or pots and pans around then. The cooked potatoes would be served simply on wooden boards in the middle of the table and be considered the main focus of the meal. When the meal was ready, the potatoes' innards would get scooped out and pounded by the men of the family with an instrument called a beetle. The wife would add ingredients like milk, butter, nettles, scallions or spring onions and chives, and this was how the champ we know today evolved. Across the country, you will find variations of champ, with nettles or sometimes even peas and leeks added, but essentially, it is made with scallions and chives and I've even seen it made with dulse seaweed.

DUBLIN CODDLE *serves* 4

Versions of this potato and onion dish seem to crop up all over the world. In France, they would make it with just potatoes and onions and call it *pommes boulangères*, and in the North of England, it relates to Lancashire Hot Pot, except that also has lamb, kidneys and sometimes black pudding in it. At the end of the day, the cheapest form of food, wherever you are in the Western world, must be potatoes and onions. And, call it what you like, it tastes great. If you're thinking of transporting a hot feast for, say, a fishing or hunting trip, then it is the perfect kind of dish, just popped into one of those Chinese takeaway containers or even in stacking tiffin boxes.

8 good-quality pork sausages

8 rashers of rindless streaky bacon

vegetable oil for frying

3 small onions, thinly sliced

1 teaspoon chopped tansy, sage or rosemary

6 baking potatoes, peeled and thinly sliced

1 litre (or enough to cover) chicken or beef stock (a good stock cube dissolved in that amount of water will do)

250ml dry cider

Preheat the oven to 220°C/ gas 7 and a hot grill. Grill the sausages and bacon until cooked and put to one side.

Heat a heavy frying pan with a couple of tablespoons of vegetable oil and fry the onions for 5–10 minutes over a medium heat until lightly coloured. Mix in the herbs and now you're ready to assemble the coddle.

Take an ovenproof casserole dish that has a lid or similar, cover the bottom with a layer of potatoes, followed by the onions with a little stock and cider, then another layer of potatoes and onions. Continue until all the onions and potatoes have been used, finishing the top with a layer of nicely overlapping potato slices.

Cook in the oven for 35–45 minutes, then arrange the sausages and bacon on the potatoes. Pour the rest of the cider over and cook for another 15–20 minutes. Turn the oven off, then wait for the old man to stumble home, tread on the cat and wake the house up. On a more practical note, this hearty hot pot is easy to keep warm and take with you on any midnight feast or festival.

CHAMP *serves* 4–6

500g floury potatoes

150–200ml milk

1 large bunch of scallions, or spring onions

2 tablespoons chopped chives

100g butter, or more if you wish

salt and freshly ground black pepper

Cook the potatoes in their skins until tender. When cool enough to handle, peel them and mash them.

While the potatoes cool, bring the milk to the boil, add the scallions, and let infuse off the heat for 3–4 minutes.

Add to the mashed potatoes with the chives and butter, season to taste and mix well.

COLCANNON

Like champ, there are many regional variations of this other traditional potato dish in homes and professional kitchens. The main difference between it and champ, however, is that colcannon is made with cooked shredded cabbage, like Savoy, or spring greens, instead of the scallions and chives. For best results and a more earthy flavour, boil your potatoes in their skins as above, mash them and mix with the cabbage, milk and butter and season. English bubble and squeak is very similar.

BOXTY *serves* 4-6

There are two main types of boxty: in the pan, which are fluffy thickish pan-fried cakes, or cooked on the griddle, sometimes called boxty pancakes. Both can be served in many ways as a breakfast dish. Here I served it with rashers of bacon and then drizzled it with honey.

150g peeled raw potatoes

250g cooked potatoes in their skins, peeled and mashed

200g plain flour

½ teaspoon bicarbonate of soda

200–300ml buttermilk (or ordinary milk)

good pinch of salt

butter, for frying

Grate the raw potatoes and mix with the mashed potatoes, flour and bicarbonate of soda, then add enough buttermilk to make a thick batter. Season with salt.

Heat a griddle or frying pan and grease it well with the butter. Drop in a quarter of the mix to make large pancakes or smaller amounts for small ones. Cook for 5 minutes on each side until golden.

TOP LEFT: boxty, TOP RIGHT: champ
BOTTOM LEFT: colcannon

Cuan Oysters

The most popular oysters in Northern Ireland are from the Cuan Sea Fisheries on Sketrick Island in Killinchy, Co Down. Jasper Parsons, proud owner of Cuan, has been supplying oysters to our restaurants for many years and, in or out of native season, his Strangford Lough pacific oysters sit comfortably in the oyster section at J. Sheekey and Scott's alongside Duchy of Cornwalls, West Mersea natives, Whitstables and fines de claires.

Jasper's marketing of his oysters is simply about the purity of the Class A waters in the Lough, which is down to the fast (up to six-knot) currents in the sea surrounding their island on Strangford Lough.

Apart from the attraction of oyster production, Strangford Lough is also one of the few marine nature reserves in the British Isles, but you don't need to make the journey to Co Down to sample their oysters; they will deliver to your door, as they do to many UK restaurants.

The Galway Oyster Festival

On all my trips to Ireland I've seen and eaten few oysters unless it was a specific oyster trip, so the build-up to the Galway Oyster Festival was really tempting, even though my scouts said the festival wasn't what it used to be.

My flight was delayed and overbooked, and anyone could have drawn the short straw to stay the night in Luton. I had my excuse and was firmly sticking to it. I overheard the Oyster Festival mentioned several times in among the now-sociable queue and my ears pricked up when the guy next to me was telling other passengers he was a world champion shucker. Sam Tamsanguan turned out to be the British Champion from Wiltons Restaurant in Jermyn Street, and had beaten our two guys from J. Sheekey at the Tabasco British Oyster Opening Championships in the Bibendum Oyster Bar a month back. I don't think I had ever met a world champion shucker before . . . what a great way to start the oyster fest.

As we were landing, over the PA system the stewardess wished Sam good luck on behalf of the passengers for his third time as British champion. It was hotting up before I even landed and I was rather concerned Mr Lowe might well be several pints of Guinness ahead before I got there, as he had already been in Ireland for a few days snapping other Celtic delicacies.

The streets of Galway are alive during the festival that celebrates the international art of oyster shucking, not forgetting the beginning of our native oyster season. We shucked and swallowed various native oysters collected from different areas of the Bay. The most interesting was the Comharcumann Sliogeisc Teo, which has remarkable red-tinged shells due to their habitat being on the broken-down coral beds and, what's more, they were still dredged with the old-fashioned curragh boats and are fished by a local cooperative collecting only 40 tonnes a year, so get consumed locally.

Irish oyster farming these days tends to be dominated by Pacific oysters, which were introduced to Ireland in the seventies because of the declining stocks of natives due to overfishing and disease. You rarely see Irish natives for sale, so we do tend to associate Pacifics with Ireland, but there are a handful of wild native, self-sustaining beds remaining, which are among the few left in Europe.

On Saturday, Championship Day, we followed the crowds across the bridge and into the corporate-looking tent – well, aircraft hanger-sized marquee – full of international oyster lovers, loading anything from lemon juice to Worcestershire sauce on to their 3-high plates of natives and balancing a Guinness in the other hand.

There seemed to be some serious shucking action going on in the back of the tent, so we checked it out and

Lough Neagh eels

Following on from the elvers in crisis story down in Gloucestershire (page 57), we now have the link to the potential and ongoing eel shortage. Not that we are a great eel-eating nation any more, but if you've ever tried to buy a live eel, you will have noticed how expensive they are. The increasing demand, especially in exports to Holland, where we end up buying most of our eels back from, just doesn't relate to the amount of elvers entering the Lough these days. Father Kennedy, the managing director of Lough Neagh's cooperative, remembers when, in a normal year before 1984, around 8 million elvers would enter the Lough after their long journey from the Sargasso sea, enough to keep everyone happy, and back in 1977 there were around 19 million. From 1985, when elvers showed a serious decline, the cooperative, who buy from around 300 fishermen, began buying in from England, as there are less than a million entering the Lough these days and its total output usually exceeds 500 tonnes. The Lough Neagh cooperative is the only wild eel fishery in Europe and, if the amount of elvers entering British and Irish rivers continues to decline, then the livelihoods of those fishermen will be in jeopardy.

it turned out the finalists were warming up by opening plates of oysters for the public oyster bar. Native oysters were being unloaded by the bucketful from a truck backed up on to the marquee. As quickly as they were dumped on the tables, they were shucked and plated and washed down with more of the black stuff.

The actual competition, with 15 international finalists, was judged on shucking 30 oysters in the quickest time, but time was not the important factor, the contestants being judged on opening technique and how perfectly the oyster lay back in the shell once it was loosened from the muscle and turned. So a quickly opened, gashed-up bivalve was not going to get the competitors anywhere.

I found myself eying up the competitors; each had their own shucking method and, seemingly, a different opening tool. The Canadian champion had an unusual method of shucking from the hinge of the oyster with a completely flat blade as if peeling an apple. Others would insert the point of the knife in the fragile side of the oyster. I hadn't realized how many types of oyster knife existed and I reckon some contestants were using their mums' kitchen knives ground down. Elastoplast on the thumb was a popular fashion accessory; good to have the plaster on before you cut yourself, I suppose.

We met up with Michael Kelly junior, European champion in the Gothenburg finals some years ago and supplier of oysters for the day. Michael was shucking a few of his own oysters from Galway Bay just to keep his hand in, as he gave us a brief history of their 55-year-old business. His father Michael senior turned up and told me he supplies Rick in Padstow and sends some all the way out to Canada. It was a becoming a bit of a social gathering around the warming-up table and we met the owner of Moran's, the famous oyster bar in Clarinbridge, which sells 50 dozen oysters a day. We later went along to check it out and, for me, it's what it's all about: perfect setting, great oysters and such a cute local little place, the perfect romantic setting for Mr Lowe and myself.

The competition got off to a great start but the first heat of five contestants saw a false start: the Norwegian was a bit keen off the mark then someone miscued and drew a bit of blood, which caused some confusion among the judges.

Each contestant arranges their 30 oysters in different ways, some in neat little overlapping rows at angles with the flat side up; and some, like our five-foot Sam, who brought a box to stand on so he could reach his oysters, just piled them up as they fell out of the box. Our Sam Tamsanguan, British Champion, got his 30 oysters shucked in good time, but not quite as good as the Frenchman, Bernard Gothier who got 5 oysters ahead in 2 minutes 29 seconds, equal with Yystein Reinsborg from Norway. Yystein had the edge, though, and his 30 were obviously a bit tidier than Bernard's, and he won the title. He was a cool guy, a bit of a Richard Gere lookalike and obviously a cool shucker with his punters.

DEEP-FRIED GALWAY BAY SHRIMPS *serves* 4

The little jewel in the Saturday market in Galway town centre was Juan's little seafood stall. It was barely a metre long, but had a great condensed selection of locally caught shellfish from the Galway Bay. A small quantity of shrimps jumping around in a basket caught my eye. These tiny shrimps are only dredged in the Bay in autumn, when the water starts to get colder They are generally sold live and should be cooked as soon as possible, either boiled, preferably in salt water, or in sea water, and served with soda bread. I prefer them deep-fried, heads, shells and all, when they take on a natural prawn cracker-like taste. Juan also had small velvet crabs, clams and local oysters, as well as a small offering of wet fish.

> 250–300g small shrimps in their shells, preferably live
>
> sea salt
>
> vegetable oil for deep-frying
>
> 80g plain flour
>
> cayenne pepper
>
> 100ml milk
>
> tartare sauce or herb mayonnaise (see below), to serve

First pre-cook the shrimps in boiling salted water for 1 minute, then drain and allow to cool.

Preheat about 8cm of oil to 160–180°C in a large heavy-based saucepan or electric deep-fryer. Season the flour with salt and cayenne pepper, then toss the prawns in the flour, shaking off any excess. Put them through the milk then back through the flour, shaking off any excess again.

Deep-fry the shrimps in the oil, a handful or so at a time, for 3-4 minutes until golden, then drain on some kitchen paper.

Serve with a mayonnaise-based sauce like tartare, or mayonnaise mixed with freshly chopped green herbs like chives, chervil, parsley and tarragon.

Co Kerry

I very rarely have a trip to the seashore without fishing the local water. When I stayed with my friend Thomas Dane in Caherdaniel a couple of years ago, I couldn't help but notice the sea urchin shells washed up on the sea shore in among the rocks, while I was out fishing off the Lamb's Head Peninsula. The fishing was a bit grim and we only caught a couple of small pollock, so I couldn't help myself but ask the guys from a diving school just near us in the tiny harbour if they would mind grabbing us some sea urchins. They give us a rather 'you must be mad' look, to say the least, and asked what we were going to do with them. 'Eat them, of course!' was our prompt reply, and then they really did think we were crazy Englishmen, as it was obviously not a local delicacy, except for the hardened seafood extremists like us.

I got on the phone to a couple of Irish chef friends, and one of them, Richard Corrigan confirmed the local sea urchins were just fine to eat. The divers got us a couple of carrier bags full and wouldn't accept any payment, so off we went back up to the house for a seafood feast. Thomas had bought some local lobsters and I got busy cleaning the sea urchins of their spines and cutting the urchins in half with a pair of scissors to reveal the delicious orange interiors.

We ate them as a starter, just raw with a teaspoon and a squeeze of lemon juice, then the following morning we used what was left. I just scrambled some local eggs with some butter and folded the orange sea urchin eggs into them at the last minute and served them back in the shells. As you probably know by now, I like to make the most of the rare pleasures in life, especially when they are free and local.

A couple of years later, I returned to Thomas's house with the kids and Clare, and armed with a bit more local knowledge. However, I had similarly small success on the fishing front, although, as usual, I tried every opportunity, including sea trout fishing on Lough Currane. We ended up going to the tiny harbour at the end of the Lamb's Head Peninsula and pleaded with a couple of local fishermen to sell us the only two lobsters they had. They had already promised them, unfortunately, but I did see a large pollock in the net, for which they wouldn't accept any money, as they probably thought I was going to use it as bait. In fact, pollock is one of my favourite fish and very sustainable, so I guess Lamb's Head must be an opportune spot for free seafood

SCRAMBLED EGGS WITH SEA URCHINS

serves 4

You will probably need to order the sea urchins in advance from your fishmonger, as they are not as common on the fishmonger's slab in this country as they are abroad, unless you know a friendly diver, that is.

4 fresh sea urchins

50g butter

6 medium eggs, beaten

salt and freshly ground white pepper

2 tablespoons double cream

Wearing a sturdy pair of gloves and using a kitchen knife, scrape away all the spines from the sea urchins and give the urchins a good wash. With a pair of scissors, make a hole just above the middle line of the sea urchin and carefully snip around so you have 2 halves. One half will be empty and the other will have orange eggs in segments.

With a teaspoon, carefully remove just the orange eggs and put them into a bowl. Discard the rest of the sea urchin from inside the shells and give the shells a good wash and scrub. Put the shells into a saucepan, cover with water, bring to the boil and simmer for a couple of minutes to sterilize them. Drain and give them a final wash, removing any membrane, then dry them off.

Melt the butter in a pan, add the beaten eggs, season and cook over a low heat, stirring, until the eggs begin to set. Stir in the double cream and cook for another 30 seconds. Stir in the sea urchin eggs, remove from the heat and spoon into the warmed shells. Serve immediately.

Derreensillagh Smokehouse

I came across Tim and Bronwyn Youard at Waterville Market at the same time I bumped into Harry Van Der Zanden (see page 220). Very conveniently, their smokehouse was right at the bottom of the farm track at the place where I was staying for the week, although it took me a few days to eventually sit them down for a chat over a few glasses of Powers whiskey at Freddie's bar and shop in Caherdaniel to pick their brains. Simon Hopkinson's name cropped up immediately, as Tim used to work for Bill Pinney at the Butley Orford Oysterage in Suffolk, and had supplied Simon with smoked eel at Bibendum for many years before he decided to move to Ireland. He had lived in Islington for many years, just near where I live and he reminisced about his young days as a chef in the kitchens of the Savoy Hotel in the 1960s.

Tim and Bronwyn's week consists of working the local markets selling their smoked salmon, hot-smoked sea trout and local mussels and oysters. Tim has a newly constructed smokehouse using an old-fashioned Scottish Pinney smoker, which is about as pure and natural as you can get. He uses oak logs from Killarney National Park and no oak chips and not a piece of electronic equipment in sight, except for the temperature gauge outside the concealed smoker. Tim and Bronwyn also smoke mackerel and haddock bought off the boats in Cahirciveen.

Clare and I had been craving for freshly cooked crab for days and when I finally managed to get to the smokehouse, Tim had just cooked some large spider crabs, which he kindly shared with us. It was heaven and, sadly, not one of the pleasures a lot of people enjoy: the meat is sweet and so different from your normal brown crab, especially with some local soda bread and freshly made mayonnaise.

The cheeses of Ireland

Derreenaclaurig cheese A stop off for provisions in the local store in Sneem on the way to Caherdaniel was my introduction to a Dutch-looking cheese I'd never come across before. The girl at the deli counter let me try the two types of the cheese, mature and not-so-mature, and carefully peeled off the label for the address, so I could go and check it out. The following day I met Harry Van Der Zanden selling his cheese in Waterville Market, in among a handful of stalls selling a mixture of bric-à-brac and local produce, from cakes to smoked fish.

Harry's house and farm are a mile outside Sneem and, surprisingly, properly and well signposted from the main Kenmare road and right to the farmhouse door. Harry makes 10 kilos of organic Dutch-style cheese a day in a cool room in his house, with bespoke handmade cheese-making gear and a smart maturing room next door. The cheeses are meticulously displayed, with bottles of his homemade sloe wine lined up beneath them on the quarry-tiled floor. The wine is purely for his own (and friends') consumption, although he does hand out a glass or two at Christmastime to his regular customers.

Harry decided to move his cheese-making from Holland to Ireland 15 years ago and when asked why, he just 'replied' with a curious cheeky grin. Harry is one of a large handful of cheese-makers who have settled in Ireland. Is it for the calm lifestyle or the Guinness? More than likely, it is for the rich pastures that provide quality milk in a world of new and quality cheese production.

Harry makes four different cheeses during his May to October cheese-making season. His popular trademark cheese Derreenaclaurig, he sells as both a young four-month-old version and a matured 10-month version. He also flavours some of them in Dutch style with cumin and one with home-grown garlic. I watched him hand-pressing his day's cheeses on a simple bespoke cheese press. Harry relies totally on organic and unpasteurized milk from his herd of 10 Jersey cows, hence his short cheese-making season, when the milk is at its best.

Corleggy goats' cheese When we visited Maja Binder's Dingle Peninsula Dairy, she insisted we take a young Corleggy cheese with us. This was Maja's favourite Irish cheese, she admitted, as she passed it to me, like some kind of tiny trophy. She told me she preferred to eat it young, when it was still soft. I must admit that before I'd even tasted it, or knew anything about it, it just had the feeling of being a great cheese, a little treasure wrapped in loose unbleached linen, tied with raffia and a label bearing the image of a farm worker with a goat's head, leaning on a piece of farm machinery.

Silke Cropp, the cheese's creator, first came to Ireland when she was a young girl and dreamt of returning there after she had gone back to her home in Germany. She did eventually end up fulfilling her dream in the early 1980s, moving to a smallholding in Corleggy, Co Cavan. It was a bit of a wreck and needed serious work doing to it. Silke decided to buy a goat, which produced far too much milk for her own consumption, so she decided to make some cheese with the excess.

Silke had no cheese-making experience, relying entirely on a book, so it was a matter of trial and error, making soft and hard cheeses washed in a sea salt brine, in between teaching art in Cavan. She would let tourists try her cheese and she proudly admits that the French loved it, which gave her the idea to make cheese to export. She bought more goats, and her cheese business took off.

By 1987, Silke was milking 120 goats around the River Erne, fed on good grass and wild herbs, and this really comes through in the cheese, and Corleggy was well and truly on the map. She started exporting cheese to her home country, Germany, and ended up selling some of her goats to her neighbours, so she could concentrate on cheese-making. Then, much to the neighbours' surprise, she started buying milk off them from the goats she'd sold them. Cheese-making took over from the teaching entirely, and she bought sheep and cows for more cheese-making.

When I got my Corleggy home, it somehow found its way to the back of the fridge and had matured into a well-flavoured hard cheese. It can be eaten between 6 weeks and 4 to 6 months, so it was still in pretty good shape, compared to the younger version we tasted in Dingle.

Aside from her passion for cheese-making, Silke also started up the Temple Bar food market with a couple of other foodie friends in the late 1990s, and the market is now well established among food lovers.

A day out to sample Inagh Farmhouse cheese Our day out to check out Siobhán Ni Ghairbhith's St Tola cheese in Inagh, Co Clare, proved to be a day of bad luck and perhaps misjudgement. We decided to stop off to see Olivier Beaujouan (see page 225) and Maja Binder (opposite) near Dingle Bay on the way and planned to return to Dingle to check out Fungi the famous bottle-nosed dolphin in the bay after the St Tola visit. An underestimated journey time, a queue at the ferry crossing and then someone breaking their ankle on the ferry slipway, forced us to postpone the trip to Co Clare and return to Dingle early, only to find that we had just missed the last dolphin trip of the day, much to the disappointment of Ellie and Lydia.

Out of the Blue was recommended as a great simple seafood restaurant, but there were no seats, so we decided to head home for pollock fishcakes left over from the previous night's dinner of roast pollock and colcannon.

Earlier in the day, we had driven through Killorglin, which seemed to be in a state of high security alert, with house driveways taped up and five temporary car parks. We discovered on the way back through that it was the three-day Puck Fair, celebrated from 10-12 August.

The first day of the Fair was referred to as 'Gathering Day', the second, 'Fair Day' and the third, 'Scattering Day'. The fair derives its name from the Gaelic word *poc*, meaning billy goat. Each year a goat is chosen, decorated with garlands and ribbons, and paraded through the town, to accompanying music. The goat is then put up on a high platform and crowned King of the Fair. On the last day, the poor old goat is carried around the town again on the shoulders of four strong men and sold off by auction.

We stopped off there briefly, although there wasn't a goat in sight, except for the statue on the bridge, but there were plenty of travelling traders selling their wares as well as gypsy fortune tellers. We headed back to Caherdaniel along the narrow windy mountainous roads and, just as we overtook a slow-moving caravan, a herd of

goats decided to cross the road right in front of us. The hire car performed well though, and kept its place on the road at 50mph, missing the leading goat by a few inches. Perhaps Puck Fair time is not a lucky time to visit a well-known producer of goats' cheese.

We did eventually get back to Co Clare on our Galway Oyster Festival trip to see Siobhán at Inagh Farm, her family home of three generations. Her cheese-making career started when she was studying as a teacher, and she worked for her neighbours, Meg and Derrick Gordon, making St Tola goats' cheese to get a bit of extra cash. She really got into cheese-making and decided to swap courses, so began studying rural business and marketing. Her interest in cheese gathered momentum and her studies gave her the idea to buy local cheeses directly from the farms and sell at local markets. She sold cheeses like St Tola, Mount Callen and Kilshanny to local restaurants, then heard Meg and Derrick were soon to retire. Her own family's farm was near to getting organic certification and she decided to take St Tola production off Meg and Derrick's hands, and move it home to Inagh Farm.

During the spring, Siobhán's excess kids and older goats get sent to Africa via a charity organization called Bo`thar, meaning 'the long road to Africa', and a couple of springs ago her best milking goat, who only has one pap, or nipplet, decided she fancied some of the African action and joined the queue and got mixed up with her friends. Fortunately Siobhán spotted her as they were about to leave and they have called her Bother ever since.

Apart from the original soft log, Siobhán has developed two other organic cheeses: a round fresh crottin and a mature version. Her latest is a feta-style cheese.

SORREL, BEETROOT AND GOATS' CHEESE SALAD *serves 4–6*

Soft goats' cheeses, like St Tola, lend themselves perfectly to a refreshing starter or main course salad. There is a great salad leaf I discovered a couple of years ago called silver sorrel, which has a small, almost heart-shaped leaf and the citrus-like flavour of the large-leaved common sorrel. Teamed with some young beetroots, this makes a great salad and a good excuse to get out the extra-virgin rapeseed oil I found in Suffolk.

1 small piece of soft goats' cheese, about 150g, at room temperature

a good handful of silver sorrel leaves, or other small salad leaves

200g baby beetroots, cooked and peeled

a few chives, snipped into 7-8cm lengths

for the dressing

2 tablespoons white wine vinegar

½ tablespoon clear runny honey

6-7 tablespoons extra-virgin rapeseed oil or olive oil

salt and freshly ground black pepper

Make the dressing by mixing all the ingredients with seasoning to taste.

Break the cheese into rough 1cm pieces and arrange on plates with the sorrel leaves and beetroot. Sprinkle generously with the dressing and scatter the chives over.

Glenilen Farm Dairy I've been on a bit of a butter mission while in Ireland, and managed to get a tip-off from John McKenna over a bit of lunch at Carmel Sommer's Good Things Café in Durrus, West Cork. Now, there's a place to go if you're in the area! Carmel used to work for Sally Clark in London and serves the best local food in the area. John reckoned the best butter in Cork was made by Alan and Valerie Kingston at Glenilen Farm, not far from where we were lunching.

We jumped in the car and John drove us up to the farm to meet Valerie, with a few little detours on the way – those farm tracks all look the same after a while. Valerie was in the garden with her kids, and Ellie and Lydia were making themselves scarce – four farms in a day was just over their limit, I think.

Alan and Valerie got married in 1997 and decided to diversify their farming, so went to West Africa on a dairy development programme. On their return in 2002, they experimented with simple cheeses like fromage frais and quark, then started making them into cheesecakes. They then produced yoghurts in old-fashioned-looking glass jars with fruit compotes. As Valerie was telling us of her products, she would keep disappearing and bring out samples; when the cheesecake arrived was when Ellie and Lydia magically reappeared.

Their dairy products and by-products are really quite special and the one that caught my eye was the butter, just cut into slabs from a large block and neatly wrapped in brown paper and tied with string. They don't produce much, 100 kilos every 3 weeks and it's made with all their own milk from their Jersey cows. I had some of it in – and melted over – my next dish of champ, and it was out of this world.

Dingle Peninsula cheese When you get a tip-off about a quality cheese-maker and a passionate French seaweed processor (if that's the right word to use, perhaps more of a gatherer), it's well worth a little detour from dolphin watching in Dingle Bay to check them out, although my daughters Ellie and Lydia were not that convinced.

Maja Binder has been making cheese in her 200-year-old stone shed, overlooking Brandon Bay on the Dingle Peninsula since 1998. She previously trained as a cheese-maker in Italy and Switzerland, which may well have something to do with her making semi-hard, Tomme de Savoie-style cheeses, using raw local cows' milk. The highly individual characteristics of the gold-medal-winning cheese are a result of a combination of daily brushing with salted whey and the old stone shed where the cheeses are matured, which has a natural flora that permeates the cheese.

Maja currently makes five cheeses, from the plain Kilcummin and the aged Beenoskee to a Dilliscus seaweed and a Beenoskee seaweed, the name coming from the hill behind the dairy.

In case you are wondering why and where the seaweed comes into it, Maja needed seaweed for her Kilcummin and Beenoskee cheeses, which are speckled through with it when cut to give an unusual taste of the sea. Olivier was the obvious forager and, say no more, there we have the current very close relationship and kids running around to prove it. The seaweed she uses is called dillisk, also known as sea grass or dulce.

Durrus cheese Jeffa Gill moved to Dublin in 1965 to study fashion, then after leaving college, she ended up doing various things connected to fashion in that sixties sort of way. Her parents were farmers and, in 1974, she bought a ruined farmhouse in Coomkeen, about 2½ miles up the hill out of Bantry. In the late 1970s, Jeffa decided to do something with the milk from the handful of Friesian cattle she reared on the farm, as delivering milk to the local creameries was an uncreative way to make a living. She found an old American cheese book that inspired her to experiment, making small amounts of cheese as a hobby. Jeffa then tempted local restaurants and shops with her cheese and thus began Durrus cheese.

Jeffa's semi-soft unpasteurized, washed-rind cheese started life much deeper than its current shape, rather like a millstone, as it was originally moulded in a drainpipe, which some small cheese-makers still use as I've discovered. The high humidity up in the hills of Coomkeen play a strong part in the natural development of the cheese and its unique ivory-tinged, coral-pink rind.

Jeffa admits to not producing all the milk from her own cows these days, as demand for her cheese is so high, but she loyally buys from a local farmer, Cornelius Buckley, winter herd and summer herd, so the cheese is made using milk from Friesians all the year round. It is made in an old raclette vat bought in Switzerland on an equipment-hunting trip as at the time there was no cheese-making equipment to be found in Ireland. Today, she has been 'Cheese Maker of the Year' in Dublin and has won a gold in the World Cheese Awards.

On the wild side – Olivier Beaujouan

I felt like I was walking in on a busy kitchen in the middle of service when I met Olivier. He actually did work in kitchens when he first moved to Ireland about 12 years ago, working as a chef in Dublin, but decided to settle for the wild life. He got inspired by Richard Mabey's wonderful book, *Food for Free* – don't we all? (And if you can actually make a living out of foraging wild food, then go for it.)

On my trip to Kerry, I couldn't resist picking wild sea vegetables on almost every trip to the beach, including sea spinach and rock samphire.
Olivier was frantically frying a large batch of chicken livers for pâté, which he sells at markets, together with lots of different types of sea vegetable preparations, from pickled konbu in a tomato dressing to a delicious seaweed tapenade made from dulce, onions, capers and olive

oil, for which he is rightly famous. Unfortunately, my pickled kelp leaked slightly in the back of the hire car and we were rather reminded of it for the whole trip. Olivier is the only producer I've come across who does such great inspiring stuff with seaweed and it's a vegetarian's dream, although I don't know that many vegetarians who would be that struck on seaweed.

Gubbeen Farm Gubbeen Farm is a perfect example of modern farming, with its main interests being the taste of the end product and maximizing production potential on their land. There are no disused barns here: each of the buildings are used or have been updated for quality artisan food production However, this has not always been the case; the Fergusons have been farming the land for five generations in a traditional way.

The minute I stepped into Giana's farmhouse kitchen, I spotted a tin of Dorset Knobs on the shelf, which Giana hadn't yet opened. I think, like many others, she just took a fancy to the tin. We piled on some of Alan and Valerie Kingston's local butter (page 223) and thick wedges of Giana's semi-soft cheese, which is ripened by its natural pink-and-white rind. While we tucked in, Giana told me about her days at the ICA in London as an exhibition organizer, and reminisced about her childhood love for Ireland, when she regularly visited her uncle's place on the island of Innisbeg. She ended up moving to Co Cork, where she met Tom when she was working as a barmaid.

With her Hungarian father who ended up in London after the war, she had moved to Andalucia and lived off the land, making goats' cheese, then later moved to

France and learned more about the great cheeses of that country; so she couldn't believe the Irish made no by-products from their milk. Her very first cheeses were simple cream cheeses, and a birthday present of a Jersey cow from her aunt, who reared them in Sussex, influenced Giana to make a new cheese.

Veronica Steele, from the equally successful Milleens Dairy, and one of the first strong personality farmhouse cheese-makers in Ireland in the early 1970s, was a guiding influence on the beginning of Gubbeen. Cheese had not been seriously made on farms in Ireland for centuries, so now was the time to make a statement and get on with it, Giana thought. So Gubbeen was to be born in 1973, just before her son Fingal in 1975, who was to become their charcuterie boy.

The significant thing about Gubbeen cheese is the bacteria. When times were difficult about 6-7 years ago, everything with raw-milk, washed-rind cheeses was under scrutiny. Tim Cogan, a professor of microbiology, visited Giana off his own back to analyse the bacteria on the rind of Gubbeen. He had been to various cheese producers across Europe and discovered that Gubbeen's listeria-free dairy was due to a unique unidentifiable airborne bacteria, or flora as it is known in the cheese business. This territorial bacteria varies from farm to farm, but this was a one-off, so he aptly named it *Microbacterium gubbeenense*. Unfortunately, dairies are becoming so sterile that these bacteria, unique to artisan cheeses, could all be lost due to over-zealous hygiene.

Giana did, however, have a scary close call at the end of the 1980s, so then started pasteurizing their milk, but without loosing too much of the character of the original cheese.

Clovisse Ferguson's Gubbeen Greens

Tom and Giana's daughter, Clovisse went to work for a couple of reputable vegetable growers in Cornwall after leaving school, then decided to return home and set up a herb garden next to brother Fingal's smokehouse. Apart from supplying Fingal with herbs for curing, marinating and flavouring sausages, she sells her organic herbs and unusual salads and veg to local places like the gourmet store in Ballydehob and the Good Things Café in Durrus. I sampled a whole plate of Ferguson's produce – ham, egg and salad – on my trip to Good Things, and it was a perfect family offering on a plate. Being a gardening nut myself, I inspected what Clovisse had growing and came across a totally new leaf called mertensia, which weirdly tasted of oysters, as if it were some sort of sea vegetable. I managed to persuade Clovisse to send me some seeds, along with her mum's giant borage plants, for which she had borrowed seeds from a rectory garden in Waterford.

Fingal Ferguson's Gubbeen Smokehouse

We wandered through the woods from the farmhouse garden to check out what Fingal was up to and, as we got close to his smokehouse (well, it's more of a charcuterie, but let's stay with smokehouse for the moment), all I could hear was heavy rock music blaring out of the mesh windows. I thought it was a bit of a strange time of day to have a party, but they are a hard-working family, so the afternoon would be as good a time as any.

Fingal greeted us and you could sense the passion in his face. I didn't really know about his products and was expecting a bit of ham and rashers of bacon. Fingal immediately talked about and led us to his Euromag, which sounded to me like some kind of porn thing, but Fingal, being the workaholic he is, would have no time for such a thing. Instead, it was one of those smart mobile charcuterie trailers that you often see in Europe, but rarely set eyes on here. It is a very clever bit of kit and well worth the 20,000 euros. It simply unfolds and transforms from a trailer into a smart EHO-approved artisan trading stand.

His smokehouse, strung up with sausages, was operated using the old-style Scottish Pinney system smoker. As he showed me around, it looked like he had been at it for decades, but this was only his fourth year trading, although his mum tells me he's been messing around with sausages for years. Jane Grigson, Fingal admitted, was a big influence in his curing recipes. He has chorizos, salamis, boerworst and several types of pancetta, as well as some of the best bacon I've tasted – meaty and thickly cut, so you can actually taste the farm-reared flavour. Everything Fingal cures and smokes comes from the farm's Old Spots and Duroc pigs, which are fed on the whey from Gubbeen cheese.

Fingal, like most other artisan producers I've come across, concentrates on selling at local markets, like Cork, Bantry, Skibbereen, Schull, etc. In true artisan spirit, Fingal explains that he'd love his drying and curing room to be made of wood, in order to retain the smoky characteristics of an old smokehouse. In this day and age, though, you need to stay one step ahead of the EHO police. If you didn't know otherwise, you could be in a top Spanish or Italian butchers shop, the way the products are hanging with little metal marker tags. Sadly, Fingal's products are not coming 'over the water' yet, but he is certainly someone to look out for.

Macroom Oat Mills

It would be a missed opportunity not to visit another Celtic oatmeal producer, especially as Donal Creedon's product is unique, and oats are an underestimated basic commodity. What, you may think, could be so unique about oats? Standing on the first floor of the original mill that Donal's family have been milling oats in since 1832, Donal confesses that he will probably be the last miller in the family, due to the economics and demand for his artisan product. Buildings like the one we were in are being bought up these days for accommodation and it seemed to me that Donal could see no future in the small business for generations to come.

Originally, his ancestors just ground wheat and then the two original brothers parted company and one started grinding oats. In the 1920s, the IRA burnt down the building that they thought was the mill, but fortunately it was the wrong building and only the store was destroyed, leaving the mill standing.

The mill is the best example of a real old-fashioned mill in the country, and was once powered by water.

Donal pointed out the hollow joists and support beams which cleverly conceal elevator belts with little buckets attached that bring the husks up top the first floor, to be processed and stone-milled, after they have been roasted on the ground floor. These old mills are known as vertical mills and are designed with the elevators concealed in the joists to minimize dust in the air.

Donal, with one other part-time worker, receives just 1 tonne of husks a day to process. On the first day, the husks are roasted and then allowed to rest for 3 days until completely dry; they are then stone-ground.

You can find Donal's oats in Neal's Yard in London and a few other shops, and Donal tells me he still eats a bowl of porridge made with them every morning. They do make great porridge, with that slightly unique toasted flavour with the odd black bit in it, but its natural. Chefs like Myrtle and Darina Allen of Ballymaloe House use them in many of their recipes, one of which appears on the back of the packet for Macroom oatmeal biscuits, but Donal says they're delicate and a bit fragile to handle.

MACROOM OATMEAL BISCUITS

Makes about 24 biscuits

- 140g Macroom oatmeal
- 140g plain white flour
- 175g butter, cut into small pieces
- 55g caster sugar (for sweet, 30g for savoury)
- pinch of salt (for savoury)

Preheat the oven to 190°C/gas 5 Mix together the oatmeal and flour, rub in the butter to a breadcrumb-like consistency and add the sugar.

Knead the mixture to a pliable dough and roll out to a thickness of about 3mm on a lightly floured table. Cut into rounds or rectangles and place on a non-stick baking sheet, or on baking parchment. Leave to rest in the fridge for 20 minutes.

Bake for 15–20 minutes, remove from the oven and leave to cool. Store in an airtight container.

Midleton Farmers' Market

Local town markets are notorious for selling junk and it's refreshing to find a market like Midleton that is entirely devoted to good-quality produce and served by the producers themselves. Tom Doorley, *The Irish Times* food and wine writer, was my tour guide and I got proper introductions to the producers. You can shop for the week here and really feel like you've been there and done it all. The market closes fairly early, so morning is your best bet to get a good look at what's on offer.

On a good day you are likely to find Myrtle Allen, Darina's mum from Ballymaloe, tending the Ballymaloe Cookery School Gardens stand, selling home-grown salads and vegetables, breads and biscuits, and pasta sauces. Frank Hederman from Belvelly Smokehouse will come with a loaded van of smoked eel, salmon, wild mussels and mackerel, and more. Declan Ryan, artisan baker of Arbutus, just can't fit enough bread into his van for the day and, when I arrived at midday, he had almost run out, except for the bag of pizza dough he handed over to Tom.

Dan and Anne Ahern rear probably the best chickens in Ireland and they fetch a similar price to their Angus beef. You can buy almost every seasonal vegetable you can think of at Tim and Fiona York's Glenribbeen Organics, like courgette flowers, squashes and pumpkins, as well as great-tasting tomatoes. At Ballintubber Farm Shop stand, you will find lots of old varieties of potatoes, romanesco broccoli and great salad leaves. If you're not into baking at home, then you shouldn't miss the homemade scones, biscuits and jams made by Wendy English and her mother.

These are a bunch of dedicated producers and they will travel for miles, like Oren Little of the Little Apple Company, who sells many varieties of apples and apple juice, and drives down all the way from Kilkenny.

Markets like this aren't just great for the local producers – shops in Midleton town have reported an increase in business with the ever-increasing popularity of the market. We even had to queue for a table at the Farmgate Café, sister to the one in Cork (see overleaf).

You will find a lot of these producers regularly doing other markets, like Bantry, Clonakilty, Kenmare, Macroom, Mahon and others. It's a way of life for them, keeping the general public in touch with great produce.

The English Market in Cork

If you want to capture all the great traditional food in Ireland under one roof, the English Market in Cork is not to be missed. Despite its deceptive name, you will come across locally grown organic vegetables and, if you're a barm brack fan, probably one of the finest in Cork is to be had at the Old Mill. At On the Pig's Back, you will find a lot of the great Irish cheeses, with a few imports slipped in among them, and cured meats made by Frank Krawczyk, as well as sausages from around the world. They also stock Arbutus breads, made by Declan Ryan, whom I met the day before in Midleton Market. There

are plenty of butchers shops, like Kathaleen Noonan's Cork Specialities, where you'll find some amazing cuts with names like bodices – a kind of cured rack of pork rib – as well as tripe, drisheen, skirts, tails, heads and lots of other cuts you just don't come across back home.

At A. O'Reily's, you will find an array of tripe cuts, and rolls of drisheen. Here, these have not been replaced with quick-cooking cuts. O'Connell's fish stand was quite impressive: Dublin Bay prawns piled high, spider crab, pollock and cod, fresh from the water.

The market reminds me of a mini version of the Boqueria in Barcelona, with shoppers and traders sitting up at high stools at coffee bars. Frank Hederman, the premier Irish smoker, has his own stand in the market, with a fine selection of smoked eels, great salmon, mussels and whatever else he fancies smoking.

We finished up our tour with a bit of lunch upstairs at the Farmgate Café on the recommendation of Tom Doorley, *The Irish Times* food and wine writer. The café has gallery seating overlooking the market, and the menu really represents what goes on downstairs. My lambs' liver and bacon, and the Irish stew were perfect, and both cooked in a homely sort of way.

It really is no wonder that the *Observer Food Magazine* voted this one of Europe's ten best covered food markets.

Black pudding

It's interesting moving around the British Isles and discovering the change in texture and flavour in artisan black pudding making. In the Kerry region, there were two particular producers of black pudding that came highly recommended by a couple of very good sources. Being an addict of the stuff, I had to check them out and, luckily, they were both en route to and from the house. Slabs of black pudding seem to be the norm over here and my idea of black pudding being forced into a sausage shape is certainly changing in favour of the slab.

My first stop was in a local supermarket called Ashes in Annascaul. It was the only supermarket in the village and seemed to resemble all the other modern all-day supermarkets and convenience stores we passed. There was a small deli counter at the back of the store and behind that was the butcher's block and mincers where the famous black pudding was made. Black and white pudding production had, sadly, finished for the day, but I

was lucky to find a packet of each on the chilled shelves. My breakfast for the next morning was 'sorted' and delicious it was too, with some leftover potatoes and cabbage, I made colcannon, with a fried egg on top.

A couple of days later I went to Sneem to visit Patrick J. Burns, an equally famous black pudding specialist. Theirs is made using their grandmother's 60-year-old recipe and uses blood and meat from their own slaughterhouse at the back of the shop. Their puddings are not made from pork either, I discovered, as they can only slaughter sheep and cows, so these puddings are completely kosher.

The texture of both was soft enough and smooth to the point of it just holding together when fried, and they were probably less spiced than those I have tried in the North of England. The great thing I've discovered with black pudding all over the world is that no two are the same and all have their characteristic texture and taste.

SPICED BEEF

Sometimes referred to as 'huntsman's beef' and at one time a popular dish all over Britain, this now only seems to be found in Ireland and, occasionally, the Midlands. For centuries, beef would have been preserved by salting and this is more than likely a development of this process when spices were imported. Spices were at one time an expensive commodity, so the introduction of spices into salting beef would have been saved for the Christmas festivities. The longer it is cured, the longer it will keep; but, with modern refrigeration, preserving is not so essential after cooking, especially at Christmastime, when you have unexpected family and guests.

Saltpetre is difficult to get hold of nowadays, as it is normally only used for charcuterie and curing, but you can find it in some independent chemists or order it by post from the Natural Casing Company (tel 012527 13545).

1.5kg-2kg piece of boned and rolled brisket, topside, or thick flank

80g sea salt

10g saltpetre

15g black peppercorns, coarsely ground

15g ground allspice

15g juniper berries, ground

50g dark brown sugar, like muscovado

About two weeks before you need it, put the beef in a close-fitting casserole, stainless steel saucepan or plastic container. Mix all of the remaining ingredients together and rub into the beef. Cover and leave in the fridge for 10–12 days, turning it once or twice a day.

Preheat the oven to 150ºC/gas 2. Wipe off all the bits of marinade from the beef, rinse out the casserole, then put the beef back in it. Put a couple of layers of foil over the pot, then fit the lid tightly. Cook for 3 hours, then remove from the oven and leave to cool for 3 hours.

Remove the beef and wipe dry with kitchen paper. Wrap the beef in clingfilm and put into a clean dish with a weight on top and refrigerate for 24 hours.

Rewrap and keep in the fridge for up to 3 weeks. Serve thinly sliced, as you would with ham with pickles, or in a sandwich.

Carrageen moss

I've had a packet of dried carrageen moss, which a friend brought back from Ireland, in my cupboard for years. In case you're wondering why I'm keeping moss in the cupboard, it's a seaweed, named after a village that once had a thriving industry in seaweed. It's generally gathered off the south and west coasts, and is sometimes referred to as Irish moss.

It is probably the most attractive-looking edible seaweed, with little fans of pink, purple and cream. Demand used to be high for it, as it contains natural gelling agents for the traditional carrageen moss pudding and blancmanges. It can also be used as a natural thickener for soups and stews. At one time, it was boiled with hot milk and honey to make a soothing drink for sore throats, and is highly recommended as a cure for stomach problems and sleeplessness.

I must say, I've never seen it mentioned on a menu anywhere and, only found one or two references in cookbooks. You occasionally see this moss drying on the seashore in places like Ballyandreen, where it's a kind of ongoing tradition, and you can get it from Frank Melvin of Carraig Fhada Seaweed in Co Sligo.

CARRAGEEN MOSS PUDDING (MUNLA CARRAIGIN) *serves 4–6*

10g dried carrageen moss

600ml milk

1 vanilla pod

1 large egg, separated

30g caster sugar

300ml rich double cream, like Jersey

Soak the carrageen in tepid water for about 10 minutes until it softens. Drain off the water and put the carrageen into a saucepan with the milk. Split and scrape the seeds of the vanilla pod into the milk and add the pod too. Bring to the boil and simmer gently for 10 minutes.

Put the egg yolk into a bowl with the sugar and mix well with a whisk. Strain the milk mixture on to the egg yolk, pushing through all the jelly-like, swollen moss with the back of a spoon. Add the cream and leave to cool, then refrigerate for 30 minutes or so until almost set.

Meanwhile, whisk the egg white until fluffy and carefully fold into the milk mixture. Cover with clingfilm and refrigerate until set.

APPLE AND GUINNESS FRITTERS *serves* 4-6

Apples are probably the fruits that crop up most in Irish recipe books. I suppose the apple is the potato of the fruit world and so user-friendly – in pies, dumplings and the traditional Irish cake. Guinness – or Smithwicks – stout makes a good batter, and why not make good use of traditional regional drinks in a pudding?

150ml stout

110g self-raising flour, plus a little extra for dusting

1 tablespoon caster sugar

vegetable oil for deep-frying

4 well-flavoured eating apples, peeled and cored

caster sugar for dusting

thick cream to serve

Whisk the stout into the flour to form a thick batter, add the sugar and leave to stand for an hour.

Preheat about 8cm of oil to 160–180°C in a large heavy-based saucepan or electric deep-fat fryer.

Dust the slices of apple in flour and shake off the excess, then dip 4 or 5 slices at a time into the batter, shake off any excess, and then drop them into the hot fat. After a minute or so, turn them with a slotted spoon so they colour evenly. When they are golden all over, remove them from the oil and drain on kitchen paper. Repeat with the rest of the apples.

Dust with caster sugar and serve with thick cream.

Gazetteer

LONDON

Andrew Casson
(honey)
07734 924 389

Faulkners
(fish and chip shop)
424-426 Kingsland Road
Dalston, London E8 4AA
020 7254 6152

F. Cooke
(pie and mash shop)
150 Hoxton Street
London N1 6SH
020 7729 7718

Neal's Yard Dairy
(British farmhouse cheeses)
Randolph Hodgson
17 Shorts Gardens, Covent Garden
London WC2H 9UP
020 7240 5700
coventgarden@nealsyarddairy.co.uk
www.nealsyarddairy.co.uk

The Two Brothers
(fish and chip shop)
297-303 Regents Park Road
Finchley, London N3 1DP
0871 3327768

BOROUGH MARKET

Neals Yard Dairy
6 Park Street, Borough Market
London SE1 9AB
020 7645 3554
retail@nealsyarddairy.co.uk
www.nealsyarddairy.co.uk

Tony Booth
(vegetables and fungi)
Units 15-16
020 7378 8666

The Wild Boar stall
(rare-breed pork, wild boar, sausage
and hams)
Peter Gott
most Fridays and Saturdays

**The Wright Brothers Oyster and
Porter House**
Ben Wright and Robin Hancock
11 Stoney Street London SE1
020 7403 9554
020 7403 9550 (for home deliveries)

THE SOUTH

**Whitstable Oyster Fishery
Company**
17-20 Sea Street, Whitstable
Kent CT5 1AN
01227 276856
www.oysterfishery.co.uk

Marsh Produce
(market gardener: veg and eggs)
Clive Ovenden
Old Hall Farm, King Street, Brookland
Romney Marsh, Kent TN29 9RJ
01797 344383

www.forager.org.uk
(wild food)
01227 700141

The Goods Shed
(farmers' market)
Station Road West, Canterbury
Kent CT2 8AN
01227 459153
greatgrub@yahoo.co.uk

Food fore thought
(salt marsh lamb)
Wickham Manor Farm
Winchelsea
East Sussex TN36 4AU
01797 225575

Ashley or Andrew Saddler
(Kentish hops)
Unit W
Paddock Wood Distribution Centre
Tunbridge, Kent
TN12 6UU
01892 835001

National Fruit Collections
Brogdale Farm, Brogdale Road
Faversham, Kent ME13 8XZ
01795 535286
01795 531710 (fax)
info@brogdale.org

Chegworth Valley Juices
Water Lane Farm, Chegworth
Harrietsham, Kent ME17 1DE
01622 859272
01622 850918 (fax)
info@chegworthvalley.com
www.chegworthvalley.com

Eastside Cheese Company
Pat Robinson
East Lodge, Tanbridge, Hill Lane
Godstone, Surrey RH9 8DD
01883 743617

Two Hoots Cheese
Two Hoots Farm
Feathercot, School Road
Barkham, Wokingham, Berkshire
01189 760401

THE SOUTH WEST

Birdwood Organic Cheesemakers
(Birdwood Blue Heaven cheese)
Melissa Ravenhill
Woefuldane Farm
Minchinhampton, Stroud
Gloucestershire GL6 9AT
01453 887065

Bollhayes Cider
Alex Hill
Bollhayes Park, Clayhidon
Cullompton, Devon EX15 3PN
01823 680230

Charles Martell
(cheeses and fruit)
Laurel Farm, Dymock
Gloucestershire GL18 2DP
01531 890637
01531 890637 (fax)

The Chough Bakery
(Cornish pasties)
3 The Strand, Padstow
Cornwall PL28 8AJ
01841 532835
01841 533361 (fax)
elaine@the chough.demon.co.uk

Denhay Farms
(cheese and ham)
Broadoak, Bridport
Dorset DT6 5NP
01308 458963

The Dorset Blueberry Farm
David Trehane
352 Hampreston, Wimborne
Dorset BH21 7LX
01202 579342
01202 579014 (fax)
info@dorset.blueberry.co.uk
www.dorset-blueberry.com

Dorset Blue Cheese Company
Woodbridge Farm, Stock Gaylard
Sturminster Newton
Dorset DT10 2BD
01963 23216

Duchy of Cornwall Oysters
Port Navas, Falmouth
Cornwall TR11 5RJ
01326 34210

Leakers Bakery
29 East Street, Bridport
Dorset DT6 3JX
01308 423296

The Lizard Pasty Shop
(Cornish pasties)
Anne Muller, Beacon Terrace
The Lizard, Helston
Cornwall TR12 7PB
01326 290889
01326 290153 (fax)

Moores Biscuit Bakery
(Dorset knobs)
Morcombelake, Bridport
Dorset DT6 6ES
01297 489 253

Netherton Farm
(Cornish Yarg cheese)
Upton Cross
Liskeard, Cornwall PL14 5BD
01579 363128/362244
01579 362666 (fax)

The Pilchard Works
Tolcarne, Newlyn, Penzance
Cornwall TR18 5QH
01736 332112

Portland Shellfish
Building 233
Portland Port Business Centre
Castletown, Portland
Dorset DT5 1PA
01305 822522

Proper Cornish Limited
(Cornish pasties)
Western House, Lucknow Road
Bodmin, Cornwall PL31 1EZ

01208 265830
01208 78713 (fax)

Severn and Wye Smokery
Richard Cook
Chaxhill, Westbury-on-Severn
Gloucestershire
01452 760190

Ticklemore Cheese
Robin Congdon
1 Ticklemore Street, Totnes
Devon TQ9 5EJ
01803 865926

THE MIDLANDS

Goodmans Geese
Little Walsgrove Home Farm
Great Witley, Worcester
Hereford and Worcester WR6 6JJ
01299 896 362
www.goodmansgeese.co.uk

Huntsman Farm
(rare-breed pork)
Richard Vaughan
Goodrich, Ross on Wye
Herefordshire HR9 6JN
01600 890296

Mrs Kings Pork Pies
Ian Hartland
Unit 30, Manvers Business Park
High Hazels Road, Cotgrave
Nottingham NG12 3JW
0115 989 4101

Neals Yard Creamery
Charlie Westhead
or Sue Davies
Caeperthy Farm, Arthur Stone Lane
Dorstone nr. Hay on Wye
Herefordshire HR3 6AX
01981 500 395 (phone and fax)
ny.creamery@virgin.net

Quenby Hall Stilton
Hungarton Road, Hungarton
Leicestershire
0116 259 5224

Sparkenhoe Farm
(Red Leicester cheese)
Jo and David Clarke
Upton, Nuneaton
Leicestershire CV13 6JX
01455 213 203

THE EAST

The Asparagus Growers Association
133 Eastgate, Louth
Lincolnshire LN11 9QG
01507 602 427
www.british-asparagus@pvga.co.uk

Childwickbury Goats Cheese
Elizabeth and David Harris
Childwickbury Estate
St Albans, Hertfordshire AL3 6JX
01727 841151

Estuary Fish Merchants
8 Cockle Sheds, High Street
Leigh-on-Sea, Essex SS9 2ER
01702 470741

Mrs Temple's Cheeses
Copys Green Farm
Wighton, Wells next the Sea
Norfolk
01328 820224

Peter Jordan
(wild mushroom forays)
info@tastymushroom
partnership.co.uk

Tavern Tasty Meats
Roger Human
The Farm Shop, The Street, Swafield
North Walsham
Norfolk NR28 0PG
01692 405444
roger@tavern.fsbusiness.co.uk
www.taverntasty.co.uk

Cookies Crab shop
The Green
Salthouse, Holt, Norfolk NR25 7AJ
01263 740352

Colchester Oyster Fishery
Pyfleet Quay
North Farm, East Mersea, Colchester
Essex CO5 8UN
mail@colchesteroysterfishery.com
www.colchesteroysterfishery.com

West Mersea Oyster Bar
Coast Road, West Mersea
Essex CO5 8LT
01206 381600

Hillfarm Oils
(rapeseed oil)
Home Farm
Heveningham, Halesworth
Suffolk IP19 0EL
01986 798660
www.hillfarmoils.com

Paul Rackham Ltd
(high-quality beef)
Philip Dale, Bridgham
Norwich NR16 2RX
01953 717176

THE NORTH

Bettys & Taylors of Harrogate Ltd
Head Office, 1 Parliament Street
Harrogate
North Yorkshire HG1 2QU
01423 877300
01423 877301 (fax)
www.bettysandtaylors.com

E. Oldroyd Hulme
(rhubarb)
Carlton, nr Wakefield
Yorkshire WF3 3RW
0113 282 2245

Higginsons Ltd
(black pudding)
Keswick House, Main St
Grange Over Sands
Cumbria LA11 6AB

L. Robson and Sons Ltd
(Craster kippers)
Neil Robson
Haven Hill,
Craster, Nr Alnwick
Northumberland NE66 3TR
01665 576223

Scotts of York Butchers
(York ham)
81 Low Petergate, York YO1
01904 622972
scottsyork@hotmail.com

Sillfield Farm
(wild boar and Cumberland
sausages)
Peter Gott
Endmoor, Kendal, Cumbria LA8 0HZ
015395 67609
015395 67483 (fax)
enquiries@sillfield.co.uk

WALES

The Anglesey Sea Salt Company
Brynsiencyn
Isle of Anglesey
Gwynedd LL61 6TQ
01248 430871

Beef Direct Limited
Brian and Fiona Thomas
Plas Coedana
Llannerch-y-medd
Ynys Mon LL71 8AA
01248 470387
info@beefdirect.net
www.beefdirect.net

Caws Cenarth Cheese,
Glyneithinog Farm
Pontseli, Boncath
Dyfed, SA37 0LH
01239 710432
cenarth.cheese@virgin.net

Gorau Glas Cheese
Margaret Davies and Catrin Roberts
Quirt Farm, Dwyran, Ynys
Mon LL61 6BZ
01248 430570

Llanboidy Cheesemakers
Sue Jones
Cilowen Uchaf, Login, Whitland
Dyfed SA34 OTJ
01994 448303

Menai Oysters
Tal y Bont Bach
Dwyran, Llanfairpwllgwyngyll
Gwynedd, LL61 6UU
01248 430878

The Lobster Pot
Church Bay, Nr Holihead
Anglesey
01407 730 341/588
www.thelobsterpot.net

SCOTLAND

Arbroath smokies
www. arbroath-smokie.co.uk

Deans of Huntley Ltd.
(shortbread)
Huntly, Aberdeenshire AB54 8JX
01466 792086
www.deans.co.uk

H. J. Errington & Co
(Lanark blue cheese)
Braehead Farm, Walston, Ogscastle
Carnwath, Lanarkshire ML11 8NF
0189 9810257

J. B. Houston
(haggis)
Stuart Houston
Greenbrae Loaning
Dumfries DG1 3DQ
01387 255528
www.jbhouston.co.uk

Mackays Ltd
(marmalade and other preserves)
21-23 Thistle Street
Carnoustie, Angus DD7 7PR
tel 01241 853 109
www.mackays.com

Montgarrie Mills
(oatmeal)
Alford, Aberdeenshire AB33 8AP
01561 377 356
sallyk@euphony.net
www.oatmealofalford.com

Rannoch Smokery
Kinloch Rannoch, by Pitlochry
Perthshire PH16 5QD
0870 160 1559
www.rannochsmokery.co.uk

Simon Howie
(meat products)
Findony, Muckhart Rd, Dunning
Perthshire, Scotland PH2 ORA
01764 684332
www.simonhowiefoods.co.uk

IRELAND

Annascaul Black Pudding
Thomas Ashe
Main St, Annascaul
00353 (0) 66 9157127

Ballintubber Farm
David and Siobhan Barry
Carrigtowhill, Co Cork
00 353 (0)21 488 3034

Ballycotton Potatoes
Willy Scannell
Ballybraher, Ballycotton, Co Cork
00 353 (0)21 4646924

Carraig Fhada Seaweed
(carrageen moss)
Frank Melvin, Co Sligo
00 353 (0)96 49042

Darina Allen
(cookery classes)
021 4646785
info@cookingisfun.ie
www.cookingisfun.ie

Derreenaclaurig Cheese
Harry Van Der Zanden
Derreenaclaurig, Sneem
Co Kerry
00 353 (0) 64 45330

Derreensillagh Smokehouse
Tim and Bronwyn Youard
Unit 1, Old Schoolhouse
Caherdaniel
00 353 (0) 877923318
derreensillagh@iolfree.ie
www.smoked-salmon-fish.com

Dingle Peninsula Cheese and
On the Wild Side
Kilcummin Beg
Maja Binder & Olivier Beaujouan
Castlegregory
Co Kerry, Ireland
00 353 (0) 66 7139028
dipcheese@yahoo.com
seatoland@hotmail.com
www.wildsidesitestogo.biz

Durrus Farmhouse Cheese
Jeffa Gill
Coomkeen, Durrus, Bantry
County Cork, Ireland
00 353 (0) 2761100
durruscheese@eircom.net
www.durruscheese.com

The Galway Oyster Festival
Áras Failte, Galway
00 353 (0) 91 522066

Glenilen Farm
(farmhouse butter)
Alan & Valerie Kingston
Drimoleage, Co. Cork
028 31179
028 31668 (fax)
www.glenilen.com

Gubeen Farmhouse Products
(cheese, greens and smoked meats)
Gubeen House
Schull, County Cork, Ireland
00 353 (0) 2827824
Gianaferguson@eircom.net
cheese@gubbeen.com
smokehouse@eirecom.net

Inagh Farmhouse Cheese Ltd
(St Tola goats' cheese)
Siobhán Ni Ghairbhith
Inagh, Co Clare, Ireland
00 353 (0) 656836633
info@st-tola.ie

Macroom Oat Mills
Massytown, Macroom
Co Cork Ireland
00 353 (0) 26 41800
macroomoatmealmills@
eircom.net

Moran's Oyster Cottage
The Weir, Kilcogan, Co. Galway
00 353 (0) 91 796113

Silke Cropp
(Corleggy goats' cheese)
Belturbet, Co Cavan, Ireland
049 9522930
www.corleggy.com

Index

Author's acknowledgments

My thanks to Clare Lattin and Ellie & Lydia Hix for putting up with all
the wild goose chases, smelly farmyard smells and endless talk about
cheese. Jason Lowe for his unrivalled passion and enthusiasm in making
this book complete. Richard and Horace Cook for fish, fishing and
dangerous dark riverbank liaisons. Charles Campion for local
knowledge, near and far. Carol Wilson for pointing me very north.
Randolph Hodgson for cheesy tip offs. Tony Booth for sharing his little
but big green book. Peter Gott for his inspiration, stories and knowledge
on pigs and beyond. Reg Johnson, my Lancashire informer. John
McKenna & Tom Doorley who supplied many inroads into Ireland. Ben
Weatherall for the shooting, fishing and a great Sunday lunch. Drew
Barwick for eastern delights. Jim Peyton for casting lessons and local
knowledge on the Dee. Kay Aschbar, my tour guide in Scotland. And a
big thank you to the team at Quadrille: Jane O'Shea for believing in my
vision, Lewis Esson for pulling it all together, Lawrence Morton for his
patience. And last but not least, Laura Hynd for organising Jason.

IRISH SEA

Ireland

Fingal Ferguson's
Gubbeen Smokehouse